# BASICS OF COMPUTER SCIENCE

# BASICS OF COMPUTER SCIENCE

Pawan Vashisht

ANMOL PUBLICATIONS PVT. LTD.
NEW DELHI - 110 002 (INDIA)

**ANMOL PUBLICATIONS PVT. LTD.**
**H.O.:** 4374/4B, Ansari Road, Daryaganj,
New Delhi-110 002 (India)
Ph.: 23278000, 23261597
**B.O.:** No. 1015, Ist Main Road, BSK IIIrd Stage
IIIrd Phase, IIIrd Block,
Bangalore - 560 085 (India)
*Visit us at*: www.anmolpublications.com

*Basics of Computer Science*



First Published, 2008

ISBN 978-81-261-3568-4

PRINTED IN INDIA

Printed at Mehra Offset Press, Delhi.

# Contents

# Preface

This book is designed to provide a comprehensive introduction to the design and analysis of computer algorithms and data structures. In terms of the computer science and computer engineering curricula, we have written this book to be primarily focused on the Junior-Senior level Algorithms (CS7) course, which is taught as a first-year graduate course in some schools.

This book owes its existence to the collaboration made possible by the Internet and the free software movement. Its three authors — a college professor, a high school teacher, and a professional programmer — have yet to meet face to face, but we have been able to work closely together and have been aided by many wonderful folks who have donated their time and energy to helping make this book better.

Author

# Preface

Chapter 1

# Introduction

## INTRODUCTION

This unit aims at introducing you to today's most commonly used electronic device – the computer. The study of this unit will highlight the characteristics and evolution of computers. It will also help you to understand the basic terminology associated with computers.

## OBJECTIVES

After studying this unit, you should be able to

- Understand the basic characteristics of computers,
- Understand how the computers evolved,
- Understand the components that make up a computer,
- Differentiate between hardware and software,
- Differentiate between system and application software,
- Understand the difference between bits and bytes,
- Classify devices as input and output devices,
- Differentiate between ROM and RAM, and
- Appreciate the use of various secondary storage devices.

## WHY COMPUTER?

The word 'Computer' literally means to 'Compute' or to 'Calculate'. Stated simply, it is an electronic device which processes information based on the instructions provided, to generate the desired output. It, therefore, requires two types of input – raw data, and the set of instructions to process or act upon the data.

This can schematically be shown in Figure.

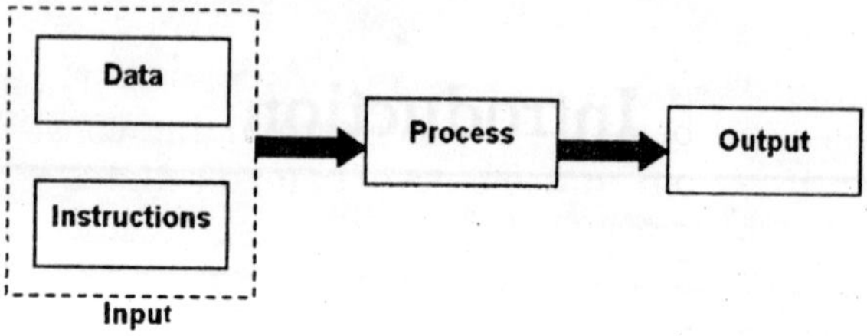


**Fig.** Processing Information

Data can be of any type – text, numeric, alpha-numeric, image, picture, sound etc. The instructions that act upon this data are also called the programme or software in computer terminology.

## CHARACTERISTICS OF COMPUTERS

The characteristics of computers that have made them so powerful and universally useful are speed, accuracy, diligence, versatility and storage capacity.

### Speed

Computers work at an incredible speed. The speed with which it performs is way beyond human capabilities. As a comparison, it can do in one minute what a human being would probably take a lifetime!

When we refer to the speed of computers, we now talk in terms of milliseconds (hundredth of a second), microseconds (millionth of a second), nanoseconds (billionth of a second), and even picoseconds (trillionth of a second). A powerful computer is capable of performing about 3-4 million simple instructions per second.

### Accuracy

In addition to being fast, computers are also accurate. Errors that may occur can almost always be attributed to human error (inaccurate data, poorly designed system or faulty instructions/programmes written by the programmer) rather than technological weaknesses. In fact, a special term GIGO (Garbage In Garbage Out) has been coined to represent a scenario where faulty results are got due to inaccurate instructions or faulty data.

### Diligence

Unlike human beings, computers are highly consistent. They do not suffer from human traits of boredom and tiredness resulting in lack of concentration. Computers, therefore, score high over human beings in performing voluminous and repetitive jobs.

### Versatility

Computers are versatile machines and are capable of performing any task as long as it can be broken down into a series of logical steps. This means that their capability is, once again, limited only by human intelligence. As is evident, in today's fast developing technology-world, it is almost inconceivable to find an area where computers are not being used. The presence of computers can be seen in every sphere – Railway/Air reservation, Banks, Hotels, Weather forecasting and many more.

### Storage Capacity

Today's computers can store volumes of data. Unlike human memory where unimportant information is relegated to the back of the mind and forgotten as time progresses, a piece of information once recorded (or stored) in the computer, can never be forgotten and can be retrieved almost instantaneously! Information can, therefore, be retained as long as desired (using secondary storage – a type of detachable memory).

Identify the characteristics of a computer that have contributed towards making it such a popular device.

## EVOLUTION OF COMPUTERS

The history of computers can be traced back to almost 2000 years ago, with the advent of abacus, a wooden rack holding two horizontal wires with beads strung on them. Numbers are represented using the position of beads on the rack. Fast and simple calculations can be carried out by appropriately placing the beads.

In 1620, an English mathematician by the name *William Oughtred* invented the slide rule – a calculating device based on the principle of logarithms. It consisted of two graduated scales devised in such a manner that suitable alignment of one scale against the other, made it possible to perform additions, compute products etc. just by inspection.

*Blaise Pascal,* a French mathematician, is usually credited for building the first digital computer in 1642. He invented the mechanical calculating machine. Numbers were entered in this machine by dialing a series of numbered wheels. Another series of toothed wheels transferred the movements to a dial, which showed the results.

In 1671, *Gottfried von Leibnitz,* a German mathematician, invented a calculating machine which was able to add and perform multiplications. He invented a special stepped gear mechanism for introducing the addend digits, which is still being used.

The prototypes made by *Pascal* and *Leibnitz* were not used in many places. It was only about a century later that *Thomas of Colmar* created the first successful mechanical calculator which could add, subtract, multiply, and divide. A lot of improved desktop calculators by various inventors followed, such that by 1890 a range of improvements like accumulation of partial results, storage of past results, and printing of results were not uncommon

## THE FIRST COMPUTER

*Charles Babbage,* a professor of mathematics at Cambridge University, England, realised that many long calculations usually consisted of a series of actions that were constantly repeated and hence could possibly be automated. By 1822, he designed an automatic calculating machine that he called the 'Difference Engine'. It was intended to be steam powered and fully automatic (including printing of result tables), commanded by a fixed instruction programme. In short, he developed a prototype of a computer which was 100 years ahead of time and is, therefore, considered as the father of modern day computers.

A step towards automated computing was the development of punched cards which were first successfully used by *Herman Hollerith,* who worked in the US Census Bureau in 1890. He along with *James Powers* developed devices that could read information that had been punched into cards, without any human help. This resulted in reduced reading errors, increased workflow and availability of unlimited memory (punched cards could be used as easily accessible memory of unlimited size).

These advantages were seen by various commercial companies and soon led to the development of improved punch-card using computers by companies like International Business Machines (IBM) and Remington.

## SOME WELL KNOWN EARLY COMPUTERS

### Mark I

After World War II there was a need felt for advanced calculations. By that time, many reliable mechanical desk calculators had been developed. *Howard A. Aiken* of Harvard University, while working on his doctorate in physics, in the year 1937, designed a machine that could automatically perform a sequence of arithmetic operations. He completed this in 1944 and named it Mark I. This machine performed a multiplication and division at an average of about four and eleven seconds respectively. The results were printed at a rate of one result per five seconds.

### ENIAC

The World War II also produced a large need for computer capacity especially for the military. New weapons were made for which trajectory tables and other essential data were needed. In 1942, Professors

*John P. Eckert* and *John W. Mauchly* at the Moore School of Engineering of the University of Pennsylvania, USA, decoded to build a high speed computer to do the job. This was called the Electronic Numeric Integrator and Calculator (ENIAC).

It used 18,000 vacuum tubes, about 1,800 square feet of floor space, and consumed about 180,000 watts of electrical power. It had punched cards I/O and its programmes were wired on boards.

ENIAC is accepted as the first successful high-speed electronic digital computer and was used from 1946 to 1955.

**EDVAC**

Fascinated by the success of ENIAC, *John Von Neumann*, a mathematician, undertook an abstract study of computation in 1945. In this he aimed to show that a computer should be able to execute any kind of computation by means of a proper programmed control. His ideas, referred to as 'stored programme technique', became essential for future generations of high-speed digital computers and were universally accepted. The basic idea behind the stored programme concept was that data as well as instructions can be stored in the computer's memory to enable automatic flow of operations.

Between 1947 and 1950, the More School personnel and the Ballistics Research Laboratory of the US army built a computer named Electronic Discrete Variable Automatic Computer (EDVAC), which was based on Von Neumann's concept of stored programme.

**UNIVAC**

The Universal Automatic Computer (UNIVAC), developed in 1951, was the first digital computer to be produced and was installed in the Census Bureau.

The first-generation stored-programme computers needed a lot of maintenance, reached 70per cent to 80per cent reliability of operations and were used for almost 10 years. EDVAC and UNIVAC fell into this group of computers and were the first commercially available computers.

## Computer Generations

Generation' in computer terminology is a 'step' ahead in technology. As you go through the history of evolution of computers, you will find that the earliest computers were big in size, consumed a lot of power and heated up quickly, due to which it had to be shut down, frequently to be cooled. They were very expensive in terms of development and maintenance.

As technology improved, computers became compact, faster and more powerful. From a user's perspective, they become user friendly and more affordable. This has largely contributed towards the popularity that computers have gained these days.

The term 'generation' was earlier used only to distinguish between varying hardware technologies but was later extended to include both hardware and software. A comparison of generations is made below.

### First Generation Computers (1940 to 1956)

The first generation of computers was characterized by vacuum tubes in the circuitry and magnetic drums for memory.

These computers were enormous in size, used great deal of electricity and were expensive to operate. They also had limited storage capacity.

First generation computers relied on machine language (binary-coded programme) to perform operations and could solve only one problem at a time. Punched cards and paper tapes were used to input data and instructions, and output was displayed on printouts.

Early computers like ENIAC, EDVAC and UNIVAC can all be classified as first generation computers.

### Second Generation Computers (1956 to 1963)

In the early 1950s, the discoveries of Transistor and Magnetic core memory changed the image of computers – from unreliable to highly reliable machines with increased capability, and higher storage capacity.

The transistor was far superior to the vacuum tube, allowing computers to become smaller in size, cheaper, reliable and more energy efficient. Though transistor still generated a great deal of heat, it was a substantial improvement over the vacuum tube.

Second generation of computers was also characterized by allowing programmers to specify instructions in symbolic (or assembly) language rather than cryptic binary machine language. High level programming languages like COmmon Business Oriented Language (COBOL) and FORmula TRANslation (FORTRAN) were also being developed at this time.

Due to the increase in the cost of expanding programming, these machines were expensive to purchase and operate. Such computers were, therefore, mostly found in large computer centres or government/private laboratories with many programmers and support professionals.

**Third Generation Computers (1964 to 1971)**

The development of Integrated Circuit by *Jack Kilby,* an engineer with Texas Instruments, in 1958, was the hallmark of the third generation of computers. Punched cards and printouts gave way to devices like keyboards and monitors making it easier for the user to interact with the computer. Computer manufacturers could provide a range of accessories like the cathode ray tube display devices, page printers, consoles etc.

Existence of an operating system allowed the device to run various applications at one time with the central programme monitoring the memory.

For the first time, computers were being widely used in business for areas like:

- Accounting
- Payroll

- Billing
- Tracking Inventory, etc.

Third generation computers were substantially smaller and cheaper than their predecessors.

Fourth Generation Computers (1971 to present)

The trend in 1970s was to move from single-purpose but powerful computers towards cheaper computer systems that could support a large range of applications.

A new revolution in computer hardware came about which could shrink the computer logic circuitry and its components using the Large Scale Integration (LSI) technology. Hundreds of components could now fit onto a single chip!

**Fig.** IC Chips

**Fig.** Intel Pentium Microprocessor Chip

In the 1980s, Very Large Scale Integration (VLSI) squeezed hundreds of thousands of components onto a single chip. This shrinking trend continued and led to the introduction of personal computers (PCs) – programmable machines that are small enough and inexpensive so that these can be purchased and used by individuals. Companies like Apple Computers and IBM introduced very successful PCs.

The IC technology was not only used to construct the processor, but also for the construction of memory. The first memory chip was constructed in 1970 and could hold 256 bits.

**Fifth Generation Computers (the Road Ahead)**

The fifth generation of computers characterized by artificial intelligence is in the process of development. The goal here is to develop devices that are capable of learning and responding to natural language input. This generation of computers is using new technologies in very large scale integration, along with new programming languages and will be capable of amazing feats, in the area of artificial intelligence, such as voice recognition.

What unique features classify computers into different generations?

## COMPONENTS OF A COMPUTER

The computer system essentially comprises three important parts – input device, central processing unit (CPU) and the output device. The CPU itself is made of three components namely, the arithmetic logic unit (ALU), memory unit, and the control unit.

In addition to these, auxiliary storage/secondary storage devices are used to store data and instructions on a long-term basis.

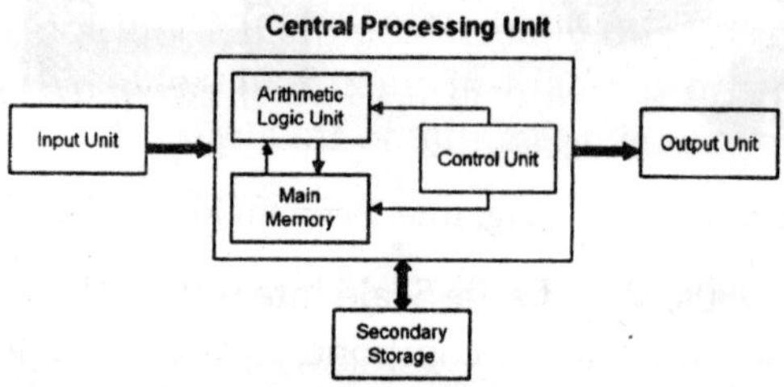


**Fig.** Schematic Representation of a Computer

### Input Unit

Data and instructions must be entered into the computer system for processing, and results obtained from computations must be displayed or recorded for the user. The input device serves the purpose of receiving data and instructions in a form that can be understood by the computer.

### Central Processing Unit

Data and instructions (programmes) are stored in the computer's memory after which all the major calculations and computations are carried out within the CPU. The CPU is also responsible for controlling the operations of various units of the computer system.

**Arithmetic Logic Unit (ALU)**

All calculations and comparisons, based on the instructions provided, are carried out within the ALU. It performs arithmetic functions like addition, subtraction, multiplication, division and also logical operations like greater than, less than and equal to.

**Main Memory**

The main memory holds data and instructions after input, till they are needed. It also holds the processed results that are awaiting output.

***Control***

The function of the control unit is to execute the instructions of a programme, one by one, in the desired sequence. It interprets each instruction and then prompts its execution by one of the units like input, output, ALU, storage.

For example, a comparison of two numbers (a logical operation) to be performed by the ALU may require loading the two numbers into the main memory which is a function performed by the control unit. It will then pass on the execution of the 'compare' function to the ALU.

**Output Unit**

The processed data, stored in the memory of the computer is sent to the output unit, which then converts it into a form that can be understood by the user. The output is usually produced in one of the two ways – on the display device, or on paper (hard copy).

**Secondary Storage**

Also termed as 'auxiliary' or 'backup' storage, it is typically used as a supplement to main storage. It is much cheaper than the main storage and stores large amount of data and instructions permanently. Hardware devices like magnetic tapes and disks fall under this category.

## HARDWARE VS SOFTWARE

The electrical, electronic, mechanical and magnetic components that make up the computer system are together termed as 'hardware'. These include components that are responsible for user input, display and mathematical processing. The CPU, disk drives, internal chips and wiring, modem, peripheral devices like the monitor, keyboard, mouse, printer, speakers etc. are together termed as computer hardware.

Computer hardware cannot perform any manipulation or calculation without being instructed as to what to do and how to do it. Programmes (or instructions) are required to tell the computer what to do. The generic term for computer programmes is 'software'. Software comes in two main types – system software and application programmes.

## SYSTEM VS APPLICATIONS SOFTWARE

System software consists of programmes that control the operations of the computer system itself. It consists of a group of programmes that control the operations of a computer equipment including functions like managing memory, managing peripherals, loading, storing, and is an interface between the application programmes and the computer. MS DOS (Microsoft's Disk Operating System), UNIX are examples of system software.

Software that can perform a specific task for the user, such as word processing, accounting, budgeting or payroll, fall under the category of application software. Such programmes run on top of an operating system (like Windows, UNIX, Linux, Macintosh) and are used to carry out specific functions. Word processors, spreadsheets, database management systems are all examples of general purpose application programmes.

## BITS AND BYTES

All information in the computer is handled using electrical components like the integrated circuits, semiconductors, all of which can recognize only two states – presence or absence of an electrical signal. Two symbols used to represent these two states are 0 and 1, and are known as BITS (an abbreviation for BInary DigiTS). 0 represents the absence of a signal, 1 represents the presence of a signal. A BIT is, therefore, the smallest unit of data in a computer and can either store a 0 or 1.

Since a single bit can store only one of the two values, there can possibly be only four unique combinations:

00 01 10 11

Bits are, therefore, combined together into larger units in order to hold greater range of values.

BYTES are typically a sequence of eight bits put together to create a single computer alphabetical or numerical character. More often referred to in larger multiples, bytes may appear as Kilobytes (1,024 bytes), Megabytes (1,048,576 bytes), Giga Bytes (1,073,741,824), TeraBytes (approx. 1,099,511,000,000 bytes), or PetaBytes (approx. 1,125,899,900, 000,000 bytes).

Bytes are used to quantify the amount of data digitally stored (on disks, tapes) or transmitted (over the internet), and are also used to measure the memory and document size.

State TRUE or FALSE

(a) All code or data is stored and processed in computers using two symbols – 0 and 1.

(b) A 'Byte' is a group of four bits and is often used to store characters.

**INPUT AND OUTPUT DEVICES**

The computer will be of no use unless it is able to communicate with the outside world. Input/Output devices are required for users to communicate with the computer. In simple terms, input devices bring information INTO the computer and output devices bring information OUT of a computer system. These input/output devices are also known as peripherals since they surround the CPU and memory of a computer system.

Some commonly used Input/Output devices are listed in table below.

| Input Devices | Output Devices |
|---|---|
| | Keyboard |
| | Mouse |
| | Joystick |
| | Scanner |
| | Light Pen |
| | Touch Screen Monitor |
| | LCD |
| | Printer |
| | Plotter |

## INPUT DEVICES

### Keyboard

It is a text base input device that allows the user to input alphabets, numbers and other characters. It consists of a set of keys mounted on a board.

**Fig.** Qwerty Keyboard Layout

#### *Alphanumeric Keypad*

It consists of keys for English alphabets, 0 to 9 numbers, and special characters like + - / * () etc.

#### *Function Keys*

There are twelve function keys labeled F1, F2, F3, ..., F12. The functions assigned to these keys differ from one software package to another. These keys are also user programmable keys.

## Special-function Keys

These keys have special functions assigned to them and can be used only for those specific purposes. Functions of some of the important keys are defined below.

### Enter

It is similar to the 'return' key of the typewriter and is used to execute a command or programme.

### Spacebar

It is used to enter a space at the current cursor location.

### Backspace

This key is used to move the cursor one position to the left and also delete the character in that position.

### Delete

It is used to delete the character at the cursor position.

### Insert

Insert key is used to toggle between insert and overwrite mode during data entry.

### Shift

This key is used to type capital letters when pressed along with an alphabet key. Also used to type the special characters located on the upper-side of a key that has two characters defined on the same key.

### Caps Lock

Cap Lock is used to toggle between the capital lock feature. When 'on', it locks the alphanumeric keypad for capital letters input only.

### Tab

Tab is used to move the cursor to the next tab position defined in the document. Also, it is used to insert indentation into a document.

**Ctrl**

Control key is used in conjunction with other keys to provide additional functionality on the keyboard.

**Alt**

Also like the control key, Alt key is always used in combination with other keys to perform specific tasks.

**Esc**

This key is usually used to negate a command. Also used to cancel or abort executing programmes.

**Numeric Keypad**

Numeric keypad is located on the right side of the keyboard and consists of keys having numbers (0 to 9) and mathematical operators (+ - * /) defined on them. This keypad is provided to support quick entry for numeric data.

**Cursor Movement Keys**

These are arrow keys and are used to move the cursor in the direction indicated by the arrow (up, down, left, right).

**MOUSE**

The mouse is a small device used to point to a particular place on the screen and select in order to perform one or more actions. It can be used to select menu commands, size windows, start programmes etc.

The most conventional kind of mouse has two buttons on top: the left one being used most frequently.

**Fig. Mouse**

### *Mouse Actions*

Left Click: Used to select an item.

Double Click: Used to start a programme or open a file.

Right Click: Usually used to display a set of commands.

Drag and Drop: It allows you to select and move an item from one location to another. To achieve this place the cursor over an item on the screen, click the left mouse button and while holding the button down move the cursor to where you want to place the item, and then release it.

## Joystick

The joystick is a vertical stick which moves the graphic cursor in a direction the stick is moved. It typically has a button on top that is used to select the option pointed by the cursor. Joystick is used as an input device primarily used with video games, training simulators and controlling robots.

**Fig.** Joystick

## Scanner

Scanner is an input device used for direct data entry from the source document into the computer system. It converts the document image into digital form so that it can be fed into the computer. Capturing information like this reduces the possibility of errors typically experienced during large data entry.

Fig. A Flat-bed Scanner

Hand-held scanners are commonly seen in big stores to scan codes and price information for each of the items.

**Light Pen**

It is a pen shaped device used to select objects on a display screen. It is quite like the mouse (in its functionality) but uses a light pen to move the pointer and select any object on the screen by pointing to the object.

Users of Computer Aided Design (CAD) applications commonly use the light pens to directly draw on screen.

**Touch Screen**

It allows the user to operate/make selections by simply touching the display screen. Common examples of touch screen include information kiosks, and bank ATMs.

**OUTPUT DEVICES**

***Monitor***

Fig. Monitor

Monitor is an output device that resembles the television screen and uses a Cathode Ray Tube (CRT) to display information. The monitor is associated with a keyboard for manual input of characters and displays the information as it is keyed in. It also displays the programme or application output. Like the television, monitors are also available in different sizes.

### *Liquid Crystal Display (LCD)*

LCD was introduced in the 1970s and is now applied to display terminals also. Its advantages like low energy consumption, smaller and lighter have paved its way for usage in portable computers (laptops).

### *Printer*

Printers are used to produce paper (commonly known as hardcopy) output. Based on the technology used, they can be classified as Impact or Non-impact printers.

Impact printers use the typewriting printing mechanism wherein a hammer strikes the paper through a ribbon in order to produce output. Dot-matrix and Character printers fall under this category.

Non-impact printers do not touch the paper while printing. They use chemical, heat or electrical signals to etch the symbols on paper. Inkjet, Deskjet, Laser, Thermal printers fall under this category of printers.

Fig. An Inkjet Printer

When we talk about printers we refer to two basic qualities associated with printers: resolution, and speed. Print resolution is measured in terms of number of dots per inch (dpi). Print speed is measured in terms of number of characters printed in a unit of time and is represented as characters-per-second (cps), lines-per-minute (lpm), or pages-per-minute (ppm).

### *Plotter*

Plotters are used to print graphical output on paper. It interprets computer commands and makes line drawings on paper using multicoloured automated pens. It is capable of producing graphs, drawings, charts, maps etc.

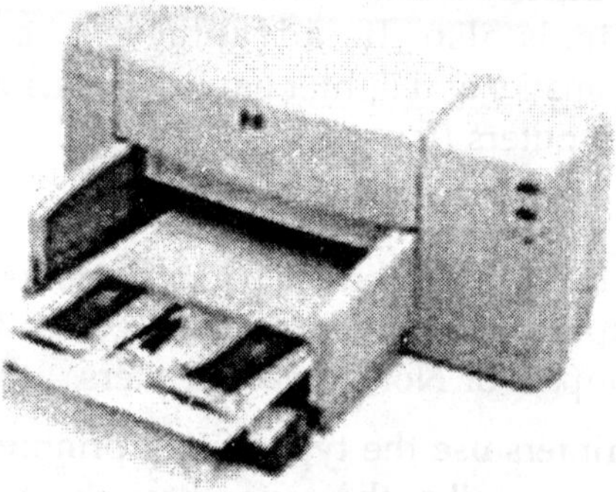

**Fig.** A Flatbed Plotter

Computer Aided Engineering (CAE) applications like CAD (Computer Aided Design) and CAM (Computer Aided Manufacturing) are typical usage areas for plotters.

### RAM/ROM

Computer's memory can be classified into two types – RAM and ROM.

RAM or Random Access Memory is the central storage unit in a computer system. It is the place in a computer where the operating system, application programmes and the data in current use are kept temporarily so that they can be accessed by the computer's processor. The more RAM a computer has, the more data a computer can manipulate.

Random access memory, also called the Read/Write memory, is the temporary memory of a computer. It is said to be 'volatile' since its contents are accessible only as long as the computer is on. The contents of RAM are cleared once the computer is turned off.

ROM or Read Only Memory is a special type of memory which can only be read and contents of which are not lost even when the computer is switched off. It typically contains manufacturer's instructions. Among other things, ROM also stores an initial programme called the 'bootstrap loader' whose function is to start the computer software operating, once the power is turned on.

Read-only memories can be manufacturer-programmed or user-programmed. While manufacturer-programmed ROMs have data burnt into the circuitry, user-programmed ROMs can have the user load and then store read-only programmes. PROM or Programmable ROM is the name given to such ROMs.

Information once stored on the ROM or PROM chip cannot be altered. However, another type of memory called EPROM (Erasable PROM) allows a user to erase the information stored on the chip and reprogram it with new information. EEPROM (Electrically EPROM) and UVEPROM are two types of EPROMs.

## SECONDARY STORAGE DEVICES

RAM is volatile memory having a limited storage capacity. Secondary/auxiliary storage is storage other than the RAM. These include devices that are peripheral and are connected and controlled by the computer to enable permanent storage of programmes and data.

Magnetic medium was found to be fairly inexpensive and long lasting medium and, therefore, became the preferred choice for auxiliary storage. Floppy disks and hard disks fall under this category. The newer forms of storage devices are optical storage devices like CDs, DVDs, Pen drive, Zip drive etc.

### Floppy Disk

These are small removable disks that are plastic coated with magnetic recording material. Floppy disks are typically

$3.5^2$ in size (diameter) and can hold 1.44 MB of data. This portable storage device is a rewritable media and can be reused a number of times.

Floppy disks are commonly used to move files between different computers. The main disadvantage of floppy disks is that they can be damaged easily and, therefore, are not very reliable.

### Hard Disk

Hard disks are made up of rigid material and are usually a stack of metal disks sealed in a box. The hard disk and the hard disk drive exist together as a unit and are a permanent part of the computer where data and programmes are saved. These disks have storage capacities ranging from 1GB to 80 GB and more. Hard disks are also rewritable and are more reliable when compared with floppies.

**Fig. A Floppy Disk**

**Fig. A Winchester Disk**

Depending on the way they are packaged, hard disks can be classified as Disk packs or Winchester disks. Disk packs are removable, in the sense that they can be removed and kept offline when not in use. They must be mounted on the disk drive before use. Winchester disks on the other hand, consist of disk platters sealed in a contamination-free container and form a permanent component of the computer.

### CD

Cmpact Disk (CD) is portable disk having data storage capacity between 650-700 MB. It can hold large amount of information such as music,

full-motion videos, and text etc. It contains digital information that can be read, but cannot be rewritten. Separate drives exist for reading and writing CDs.

Since it is a very reliable storage media, it is very often used as a medium for distributing large amount of information to large number of users. In fact today most of the software is distributed through CDs.

### DVD

Digital Versatile Disk (DVD) is similar to a CD but has larger storage capacity and enormous clarity. Depending upon the disk type it can store several Gigabytes of data (as opposed to around 650MB of a CD). DVDs are primarily used to store music or movies and can be played back on your television or the computer too. They are not rewritable media.

Chapter 2

# Fundamentals of Computer

Richard Hamming, a former researcher at Bell Labs, once observed that a change of an order of magnitude in quantity causes a change in quality. A racing car that can go 1000 km/hour in the Nevada desert is a fundamentally different machine than a normal car that goes 100 km/hour on a highway. Similarly, a 100-story skyscraper is not just a scaled up 10-story apartment building. So, too, with computers.

| Type | Price | Example Application |
|---|---|---|
| Disposable computer | 1 | Greeting cards |
| Embedded computer | 10 | Watches, toys, appliances |
| Palmtop computer | 100 | Home video games, PDA |
| Personal computer | 1K | Desktop or laptop computer |
| Server or workstation | 10K | Network server, professional use |
| Workstation clusters | 100K | Departmental mini-supercomputers |
| Mainframe computer | 1M | Batch data processing in a bank |
| Supercomputer | 10M | Weather prediction |

## DISPOSABLE COMPUTER

Single chips, perhaps glued to the inside of greeting cards, play tunes such as "Happy Birthday" or "Here Comes the Bride".

## SMART CARDS

A smart card is a credit-card sized plastic card with an embedded computer chip. The chip can either be a microprocessor with internal memory or a memory chip with non-programmable logic. The chip connection is either via direct physical contact or remotely via a contactless electromagnetic interface.

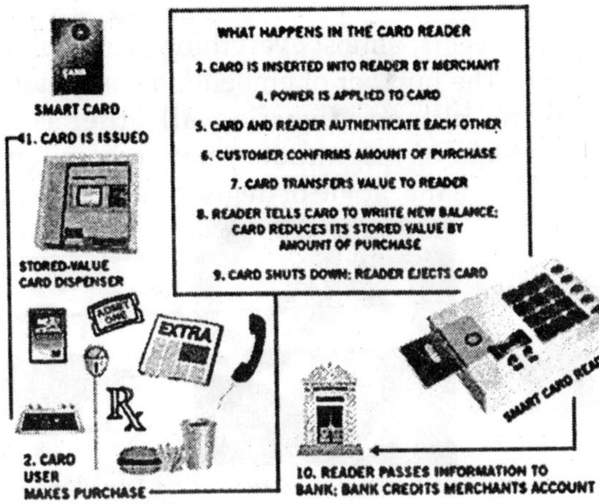


## ACTIVE BADGES

The Active Badge system provides a means of locating individuals within a building by determining the location of their Active Badge. This small device worn by personnel transmits a unique infra-red signal every 10 seconds.

## EMBEDDED COMPUTERS

Computers embedded inside telephones, microwave ovens, cameras, CD players, toys, dolls, and a thousand other devices.

Within a few years, almost everything electrical will have a computer in it. The number of embedded computers will be measured in the billons, dwarfing all other computers combined by orders of magnitude. These computers hold a processor, less than a megabyte of memory, and I/O capability.

ABS Computer

Airbag computer

Digital camera

## PALMTOP COMPUTERS

Computers the size of a credit card, cell-phone, or calculator. Portable digital assistants, limited graphical display.

These systems typically contain a few megabytes of memory, a small display, and a touch sensitive input area or limited keyboard.

## PERSONAL COMPUTERS

Personal computers, including both desktop and notebook devices, that are most associated with the word computer.

Personal computers come with many megabytes of memory, hard disks in the gigabytes, DVD or CD drives, keyboard, pointing devices, full-size display, multimedia, and communication devices.

## SERVER OR WORKSTATION

High-performance computers, often with multiple processors, with gigabytes of memory, terabytes of disk space, and high-speed networking capability.

The Sun Ultra™ 80 workstation brings multiprocessing power, industry-standard PCI I/O, and dual-UPA graphics capability to the desktop. This next-generation workstation uses the processing power of UltraSPARC™ -II processors, PGX32™ and Sun Elite3D and Expert3D graphics technology, UltraSCSI disks, and the innovative high-performance peripheral component interconnect (PCI) I/O bus. With the tower system enclosure, Sun Ultra 80 workstation provides all the modular and expandable features that users have grown to expect from Sun Workstation™ systems. Sun's commitment to high-performance computing means the Ultra 80 workstation delivers increasing levels of performance and preserves 100 percent binary compatibility with application software.

## WORKSTATION CLUSTERS

Standard workstations connected by advanced networks, and running special software that allow all the machines to work together on a single problem or application.

Included here are "farms" of network servers, graphics rendering machines, and enterprise-support systems.

Clusters scale easily from a handful of machines to thousands of them.

**Avalon**

Avalon is a 140 processor Alpha Beowulf cluster constructed entirely from commodity personal computer technology. It is a co-operative venture of the Los Alamos National Laboratory Centre for Nonlinear Studies and Theoretical Division.

## MAINFRAMES

Room-size computers with massive storage systems, extensive I/O capability, and capable of handing enormous numbers of transactions.

These are the direct descendants of the corporate computing facilities first acquired decades ago. While extremely expensive, they are often kept running because of the enormous investment in software, data, operating procedures, and personnel that they represent.

Mainframes are notorious as the source of the Year 2000 problems caused by COBOL or FORTRAN programmes written in the 1960s and 1970s by programmers who never envisioned their software lasting three or four decades.

### UNISYS ES7000 SERVER

A CMP-based ES7000 contains numerous "cells" to form a powerful, reliable, agile, and cost-effective Intel® mainframe. These cells can be configured flexibly to create a server with:

- as many as 32 CPUs
- 4 crossbar intra-connects
- 256MB of third-level cache
- 64GB of memory
- 96 PCI adapters

with partitions running up to eight operating systems

**Supercomputers**

Supercomputers have extremely fast CPUs, disks and networks. Typically they are highly parallel machines, similar to workstation clusters, but with faster components and specialized processors.

Supercomputers are used to solve computationally intensive problems in science and engineering, such as modeling climate systems, modeling fluid-flow systems such as aircraft structures, synthesizing new molecules for medical or genetic studies, and simulating large economics systems.

**Ohio Supercomputer Centre**

The CRAY SV1 computer system at the Ohio Supercomputer Centre (OSC) is a powerful parallel vector processor (PVP) super-computer that features 16 (500 MHz) vector processors and 32 Gbytes of physical RAM for large memory jobs. Serial jobs, auto-tasked and parallel jobs are scheduled on the 16 single streaming processors (SSP). Four of the SV1 SSP processors can be combined into one multi-streaming processor (MSP). Multi-streaming is a feature that automatically divides loop iterations among the four CPUs. You may get speedup factors of up to four on loops to which this technique can be applied.

Chapter 3

# Operating Systems

## OPERATING SYSTEMS I

A batch system is one in which jobs are bundled together with the instructions necessary to allow them to be processed without intervention.

Often jobs of a similar nature can be bundled together to further increase economy

The basic physical layout of the memory of a batch job computer is shown below:

Monitor (permanently resident)

User Space

(compilers, programmes, data, etc.)

The monitor is system software that is responsible for interpreting and carrying out the instructions in the batch jobs. When the monitor started a job, it handed over control of the entire computer to the job, which then controlled the computer until it finished.

A sample of several batch jobs might look like:

```
JOB user_spec        ; identify the user for accounting purposes
FORTRAN              ; load the FORTRAN compiler
ource programme cards
LOAD                 ; load the compiled programme
RUN                  ; run the programme
```

```
Data cards
EOJ                 ; end of job
JOB user_spec       ; identify a new user
LOAD application
RUN
data
EOJ
```

Often magnetic tapes and drums were used to store intermediate data and compiled programmes.

1. Advantages of batch systems
   - a Move much of the work of the operator to the computer
   - b Increased performance since it was possible for job to start as soon as the previous job finished
2. Disadvantages
   - a turn-around time can be large from user standpoint
   - b more difficult to debug programme
   - c due to lack of protection scheme, one batch job can affect pending jobs (read too many cards, etc)
   - d a job could corrupt the monitor, thus affecting pending jobs
   - e a job could enter an infinite loop

As mentioned above, one of the major shortcomings of early batch systems was that there was no protection scheme to prevent one job from adversely affecting other jobs.

The solution to this was a simple protection scheme, where certain memory (e.g. where the monitor resides) were made off-limits to user programmes. This prevented user programmes from corrupting the monitor.

To keep user programmes from reading too many (or not enough) cards, the hardware was changed to allow the computer to operate in one of two modes: one for the monitor and one for the user programmes. IO could only be performed in monitor mode, so that IO requests from the user programmes were passed to the monitor. In this way, the monitor could keep a job from reading past it's on $EOJ card.

To prevent an infinite loop, a timer was added to the system and the $JOB card was modified so that a maximum execution time for the job was passed to the monitor. The computer would interrupt the job and return control to the monitor when this time was exceeded.

## SPOOLING BATCH SYSTEMS

One difficulty with simple batch systems is that the computer still needs to read the the deck of cards before it can begin to execute the job. This means that the CPU is idle (or nearly so) during these relatively slow operations.

Since it is faster to read from a magnetic tape than from a deck of cards, it became common for computer centres to have one or more less powerful computers in addition to there main computer. The smaller computers were used to read a decks of cards onto a tape, so that the tape would contain many batch jobs. This tape was then loaded on the main computer and the jobs on the tape were executed. The output from the jobs would be written to another tape which would then be removed and loaded on a less powerful computer to produce any hardcopy or other desired output.

It was a logical extension of the timer idea described above to have a timer that would only let jobs execute for a short time before interrupting them so that the monitor could start an IO operation. Since the IO operation could proceed while the CPU was crunching on a user programme, little degradation in performance was noticed.

Since the computer can now perform IO in parallel with computation, it became possible to have the computer read a deck of cards to a tape, drum or disk and to write out to a tape printer while it was computing. This process is called spooling: Simultaneous Peripheral Operation OnLine.

Spooling batch systems were the first and are the simplest of the multiprogramming systems.

One advantage of spooling batch systems was that the output from jobs was available as soon as the job completed, rather than only after all jobs in the current cycle were finished.

## MULTIPROGRAMMING SYSTEMS

As machines with more and more memory became available, it was possible to extend the idea of multiprogramming (or multiprocessing) as used in spooling batch systems to create systems that would load several jobs into memory at once and cycle through them in some order, working on each one for a specified period of time.

Monitor

(more like a operating system)

User programme 1

User programme 2

User programme 3

User programme 4

At this point the monitor is growing to the point where it begins to resemble a modern operating system. It is responsible for:

- Starting user jobs
- Spooling operations
- IO for user jobs
- Switching between user jobs
- Ensuring proper protection while doing the above

As a simple, yet common example, consider a machine that can run two jobs at once. Further, suppose that one job is IO intensive and that the other is CPU intensive. One way for the monitor to allocate CPU time between these jobs would be to divide time equally between them. However, the CPU would be idle much of the time the IO bound process was executing.

A good solution in this case is to allow the CPU bound process (the background job) to execute until the IO bound process (the foreground job) needs some CPU time, at which point the monitor permits it to run. Presumably it will soon need to do some IO and the monitor can return the CPU to the background job.

## TIMESHARING SYSTEMS

Back in the days of the "bare" computers without any operating system to speak of, the programmer had complete access to the machine. As hardware and software was developed to create monitors, simple and spooling batch systems and finally multiprogrammed systems, the separation between the user and the computer became more and more pronounced.

Users, and programmers in particular, longed to be able to "get to the machine" without having to go through the batch process. In the 1970s and especially in the 1980s this became possible two different ways.

The first involved timesharing or timeslicing. The idea of multiprogramming was extended to allow for multiple terminals to be connected to the computer, with each in-use terminal being associated with one or more jobs on the computer. The operating system is responsible for switching between the jobs, now often called processes, in such a way that favoured user interaction. If the context-switches occurred quickly enough, the user had the impression that he or she had direct access to the computer.

Interactive processes are given a higher priority so that when IO is requested (e.g. a key is pressed), the associated process is quickly given control of the CPU so that it can process it. This is usually done through the use of an interrupt that causes the computer to realise that an IO event has occurred.

It should be mentioned that there are several different types of time sharing systems. One type is represented by computers like our VAX/VMS computers and UNIX workstations. In these computers entire processes are in memory (albeit virtual memory) and the computer switches between executing code in each of them. In other types of systems, such as airline reservation systems, a single application may actually do much of the timesharing between terminals. This way there does not need to be a different running programme associated with each terminal.

## PERSONAL COMPUTERS

The second way that programmers and users got back at the machine was the advent of personal computers around 1980. Finally computers became small enough and inexpensive enough that an individual could own one, and hence have complete access to it.

## REAL-TIME, MULTIPROCESSOR, AND DISTRIBUTED/NETWORKED SYSTEMS

A real-time computer is one that execute programmes that are guaranteed to have an upper bound on tasks that they carry out. Usually it is desired that the upper bound be very small. Examples included guided missile systems and medical monitoring equipment. The operating system on real-time computers is severely constrained by the timing requirements.

Dedicated computers are special purpose computers that are used to perform only one or more tasks. Often these are real-time computers and include applications such as the guided missile mentioned above and the computer in modern cars that controls the fuel injection system.

A multiprocessor computer is one with more than one CPU. The category of multiprocessor computers can be divided into the following sub-categories:

- Shared memory multiprocessors have multiple CPUs, all with access to the same memory. Communication between the the processors is easy to implement, but care must be taken so that memory accesses are synchronized.
- Distributed memory multiprocessors also have multiple CPUs, but each CPU has it's own associated memory. Here, memory access synchronization is not

a problem, but communication between the processors is often slow and complicated.

**Related to Multiprocessors are the Following:**

- Networked systems consist of multiple computers that are networked together, usually with a common operating system and shared resources. Users, however, are aware of the different computers that make up the system.
- Distributed systems also consist of multiple computers but differ from networked systems in that the multiple computers are transparent to the user. Often there are redundant resources and a sharing of the workload among the different computers, but this is all transparent to the user.

## UNIX OPERATING SYSTEM OVERVIEW

UNIX was developed at Bell Labs in the early 1970s. The first version was written by Ken Thompson in assembler for the PDP- 7 minicomputer. This was soon followed by a version for the PDP-ll, written in a new language called C that was devised and implemented by Dennis Ritchie. In 1974, Ritchie and Thompson published a landmark paper about UNIX (Ritchie and Thompson, 1974). For the work described in this paper they were later given the prestigious ACM Turing Award (Ritchie, 1984; Thompson, 1984). The publication of this paper stimulated many universities to ask Bell Labs for a copy of UNIX. Since Bell Labs' parent company, AT&T, was a regulated monopoly at the time and was not permitted to be in the computer business, it had no objection to licensing UNIX to universities for a modest fee.

In one of those coincidences that often shape history, the PDP-11 was the computer of choice at nearly all university computer science departments, and the operating systems that came with the PDP-l1 were widely regarded as being dreadful by professors and students alike. UNIX quickly filled the void, not in the least because it was supplied with the complete source code, so people could, and did, tinker with it endlessly.

One of the many universities that acquired UNIX early on was the University of California at Berkeley. Because the complete source code was available, Berkeley was able to modify the system substantially. Foremost among the changes was a port to the V AX minicomputer and the addition of paged virtual memory, the extension of file names from 14 characters to 255 characters, and the inclusion of the TCP/IP networking protocol, which is now used on the Internet (largely due to the fact that it was in Berkeley UNIX).

While Berkeley was making all these changes, AT&T itself continued to develop UNIX, leading to System III in 1982 and then System V in 1984. By the late 1980s, two different, and quite incompatible, versions of UNIX were in widespread use: Berkeley UNIX and System V. This split in the UNIX world, together with the fact that there were no standards for binary programme formats, greatly inhibited the commercial success of UNIX because it was impossible for software vendors to write and package UNIX programmes with the expectation that they would run on any UNIX system (as was routinely done with MS-DOS). After much bickering, a standard called POSIX (Portable Operating System-IX) was created by the IEEE Standards Board. POSIX is also known by its IEEE Standards number, PlO03. It later became an International Standard.

The POSIX standard is divided into many parts, each covering a different area of UNIX. The first part, PlO03.l, defines the system calls; the second part, PlO03.2, defines the basic utility programmes, and so on. The PlO03.l standard defines about 60 system calls that all conformant systems must support. These are the basic calls for reading and writing files, creating new processes, and so on. Nearly all UNIX systems now support the PlO03.l system calls. However many UNIX systems also support extra system calls, especially those defined by System V and/or those in Berkeley UNIX. Typically these add up to perhaps 100 system calls to the POSIX set. The operating system for the UltraSPARC II is based on System V and is called Solaris. It also supports many of the Berkeley system calls.

A rough breakdown of the Solaris system calls by category is given in Fig. 629. The file and directory management system calls are largest and the most important categories. Most of these come from PIO03.l. A relatively large fraction of the others are derived from System V.

| Category | Some examples |
|---|---|
| File management | Open, read, write, close, and lock files |
| Directory management | Create and delete directories; move files around |
| Process management | Spawn, terminate, trace, and signal processes |
| Memory management | Share memory among processes; protect pages |
| Getting/setting parameters | Get user, group, process ID; set priority |
| Dates and times | Set file access times; use interval timer; profile execution |
| Networking | Establish/accept connection; send/receive message |
| Miscellaneous | Enable accounting; manipulate disk quotas; reboot the system |

One area that is largely due to Berkeley UNIX rather than System V is networking. Berkeley invented the concept of a socket, which is the endpoint of a network connection. The four-pin wall plugs to which telephones can be connected served as the model for this concept. It is possible for a UNIX process to create a socket, attach to it, and establish a connection to a socket on a distant machine. Over this connection it can then exchange data in both directions, typically using the TCP/IP protocol. Since networking technology has been in UNIX for decades and is very stable and mature, a substantial fraction of the servers on the Internet run UNIX.

Since there are many implementations of UNIX, it is difficult to say much about the structure of the operating system since everyone is somewhat different from all the others. However, in general, Fig. 6-30 applies to most of them. At the bottom, there is a layer of device drivers that shield the file system from the bare hardware. Originally, each device driver was written as an independent entity, separate from all the others. This arrangement led to a lot of duplicated effort, since many drivers must deal with flow control, error handling, priorities, separating data from control, and so on. This observation led Dennis Ritchie to develop a framework called streams for writing drivers in a modular way. With a stream, it is possible to establish a two-way connection from a user process to a hardware device and to insert one or more modules along the path. The user process pushes data into the stream, which then is processed or transformed by each module until it gets to the hardware. The inverse processing occurs for incoming data.

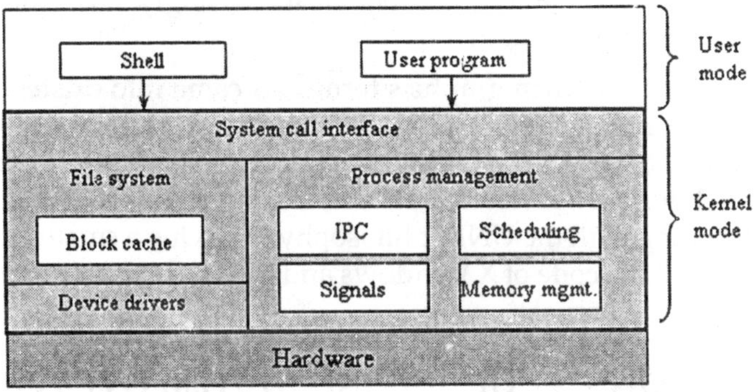


**Figure.** The structure of a typical UNIX system.

On top of the device drivers comes the file system. It manages file names, directories, disk block allocation, protection, and much more. Part of the file system is a block cache, for holding the blocks most recently read in from disk, in case they are needed again soon. A variety of file systems have been used over the years, including the Berkeley fast file system.

The other part of the UNIX kernel is the process management portion. Among its various other functions, it handles IPC (InterProcess Communication), which allows processes to communicate with one another and synchronize to avoid race conditions. A variety of mechanisms are provided. The process management code also handles process scheduling, which is based on priorities. Signals, which are a form of (asynchronous) software interrupt, are also managed here. Finally, memory management is done here as well. Most UNIX systems support demandpaged virtual memory, sometimes with a few extra features, such as the ability of multiple processes to share common regions of address space.

From its inception, UNIX has tried to be a small system, in order to enhance reliability and performance. The first versions of UNIX were entirely text-based, using terminals that could display 24 or 25 lines of 80 ASCII characters. The user interface was handled by a user-level programme called the shell, which offered a command line interface. Since the shell was not part of the kernel, adding new shells to UNIX was easy, and over time a number of increasingly sophisticated ones were invented.

Later on, when graphics terminals came into existence, a windowing system for UNIX, called X Windows, was developed at M.I.T. Still later, a full-fledged GUI (Graphical User Interface), called Motif, was put on top of X Windows. In keeping with the UNIX philosophy of having a small kernel, nearly all the code of X Windows and Motif runs in user mode, outside the kernel.

## WINDOWS NT OPERATING SYSTEM OVERVIEW

When the original IBM PC was launched in 1981, it came equipped with a 16-bit real-mode, single-user, command-line oriented operating system called MS-DOS 1.0. This operating system consisted of 8 KB of memory resident code. Two years later, a much more powerful 24-KB system, MS-DOS 2.0, appeared. It contained a command line processor (shell), with a number of features borrowed from UNIX. When IBM released the 286-based PC/AT in 1984, it came equipped with MS-DOS 3.0, by now 36 KB. Over the years, MS-DOS continued to acquire new features, but it was still a command-line oriented system.

Inspired by the success of the Apple Macintosh, Microsoft decided to give MS-DOS a graphical user interface that it called Windows. The first three versions of Windows, culminating in Windows 3.x, were not true operating systems, but graphical user interfaces on top of MS-DOS, which was still in control of the machine. All programmes ran in the same address space and a bug in anyone of them could bring the whole system to a grinding halt.

The release of Windows 95 in 1995 still did not eliminate MS-DOS, although it introduced a new version, 7.0. Together, Windows 95 and MS-DOS 7.0 contained most of the features of a full-blown operating system, including virtual memory, process management, and multiprogramming. However, Windows 95 was not a full 32-bit programme. It contained large chunks of old 16-bit code (as well as some 32-bit code) and still used the MS-DOS file system, with nearly all its limitations. The only major change to the file system was the addition of long file names in place of the 8 + 3 character file names allowed in MS-DOS.

Even with the release of Windows 98 in 1998, MS-DOS was still there (now called version 7.1) and running 16-bit code. Although a bit more functionality migrated from the MS-DOS part to the Windows part, and a disk layout suitable for larger disks was now standard, under the hood, Windows 98 was not very different from Windows 95. The main difference was the user interface, which integrated the desktop, the Internet, and television more closely. It was precisely this integration that attracted the attention of the U.S. Dept. of Justice, which then sued Microsoft claiming that it was an illegal monopoly.

While all these developments were going on, Microsoft was also busy with a completely new 32-bit operating system being written from the ground up. This new system was called Windows New Technology, or Windows NT. It was initially hyped as the replacement for all other operating systems for Intel-based PCs, but it was somewhat slow to catch on and was later redirected to the upper end of the market, where it found a niche. It is gradually becoming more popular at the low end as well.

NT is sold in two versions: server and workstation. These two versions are nearly identical and are generated from the same source code. The server version is intended for machines that run as LAN-based file and print servers and has more elaborate management features than the workstation version, which is intended for desktop computing for a single user. The server version has a variant (enterprise) intended for large sites. The various versions are tuned differently, each one optimized for its expected environment. Other than these minor differences, all the versions are essentially the same. In fact, nearly all the executable files are identical for all versions. NT itself discovers which version it is by looking at a variable in an internal data structure (the registry). Users are forbidden by the license from changing this variable and thus converting the (inexpensive) workstation version into the (much more expensive) server or enterprise versions. We will not make any further distinction between these versions.

MS-DOS and all previous versions of Windows were single-user systems. NT, however, supports multiprogramming, so several users can work on the same machine at the same time. For example, a network server may have multiple users logged in simultaneously over a network, each accessing its own files in a protected way.

NT is a true 32-bit multiprogramming operating system. It supports multiple user processes, each of which has a full 32-bit demand-paged virtual address space. In addition, the system itself is written as 32-bit code everywhere.

One of NT's original improvements over Windows 95 was its modular structure. It consisted of a moderately small kernel that ran in kernel mode, plus a number of server processes that ran in user mode. User processes interacted with the server processes using the client-server model: a client sent a request message to a server, and the server did the work and returned the result to the client via a second message. This modular structure made it easier to port it to several computers besides the Intel line, including the DEC Alpha, IBM PowerPC, and SGI MIPS. However, for performance reasons, starting with NT 4.0, pretty much all of the system was put back into the kernel.

One could go on for a long time both about how NT is structured internally and what its system call interface is like.

Since our primary interest here is the virtual machine presented by various operating systems (i.e., the system calls), we will give a brief summary of the system structure and then move on to the system call interface.

The structure of NT is illustrated in Fig. 6-31. It consists of a number of modules that are structured in layers and work together to implement the operating system. Each module has some particular function and a well-defined interface to the other modules. Nearly all the modules are written in C, although part of the graphics device interface is written in C++ and a tiny bit of the lowest layers are written in assembly language.

At the bottom is a thin layer called the hardware abstraction layer. Its job is to present the rest of the operating system with abstract hardware devices, devoid of the warts and idiosyncracies with which real hardware is so richly endowed. Among the devices modeled are off-chip caches, timers, I/O buses, interrupt controllers, and DMA controllers. By exposing these to the rest of the operating system in idealized form, it becomes easier to port NT to other hardware platforms, since most of the modifications required are concentrated in one place. User mode

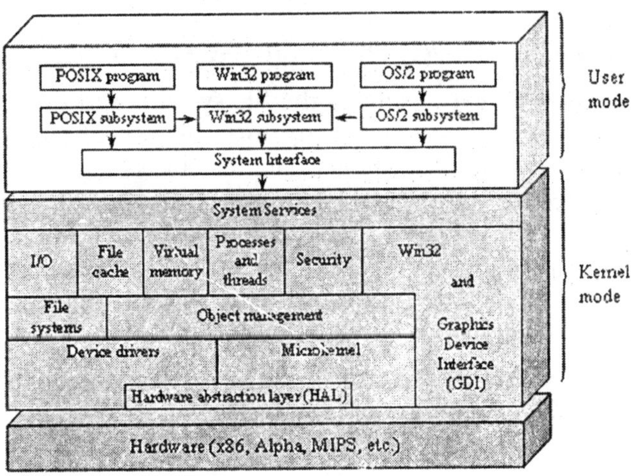


**Figure.** The structure of Windows NT.

Above the hardware abstraction layer is a layer containing the microkernel. and the device =drivers. The microkernel and all the device drivers have direct access to the hardware when needed, as they contain hardware-dependent code.

The microkernel supports the primitive kernel objects, interrupt, trap, and exception handling, process scheduling and synchronization, multiprocessor synchronization, and time management. The purpose of this layer is to make the rest of the operating system completely independent of the hardware, and thus highly portable. The micro kernel is permanently resident in main memory and is not preemptable, although it can temporarily give up control to service I/O interrupts.

Each device driver can control one or more I/O devices, but a device driver can also do things not related to a specific device, such as encrypting a data stream or even just providing access to kernel data structures. Since users can install new device drivers, they have the power to affect the kernel and corrupt the system. For this reason, drivers must be written with great care.

Above the microkernel and device drivers is the upper portion of the operating system, called the executive. The executive is architecture independent and can be ported to new machines with relatively little effort. It consists of three layers.

The lowest layer contains the file systems and the object manager. The file systems support the use of files and directories. The object manager handles objects known to the kernel. These include processes, threads (lightweight processes within an address space), files, directories, semaphores, I/O devices, timers, and many others. It also manages a namespace in which newly created objects can be placed so they can be referred to later.

The next layer consists of six major parts, as shown in Fig. 6-31. The I/O manager provides a framework for managing I/O devices and provides generic I/O services. It uses the services of the file system, which in turn uses the device drivers, as well as the services of the object manager.

The cache manager keeps the most recently used disk blocks in memory to speed up access to them in the (likely) event that they are needed again. Its job is to figure out which blocks are probably going to be needed again and which ones are not. It is possible to configure NT with multiple file systems, in which case the cache manager works for all of them, so each one does not have to do its own cache management. When a block is needed, the cache manager is asked to supply it. If it does not have the block, the cache manager calls upon the appropriate file system to get it. Since files can be mapped into processes' address spaces, the cache manager must interact with the virtual memory manager to provide the necessary consistency.

The virtual memory manager implements NT's demand-paged virtual memory architecture. It manages the mapping of virtual pages onto physical page frames. It thereby enforces the protection rules that restrict each process to only access those pages belonging to its address space and not to other processes' address spaces (except under special circumstances). It also handles certain system calls that relate to virtual memory.

The process and thread manager handles processes and threads, including their creation and destruction. It is concerned about the mechanisms used to manage them, rather than policies about how they are used.

The security manager enforces NT's elaborate security mechanism, which meets the U.S. Dept. of Defence's Orange Book C2 requirements. The Orange Book specifies a large number of rules that a conforming system must meet, starting with authenticated login through how access control is handled to the fact that virtual pages must be zeroed out before being reused.

The graphics device interface handles image management for the monitor and printers. It provides system calls to allow user programmes to write on the monitor or printers in a device-independent way. It also contains the window manager and hardware device drivers. In versions of NT prior to NT

4.0, it was in user space but the performance was disappointing, so Microsoft moved it into the kernel to speed it up. The Win32 module also handles most of the system calls. It, too, was originally in user space but was also moved to the kernel to improve performance.

On the top of the executive is a thin layer called system services. Its function is to provide an interface to the executive. It accepts the true NT system calls and calls other parts of the executive to have them executed.

Outside the kernel are the user programmes and the environmental subsystems. The environmental subsystems are provided because user programmes are not encouraged to make system calls directly (although they are technically capable of it). Instead, each environmental subsystem exports a (different) set of function calls that user programmes can use. Three environmental subsystems are shown in Fig. 6-31: Win32 (for NT or Windows 95/98 programmes), POSIX (for UNIX programmes that have been ported), and OS/2 (for OS/2 programmes that have been ported).

Windows applications use the Win32 functions and communicate with the Win32 subsystem to make system calls. The Win32 subsystem accepts the Win32 function calls and uses the system interface library module to make the necessary true NT system calls to carry them out.

There is also a POSIX subsystem, which provides minimal support for UNIX applications. It supports only the P1003.l functionality and little else. It is a closed subsystem, meaning that its applications cannot use the facilities of the Win32 subsystem, which greatly restricts what they can do. In practice, porting any real UNIX programme to NT using this subsystem is nearly impossible. It was included only because parts of the U.S. government require operating systems for government computers to be PlOO3.1 compliant. This subsystem is not selfcontained so it uses the Win32 subsystem for some of its work, but without exporting the full Win32 interface to its user programmes.

The OS/2 subsystem is similarly limited in functionality and may be dropped in some future release. It also uses the Win32 subsystem. There is also an MS-DOS environmental subsystem (not shown in the figure).

Having looked briefly at the structure of NT, let us now turn to our main subject, the services offered by NT. This interface is the programmer's main connection to the system. Unfortunately, Microsoft has never made the complete list of NT system calls public, and it also changes them from release to release. Under such conditions, writing programmes that make system calls directly is nearly impossible.

What Microsoft has done is define a set of calls called the Win32 API (Application Programming Interface) that are publicly known. These are library procedures that either make system calls to get the work done, or, in some case, do the work right in the user-space library procedure or in the Win32 sub system. The Win32 API calls do not change with new releases, to promote stability. However, there are also NT API calls that may change between releases of NT. Although the Win32 API calls are not all NT system calls, it is better to focus on these here rather than the true NT system calls because the Win32 API calls are well documented and more stable over time.

The Win32 API philosophy is completely different from the UNIX philosophy. In the latter, the system calls are all publicly known and form a minimal interface: removing even one of them would reduce the functionality of the operating system. The Win32 philosophy is to provide a very comprehensive interface, often with three or four ways of doing the same thing, and including many functions that clearly should not be (and are not) system calls, such as an API call to copy an entire file.

Many Win32 API calls create kernel objects of one kind or another, including files, processes, threads, pipes, etc. Every call creating a kernel object returns a result called a handle to the caller. This handle can be subsequently used to perform operations on the object. Handles are specific to the process that created the object referred to by the handle. They cannot be passed directly to another process and used there (just as UNIX file descriptors cannot be passed to other processes and used there). However, under certain circumstances, it is possible to duplicate a handle and pass it to other processes in a protected way, allowing them controlled access to objects belonging to other processes. Every object also has a security descriptor associated with it, telling in detail who may and may not perform what kinds of operations on the object.

NT is sometimes said to be object-oriented because the only way to manipulate kernel objects is by invoking methods (API functions) on their handles. On the other hand, it lacks some of the most basic properties of object-oriented systems such as inheritance and polymorphism.

number of exceptions. For example, Windows 95/98 do not have any security, so those API calls that relate to security just return error codes on Windows 95/98. Also, NT file names use the Unicode character set, which is not available on Windows 95/98.

There are also differences in parameters to some API function calls. On NT, for example, all the screen coordinates given in the graphics functions are true 32-bit numbers; on Windows 95/98, only the low-order 16 bits are used (for backward compatibility with Windows 3.1). The existence of the Win32 API on several different operating systems makes it easier to port programmes between them but also points out more clearly that it is somewhat decoupled from the actual system calls. Some of the differences between Windows 95/98 and NT are summarized in Figure.

| Item | Windows 95/98 | NT 5.0 |
|---|---|---|
| Win32 API? | Yes | Yes |
| Full 32-bit system? | No | Yes |
| Security? | No | Yes |
| Protected file mappings? | No | Yes |
| Private address space for each MS-DOS programme? | No | Yes |
| Plug and play? | Yes | Yes |

| | | |
|---|---|---|
| Unicode? | No | Yes |
| Runs on | Intel 80x86 | 80x86, Alpha |
| Multiprocessor support? | No | Yes |
| Re-entrant code inside aS? | No | Yes |
| Some critical as data writable by user? | Yes | No |

# OPERATING SYSTEMS II

## INTRODUCTION

- The CPU is essentially a glorified calculator;
  - That main-memory is a large collection of 'pigeon-holes' each of which can hold one number; each number can represent:
    - » An actual numeric quantity;
    - » A text character coded as a number;
    - » etc....
    - » An instruction to be executed by the CPU;
- That a disk or other magnetic memory is a place to store:
    - » Pieces of memory that need to be stored after the computer is switched off - non-volatile storage;
    - » Later we will see that a disk can also be used to hold pieces of (main) memory that have got too big for the physically available memory size, i.e. virtual memory on disk.

### Software

Without software, the system in Figure just sits there quietly, doing nothing!. It must be programmed with appropriate software.

Roughly speaking, software can be divided into two categories:

**System Software**

Operating system and utilities;

**Application Software**

e.g. wordprocessing, spreadsheets,..., including user-developed software.

The divide, between system and application, can be somewhat blurred. In general, the more general purpose and *ordinary* the function performed - like copying or deleting files, or compiling or assembling programmes - the closer to system software; the more special purpose - like a database management system - the closer to application category.

Originally, the system software was likely to be developed by the computer *hardware* manufacturer; however, since the 1980s, the PC revolution has turned this on its head. This chapter is concerned primarily with the operating system - which is definitely system software.

## WHAT DOES AN OPERATING SYSTEM DO?

The system software, particularly the operating system, mediates between the user (and the application software) and the hardware. Thus, though in reality (hardware) a disk may be lots of circles with bits (1 or 0) arranged along their circumference, that is very difficult for a programmer or user to handle. For example, instead of clicking on FILE/SAVE, you would have to concoct some machine code to do: 'save the first 128 bytes on circle 22, head 2, sector 4 and save the second 128 bytes on...', all the time checking, and updating your list of occupied sectors. The operating system handles the whole filing system for you. You just give the file name and it does the rest.

From the point of view of a user at the keyboard, the operating system makes the computer act 'intelligent' and alive. From the programmer point of view, it provides several services. The user of the service can be an application programme - via invocation of a service function, e.g. System.output.println(); - or a human user - via the operating systems human-interface,

With Windows NT and Linux, we are moving away from single-user operating systems to multi-tasking - where, for example, the user can set the computer to compiling a large file, while he/she starts to edit another file.

Microsoft Windows-95/98 offers some multi-tasking features. Windows NT is truly multi-tasking.

Since the late 1960s, operating systems on large computers have been multi-user; they allow a large number of users to use a single computer at one time, with each having the sensation of being the sole user of the machine. In the multi-user case, in addition to normal operating system duties, the operating system must:

- Allocate the CPU on a fair basis, and so that users, or a singles user's separate programmes, do not notice much delay;
- Keep each programme, or bits of them, in memory at once - a difficult juggling trick;
- Keep each programme from interfering with another program's memory, whether maliciously or by error;
- Manage a private area of disk for each user/ programme;
- Perform accounting tasks (perhaps) - so that users can be charged for the use of each service.

## VIRTUAL MACHINE LEVELS AND THE OPERATING SYSTEM

The multilevel view of a computer. At each level there is a different virtual machine which obeys its own language.Figure recalls this view.

Except for levels 0 and 1 each level is, in fact, virtual, in the sense that it is created by a computer programme or interpreter.

The operating system also provides a higher-level abstraction for parts of the underlying hardware, e.g. a hierarchical file directory structure as an abstraction for a complex system of spinning disks, controllers etc.

It would be a good idea, at this stage, for you to get these different levels clear in your head. You should also convince yourself of the value of working at the highest level possible - employing the highest level of abstraction possible. If you need more convincing, consider reworking your last Java assignment in assembly language! Employing a higher level of abstraction is like a walker being able to take 10, 20 or maybe 500 steps at a time - for no extra effort; or, like travelling across the Atlantic by air, rather than swimming or rowing a boat.

## HISTORICAL DEVELOPMENT OF OPERATING SYSTEMS

Computers were treated as electronic instruments and could only be programmed using binary codes (machine code). The methods of inserting the codes varied: switches, paper tape, punched cards or, at the beginning, *patched* in with wires which connected High or Low voltages to indicate '1' or '0'.

## OPEN SHOP

By this time (say 1959) there were compliers - like FORTRAN. Users would run their own programmes - much like users of personal computers do nowadays. Users booked the machine for (say) 1/2 hour at a time. Programmes were prepared off-line - onto punched cards - computers were too expensive for such menial tasks.

It was up to the new user to load whatever programme was required onto the machine - from cards; executable and source code were both on cards.

You may be able to imagine the following scenario if you think of an organisation with a single small, slow microcomputer, with one floppy drive, no hard disk and no resident operating system.

1. At the appointed hour, you would charm/threaten/ cajole the previous user out of the computer room.
2. First, the FORTRAN compiler had to be loaded - a huge deck of cards - via the card reader; note: before this there was no software in the computer, except

for a small card reader programme. Such a programme was sometimes called a 'bootstrap' or card-loader - these were the great-great-grand-daddy of todays operating systems; a typical card-loader occupied, maybe, 50 to 100 bytes of memory.

3. Then your new source was read in, and compiled.
4. If there were compiler errors, you noted them and left the computer room. The next user took over - or the computer lay idle until the next half-hour slot began. You would then book another 1/2 hour (maybe the next free was 2 days away - or, you could come in in the middle of the night), try to locate the error, and retype the offending card(s); NB. there was no editing facility in the computer.
5. If there were no compilation errors, the machine would punch the object code onto cards.
6. The next stage was to link and load the object code with the library of system subroutines - also object code. To do this, the linker programme, followed by library, followed by users object code, had to be read in via the card reader.
7. If no linker errors - they were plentiful - you ended up with a programme in the computers memory, ready to execute.
8. Now, you could either run the programme - by putting the start address into the PC register, via switches, or punch out the executable programme - the equivalent of a '.exe' file.
9. If the programme ran correctly (and, you didn't run out of time) you left to celebrate. Otherwise, you noted the error - very difficult, if the programme just crashed. Big installations had line printers, which allowed printing of a full dump of the memory - in Hex or Octal - at the time of crashing. If you had no line printer, you noted the contents of a few memory locations using the console switches and lights - you

could dial any memory location using switches and examine the contents on a light panel (one switch for every address bit and one light for every data bit). Or, in desperation, you could try to 'patch' the machine code to try to get it to do something.

Clearly, much time was wasted:

- Loading programmes;
- Idle time, if a user did not take an allocated time slot;
- Users scratching their heads wondering what was wrong with a programme;
- etc....- but, note, no computer games!

All this on a machine that costed a few million pounds.

Side-bar: In 1960, an average programmer salary was about £1500, a computer cost around £1,500,000: ratio person annual salary to computer capital cost, 1 to 1000. Today, salary £30,000, powerful PC, £1000: ratio 30 to 1. Thus, compared to 1960, computers are times the cost; or programmers 30,000 times more expensive!

**OPERATOR SHOP**

The next stage was to hire an operator. The operator performed all interaction with the computer. Users submitted 'jobs' on cards, and received the results back on line printer paper.

The operator was more skilled and quicker at operating the computer.

Also, similar jobs could be batched, e.g. all the FORTRAN compilations - allowing the FORTRAN compiler programme to be loaded only once, followed by all the linking, etc.

Furthermore, the operator could assert priority:

- To a user who was prepared to pay more;
- To a small job, or one which used an already loaded programme;
- Also, the operator could halt jobs that ran too long.

These are all feature that can be seen in modern operating systems.

## OFF-LINE INPUT-OUTPUT AND RESIDENT MONITOR

Reading cards was not much of a job for a X million pound computer!

Better to create - on a cheaper *satellite* machine - a magnetic tape, that contained many jobs, and get the expensive machine to work its way through the tape. Maybe there were two tape decks - one to replace the card input, one to replace the card output. Also the system software (compiler, linker/loader) could be kept on a tape.

Most significant, however, from an operating systems point of view, was the addition of a small resident monitor programme which remained in memory all the time and which ran each job in turn. This was the great-grandfather of today's OSs. The term operating system crept in because of the similarity of the resident monitor's role to that of a human operator.

The previous instructions to the operator (in English) now had to be coded for the resident monitor. These instructions had to be punched on cards — a typical convention was to precede resident monitor commands with an asterisk, '*', to distinguish them from source programme statements, or data; i.e. the resident monitor had a rudimentary command language interpreter.

A typical resident monitor was IBM's FORTRAN Monitor System - FMS — that ran on the IBM 709.

## SPOOLING SYSTEMS AND SCHEDULERS

Early resident monitor systems used polled input-output, to read from and write to their magnetic tapes; thus, when they needed input, or needed to output, the CPU gave up all other activity and attended to the tape. Polled i-o is very inefficient inefficient; most of the time is wasted waiting for 'status-ready' and things like that. Therefore, the next elaboration was to add software to the resident monitor to allow it, simultaneously, to read from tape, do CPU processing, and, perhaps, write to an output tape or printer.

For slower devices like tapes, interrupt driven device drivers, were sufficient.

Eventually, disks were added to the main machine. The off-line tape preparation machines would be dispensed with, since the card jobs could be read-in on the main machine (using interrupts) and placed on disk to await execution. In addition, running jobs could write to disk files (faster), with the disk files being printed fairly independently.

A primitive scheduler was added to the resident monitor:

- When a job was read-in from cards (or tape), its name and characteristics were placed in a queue;
- The scheduler was run at the end of each job, to select the next job from the queue and set it running.

Operators tasks are now limited to:

- Mounting tapes - for large data files, too big for cards - only very privileged users were allowed to keep data on the disk;
- Restarting the resident monitor when it crashed, or a user programme crashed it;
- Loading cards;
- Unloading printer paper.

This mode of running was called spooling: simultaneous peripheral operations on line - spool.

The operation is somewhat evocative of a spool of thread:

- Jobs wound on to the outside;
- Scheduler winds them off from the inside;
- Ditto with the output: CPU winds output data on; interrupt driven printer programme winds them off — onto line-printer paper.

Spooling systems are the grand-daddies of modern OSs.

## MULTIPROGRAMMING

Nevertheless, spooling doesn't totally remove I/O waiting. Consider a programme which is doing a stock update, and the stock files is on mag. tape: very often the CPU has to issue a *read-from-tape* and can do nothing until the data arrives.

The job is then said to be input-output bound - no amount of interrupt handling can help in this case.

Multiprogramming comes to the rescue.

If the memory is big enough - or the jobs small enough:

- You can place a number of them in memory at once;
- When one becomes I/O bound, transfer to another (*).

(*) However, using only the simple rule: CPU bound jobs are favoured. The problem with this rule is that a big number crunching programme with no I/O could hog the CPU for ever.

Thus, the scheduler becomes a good deal more complicated. CPU time is one of the main resources that jobs are in competition for - implementing policies for sharing such resources is a big part of an operating system's task.

Multiprogramming also introduces competition for memory space. Also, the resident monitor and other programmes must be protected from malicious or faulty programmes that try to write to parts of memory not owned by them.

What we have just described is called batch multiprogramming: each user job may be considered to batch together a set of steps - e.g. compile-pass1...-pass2...link...run. Each step is independent - provided its results are stored safely on disk.

Thus, the resident monitor can schedule each (sub)task independently.

The term process is used to mean an executing programme that performs a subtask; more about processes later.

At this stage the resident monitor has become a true operating system, albeit still batch.

In addition to queuing and running processes, the OS provides services to the process via service calls. Programmes and processes can no longer access input-output devices directly - they must - in the terminology of multi-level machines - execute an OS machine level instruction that does that for them.

Of course, two processes may require the same resource at the same time, e.g. tape, printer; CPU time and memory are also resources that are in heavy demand. The business of granting resources in a fair way is not a trivial one.

## INTERACTIVE MULTIPROGRAMMING AND TIME-SHARING

The batch multiprogramming described above was fine for the computers - but not for people - if programmers can be considered people, which, in organisations, is rare! In developing a programme you could spot an error five seconds after getting your batch job back from the machine, and have to wait a day to get another try. Programmers needed quicker response.

Interactive multiprogramming or time-sharing was the solution.

Instead of interacting, indirectly, via cards and printout, each user has an on-line interactive terminal. They also have access to the disk - perhaps their own directory - to store programmes and data between sessions.

The whole basis of time-sharing is that there may be 5, 10 or 100 users connected to a single computer - with one CPU - with each of them getting the impression that she/he is the sole occupant. Of course, if all these users are running heavily CPU intensive programmes (number crunching), the impression of having a machine to yourself quickly subsides. However, that will rarely be the case; at any instant, out of 20 connected users, 7 might be editing (requires little or no CPU time), 10 might be thinking about what to do next, and only 3 doing anything that really exercises the CPU — e.g. compiling or running programmes.

Incidentally, operating systems have ways of discouraging heavy CPU and memory users from peak interactive times. For these users, a form of batch service is offered. The user submits a job to a batch queue much the same way as before - except the job is specified

(1) Interactively

(2) In a disk file, and

(3) The inputs and outputs also use disk files.

The batch queue is treated differently from the queue associated with the interactive users - it is probably only given a chance at night, or when the interactive use gets very slack.

Massachusetts Institute of Technology (MIT) were the first to demonstrate a time-sharing system - about 1960; that was CTSS. It ran on a converted IBM 7094. But, on machines whose hardware was meant to run one programme/user at a time, time-sharing was not easy — see later.

**Multics**

The next step was MIT, Bell Labs. and General Electric co-operating in producing MULTICS (MULTiplexed Information and Computing Service). MULTICS was way ahead of its time. For the companies involved, maybe too far ahead, for it was costly to produce, and was not commercially successful.

But, MULTICS was enormously influential on the technical development of operating systems. MULTICS begat UNIX. Scratch the surface of most modern operating systems and you will find some MULTICS or UNIX influence.

**Minicomputers**

Up to 1961 computers were a bit like electricity generating plants — they took up whole buildings or, at least, floors or rooms. They cost $millions.

In 1961 Digital Equipment Corporation (DEC) introduced the PDP-1. The PDP-1 had 4K of 18-bit words. It cost a mere $ 120,000. For some jobs it was nearly as fast as an IBM 7094 - the 7094 cost $2 million). Personal computing was on the horizon.

A whole family of PDPs, so-called mini-computers were developed, leading to the PDP-8 - the first true personal, or, at least, laboratory computer - and the PDP-11.

## UNIX

After Bell Labs. dropped out of the MULTICS project, Ken Thompson, one of the MULTICS team at Bell Labs., wrote a single user version of MULTICS for a PDP-7. It was written in assembly language. It was called UNIX - as a pun on Multics.

Note that the PDP-7 had 4K memory.

Yet this early UNIX featured:

- A file system;
- A process control mechanism;
- File utilities;
- A command interpreter.

Next step: UNIX was ported onto a PDP-11/20 and later a PDP-11/45.

But, besides its power and elegance, the next step was to ensure UNIX's fame and fortune. Dennis Ritchie joined the team and developed the C programming language. Around 1972, a new version of UNIX was written, almost entircly in C. Now UNIX could be ported onto any machine that had a C compiler.

## HISTORY OF OPERATING SYSTEMS - GENERATIONS, SUMMARY

This section summarises OS history in the form of generations.

## 1ST GENERATION (1945-1955): VACUUM TUBES AND PLUGBOARDS

- Plugboards;
- Vacuum Tubes;
- Machine language;
- The computer is the eighth wonder of the world!

## 2ND GENERATION 1955-1965): TRANSISTORS AND BATCH SYSTEMS

- Transistors: greater reliability, smaller, less power, faster than vacuum tubes - all the factors you want in a computer;
- PDP-1 from DEC - interactive computing;
- PDP-1 from DEC - cheap(ish) computing;
- PDP-8 from DEC - personal computing;
- jgc in short pants;-)

## 3RD GENERATION (1965-1980): ICS, MULTIPROGRAMMING AND TIMESHARING

- People becoming more important than the computer;
- OS written in a high-level language.

## 4TH GENERATION (1980-1991): PCS AND DISTRIBUTED COMPUTING

- Ordinary people using computers;
- computers become a consumer item;
- Need for *user-friendly* operating systems and software - people are no longer prepared to go to college for three years just to learn how to use a computer;
- Networks of PCs replace mainframes.

## THE FUTURE (1993- )

- World-wide-web;
- Left as exercise for student.

## PREVIEW OF THE WORK OF A TIME-SHARING OPERATING SYSTEM

If each task required nothing but CPU time then multiprogramming would have little advantage over running tasks consecutively. Figure shows two tasks labelled A and B, each of which requires different resources (VDU, disk and CPU) in the order in which they are shown.

If task A were allowed to run to completion before task B was started, valuable processing time would be wasted. We show below how the tasks may be scheduled to make more efficient use of resources, each step takes one unit of time, and they are done entirely sequentially, then the total time is 10 steps. Contrast Figure - timeshared -, which takes just 6 steps. It is worth noting that if the CPU is to be available to one task while another is accessing a disk or using a printer, then these devices must be capable of autonomous operation, i.e. they must either be able to transfer data by DMA without the active intervention of the CPU or must be able to receive a chunk of data at high speed from the CPU and process it at their leisure.

The next chapter will look at some of the details of how a time-sharing operating system schedules many tasks, and allocates resources to them in a fair or otherwise optimal manner.

This comes down to:

- CPU allocation;
- I/O resource allocation, i.e. disks, printers, tapes;
- Memory resource allocation, i.e. virtual memory.

## OPERATING SYSTEMS

The operation - in the sense of 'driving' them - of computers evolved through users operating them, to operators, and finally through various sophistications of operating system software to timesharing operating systems.

First, we give a demonstration of the effect of multiprogramming.

Assume that the jobs/processes/programmes are in memory to start with, that they do some computation (taking 10 millisec) which results in the requirement to read a particular record from a disk file (taking 10 millisec), finally they do some more computation (again 10 millisec). Viewed as executions of single programmes this may not appear too useful - where do the results go to - but, in fact, the jobs are quite typical of what would be encountered by a timesharing during the execution lifetime of three processes

Figure shows how the jobs would have to run on a single user system like MS-DOS. The computer is *I/O blocked* during each disk input - regardless of whether the input is by polled I/O, interrupts, or DMA.

Figure shows the effect of multiprogramming; when one process become I/O bound, the CPU can do processing for another. Thus, a 90 millisec of computer usage can be reduced to 60; add more jobs and you get a greater increase in efficiency. NB. in this case, you are concerned with the method of I/O transfer - ideally the CPU asks for the data, and receives an interrupt when they are placed in memory.

The work that a modern timesharing operating system performs is a good deal more complex than that of, for example, a simple resident monitor - or even a single user OS like MS-DOS. Nevertheless, like all complex systems, the analysis of operating systems responds to breaking them into subsystems/components.

The following functions are required:

1. Dispatching or scheduling. Switching the processor from one process to another; allowing jobs to enter queue.
2. Interrupt handling.
3. Resource allocation. Allocation of the computer's resources to processes: memory, I/O devices, CPU time.
4. Resource protection. Ensuring that no process can access any resource which has not been allocated to it.

5. Provision of (virtual) I/O and other services.
6. Provision of a file system - to processes, and to human users.
7. Analysing and decoding user commands - and requests from programmes, and converting these into procedure and programme names.

We shall now briefly look at a selection of topics that pertain to these requirements.

## PROCESSES

### General

The concept of a process is central - first used by MULTICS. Sometimes referred to as a task. Definition can be difficult: 'a programme in execution' may be the best.

During its life, a process goes through a series of discrete states:

- Running - if it currently has the CPU resource;
- Ready - if it could use the CPU if the CPU were available;
- Blocked - if it is waiting for some event to happen before it can proceed.

When a job is admitted to the system, a corresponding process is created and placed at the back of the queue and it is marked ready; alternatively, there may be separate queues. It gradually moves to the top of the ready list - see scheduling/ dispatching below; when the CPU becomes available the process makes a state transition from ready to running. Strictly speaking this is dispatching.

To prevent any one process, say process A, monopolising the system - i.e. to provide time-sharing it must be possible possible to stop the process after it has consumed its allocated amount of CPU time. This is done via an interrupting clock (hardware) which allows a specified time quantum - a time-slot to pass; if process A is still using the CPU the clock generates an interrupt, causing the system to regain control.

Process A now makes the state transition back to ready, i.e. A is put back in the ready queue.

The next process, process B, say, on the ready queue is now put into the running state; and so on....

If a running process initiates an I/O operation before its time-slot expires then the process is forced to release the CPU; it enters the blocked state and releases the CPU.

If a process is in the blocked state and the event for which it is waiting completes, then the process makes the transition from blocked to ready.

## PROCESS CONTROL BLOCK (PCB)

Because of this 'switching on and off' of processes is is necessary to have housekeeping information associated with each process. A process control block PCB which is a record containing important current information about the process, for example: current state of the process, unique identification of the process, the process's priority, open files and I/O devices, use of main memory and backing store, other resources held, a register save area.

## THE KERNEL

All of the operations involving processes are controlled by a portion of the OS called its nucleus, core or kernel. The kernel represents only a small portion of the code of the entire OS but it is intensively used and so remains in primary storage while other portions may be transferred in and out of secondary storage as required.

One very important function of the kernel is interrupt processing. In large multi-user systems, the kernel is subjected to a constant barrage of interrupts. Clearly, rapid response is essential: to keep resources well utilised, and to provide acceptable response times for interactive users.

In addition, while dealing with an interrupt, the kernel disables other interrupts. Thus, to prevent interrupts being disabled for long periods of time, the kernel is designed to do the minimum amount of processing possible on each interrupt and to pass the remaining processing to an appropriate system process.

The kernel of a sophisticated OS may contain code to perform:

- Interrupt handling;
- Process creation and destruction;
- Process state switching and dispatching;
- Inter process communication;
- Manipulation of PCB;
- Support of I/O activities;
- Support of memory allocation and deallocation;
- Support of the file system;
- Support of system accounting functions.

Supporting hardware and microcode is often provided - even for portable operating systems like UNIX.

The kernel has privileges that allow it to do things that normal processes cannot do, e.g. access I/O devices. Privilege is usually conferred by the processor state, i.e. privilege level is stored in hardware, so a process has a different processor state from the kernel. In the original Intel 8086/88 and 80286, there was limited support for processor states; however, in the 80386 and after, full time-sharing was supported.

## SCHEDULING

The goal of scheduling (the method by which processor time is managed) is to provide good service to all the processes that are currently competing for resources, including the CPU.

Three type of scheduling may be identified: long term scheduling, medium term scheduling, and short term scheduling.

We will be concerned only with short-term scheduling - also called dispatching, which decides how to share the computer among all the processes that currently want to compute. Such decisions may be made frequently - tens of times per second.

There are several competing goals that scheduling policies aim to fulfill - one is *good throughput*. For short term scheduling, this minimizes the number of process switches. Another goal is good (quick) service.

### Scheduling Objectives

Some of the - often conflicting - objectives of a good scheduling algorithm/policy are:

1. Be fair - all processes should be treated equitably;
2. Maximize throughput and service, i.e. as many processes as possible per unit time;
3. Maximize the number of interactive users receiving acceptable response times;
4. Be predictable - a given job should run in about the same amount of time regardless of the load on the system;
5. Balance resource use - processes using underutilized resources should be favoured;
6. Achieve a balance between response and utilization;
7. Avoid indefinite postponement - as a process waits for a resource its priority should grow (aging);
8. Enforce priorities;
9. Give preference to processes holding key resources;
10. Give better service to processes exhibiting desirable behaviour e.g. low paging rates,
11. Degrade gracefully under heavy loads.

Thus, scheduling may appear to be a complex problem.

## SCHEDULING POLICIES, ALGORITHMS

### First Come, First Served (FCFS)

Under FCFS, the short term scheduler runs each process until it either terminates or leaves because of I/O or resource requests. Processes arriving wait in the order that they arrive.

FCFS is non-preemptive, so a process is never blocked once it has started to run until it leaves the domain of the short term scheduler.

FCFS is usually unsatisfactory because of the way that it favours long (greedy) processes - like the person in the bank queue in front of you with the weeks takings from a shop!

## Round Robin (RR)

The intention is to provide good response ratios for short as well as long processes. This policy services (allocates CPU to) a process for a single time slot (length = q), where q = between 1/60 and 1 second; if the process is not finished it is interrupted at the end of the slot and placed at the rear of the ready queue and will wait for its turn again. New arrivals enter the ready queue at the rear.

RR can be tuned by adjusting q. If q is so high that it exceeds the service requirements for all processes, RR becomes the same as FCFS. As q tends to 0, process switching happens more frequently and eventually occupies all available time. Thus q should be set small enough so that RR is fair but high enough so that the amount of time spent switching processes is reasonable.

RR is preemptive, i.e. it will stop a process, if the process has not completed before the end of its time-slot.

## SHORTEST PROCESS NEXT (SPN)

SPN (like FCFS) is non-preemptive. It tries to improve response for short processes over FCFS. But, it requires explicit information about the service time requirements for each process. The process with the shortest time requirement is chosen.

Unfortunately, long processes wait a long time or suffer starvation. Short processes are treated very favourably.

## CONCLUSION

- Preemption is worth the extra switching cost. Since context must switch at every interrupt from the running process back to the kernel, it does not usually cost much extra for the kernel to make a decision and allow a different process to run.

- The time-slot should be large enough so that preemption cost does not become excessive, e.g.. if a process switch costs 100 microseconds, the quantum should be about 100 times as long.
- Some policies are more expensive than others to implement. FCFS only requires a queue for the ready list.
- Many OSs use a hybrid policy, with RR for short processes and some other method for long.
- Space management affects scheduling. Processes that need a substantial amount of memory are often given larger time-slots so that they can get more work done while they are occupying main store.

## MEMORY MANAGEMENT

Data that is currently accessed most frequently should be in the highest level of storage hierarchy. Each offers about an order of magnitude faster access than its lower neighbour.

The relationship between each layer and the one below it can be considered as similar to that between cache and main memory - cache. If we need to cache an item from a higher level then access is significantly slower. We call such a situation a cache miss. In contrast a cache hit is when we find the data we need in a cache and need not turn to the associated slower memory.

## PHYSICAL AND VIRTUAL STORE

The OS must arrange main memory so that processes remain ignorant of each other and still share main memory. A guiding principle is that the more frequently data are accessed, the faster the access should be. If swapping in and out of main storage becomes the dominant activity, then we refer to this situation as thrashing. Physical store is the hardware memory on the machine, usually starting at physical address 0. Certain locations may be reserved for special purposes; the kernel may reside in in the low addresses. The rest of physical store may be partitioned into pieces for the processes in the ready list.

Each process has its own virtual memory - the memory perceived by the process. As far as the process is concerned all address references refer to virtual space. Each process' virtual memory is limited only by the machine address size.Virtual memory can also be very useful even in a single user system - if the computer has a larger address space than physical memory, and if programmes need a large amount of memory; compare overlaying - in which the programmer takes responsibility for segmenting the programme into memory sized chunks.

## CHOICE OF PAGE SIZE

The choice of page size determined at the design stage is a trade- off between various considerations:

- Overhead space - least with large pages, since page tables have fewer entries.
- Internal waste - smallest with small pages.
- Cold start faults - lower with large pages. These are the faults needed to bring the programme into main store the first time. With larger pages there are fewer total pages, hence fewer cold start faults.
- Page fault rate - generally lower with small pages, assuming that a fixed amount of main store is available.
- Efficiency of transfer between main memory and disk store - best with large pages, since they take about the same amount of time to transfer as small pages.

Larger pages are usually better, unless they become so large that too few processes in the ready list can have pages in main store at the same time. Common page sizes are from 512 bytes to 4K bytes but can be as large as 8K.

## PAGE REPLACEMENT POLICIES

The storage manager must decide to keep some pages in main store and other pages in secondary store - unless virtual space requirements are less than the available physical space.

These decisions may be made at any time but when a page fault occurs a decision must be made; the process that suffered the page fault cannot continue until the appropriate page is swapped in.

A page replacement policy (PRP)/algorithm is used to decide which page frame to vacate ie. swap out its page.

Some commonly quoted strategies are:

Note: pages being heavily used should be preserved. One goal is to minimize the number of page faults. Swapping can reach a level at which all processes present need to swap so no progress can be made. If this persists, the OS is spending all its time transferring pages in and out of main store - known as thrashing.

## FIRST IN, FIRST OUT (FIFO)

Also called longest resident.

When a page frame is needed, the page that has been in main store for the longest time is chosen. This policy tends to save recently used pages which have a higher probability of being used again soon. However a frequently used page still gets swapped out when it gets to be old enough, even though it will have to be brought in immediately.

## LEAST RECENTLY USED (LRU)

This method is based on the assumption that the page reference pattern in the recent past is a mirror of the pattern in the near future. Pages that have been accessed recently are likely to continue to be accessed and ought to be kept in main store. It is expensive to implement exactly since in order to find the page least recently used, either a list of pages must be maintained in use order or each page must be marked with the time it was last accessed.

# Chapter 4

# Processing Unit

A CPU and memory aren't much use without a keyboard and screen, and a disk drive, i.e. a useful computer is actually a computer system.

Figure shows the organisation of a simple computer system with one CPU, memory and three input-output (I/O) devices - *peripherals*: a disk and a keyboard & screen. As always, the components are connected by a system bus - this is the same as the bus mentioned above; communication with peripherals can be done in a manner similar to memory reading/writing.

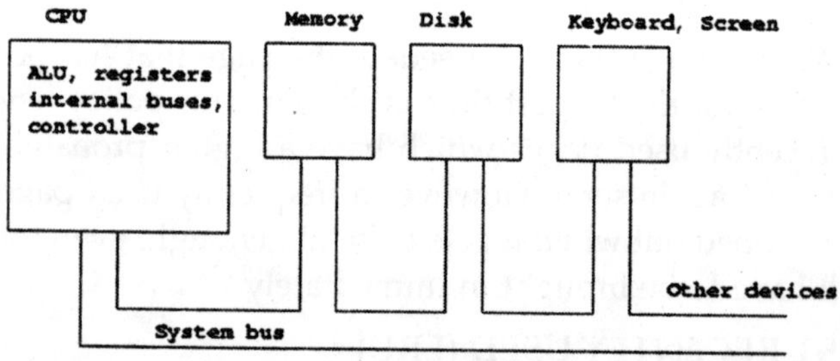


Figure: Organisation of a Simple Computer System

Figure shows main memory; it is essentially a sequential collection of cells, each of which, typically, can store eight binary digits - bits - BInary digiTs. Each bit is like a *sub-cell* that can be '0' or '1'. Bits have much in common with light-bulbs - they are either on - value 1, or off - value 0.

We commonly term a collection of eight bits a byte.

Each cell has an address.

Addresses run from 0 to N-1, where N is the size of the memory; on a typical PC these days, N is 64 Mega(bytes) - Mega = million, well actually 1048576 = $2^{20}$.

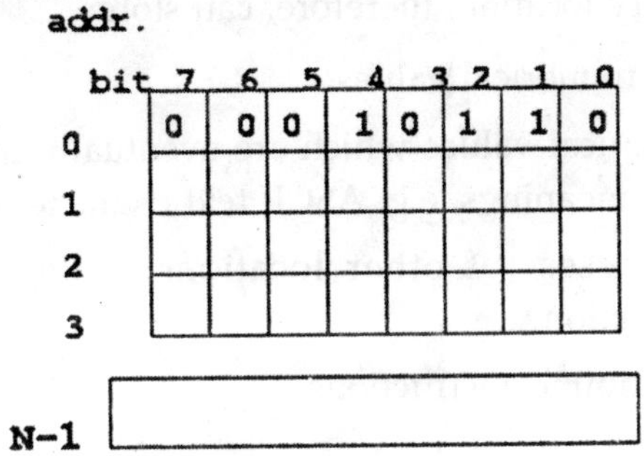


**Figure:** Memory

## Numeric Values

Each bit is a single binary value: you can count only from 0 to 1 with it; however, a collection of eight bits, properly interpreted, allows you to count from 0 up to 255; and 16 bits, 0...65535 (64K - 1). The byte shown in address 0 of Figure contains 0001 0101 which is decimal (base-10) 22, hexadecimal (base-16) 15, or octal (base-8) 025..

Essentially, Figure conforms to the so-called von Neumann computer architecture, which has five basic parts:

1. The arithmetic-logic unit (ALU).
2. The control unit. The ALU and the control unit comprise the CPU.
3. The memory.
4. Input equipment.
5. Output equipment.

As we have already said, memory may contain, in addition to data, programme instructions - coded as numbers. One major breakthrough of the von Neumann architecture was that data - the things that are processed - and instructions - that describe the processing to be done - are both numbers, and both reside in the same memory.

However, *inside the machine*, there is nothing to distinguish data from instructions, nor, for that matter, data from addresses - except in how they are used.

A memory location, therefore, can store:

- True numerical values.
- Numerical values which are eventually translated to other meanings, e.g. ASCII text character codes.
- Addresses (of other locations, cells) - pointers, indirection.
- Programme instructions.

## CENTRAL PROCESSING UNIT

### INTRODUCTION

As indicated, the CPU consists of an Arithmetic-Logic-Unit (ALU) - the calculator, and a controller - to do the fetching and executing of the programme instructions; in addition, we need a few local memory registers - for storage of temporary data, and buses to transfer data and addresses throughout the CPU.

### ARITHMETIC LOGIC UNIT - ALU

The ALU is the calculator part. The ALU takes the contents of ALU input buses A and B and combines them in some way (add, subtract, logical OR, etc.) and passes the result onto a C data bus. Let us assume that this is a 16-bit machine, i.e. the buses and ALU take 16-bit numbers - they are 16-bits wide.

A simple ALU is shown in Figure . It has a number of functions which are selected by function selection control lines F; the control lines are equivalent to selecting the operation on a calculator, e.g. add, subtract. Two condition flags are output: N, set to 1 if last operation caused a negative result; Z, last operation, if a zero result; result flags are important for constructing conditional instructions (if, else).

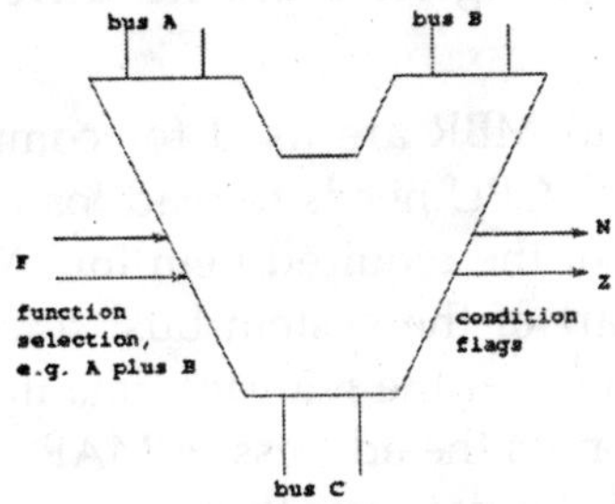


**Figure:** Arithmetic and Logic Unit (ALU)

## SIMPLIFIED CPU

Figure gives a view of a simplified CPU - but not so simplified that we cannot describe how an actual programme might operate in it; with few additions figure would actually work. The major thing we have left out is control.

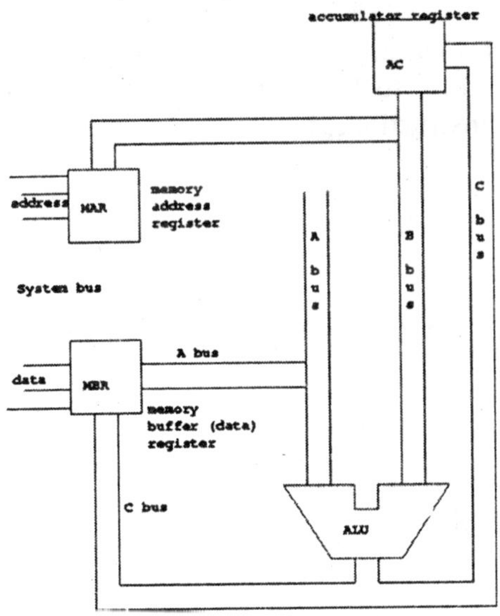


**Figure:** Central Processing Unit

In addition to the buses - both internal and system - the system bus is one on the far left), and ALU, all mentioned before, we have just three new items: the memory address register (MAR), the memory buffer register (MBR), and the accumulator register(AC).

Conceptually, registers are no different from main memory cells.

The MAR and MBR are used for communicating with memory: when the CPU needs to read load from memory, it puts the address of the required item into MAR, asserts *read* on the control part of the system bus, some time later, the system bus will transfer the relevant data item into the MBR; for write store, it puts the address in MAR, the data in MBR, and asserts *write,* the data are then copied into the relevant memory location.

The AC is used as a general holding register for operand (input) data and results.

All will become clear if we return to the example programme statement:

z = x + y;

As in the introduction, assume that z corresponds to location 2, x to 0, and y to 1. The programme, as it would appear in machine instructions, is:

P1.

Load contents of location 0 (x, 22) into AC.

P2.

Add contents of 1 (y, 33) to AC, with result going to AC.

P3.

Store contents of AC in location 2 (z).

## VIRTUAL MACHINES, ABSTRACTION, LEVELS OF CONCERN

Here, and in other modules, you will frequently encounter the term *abstraction,* most often in the context of an antidote to *complexity*. It crops up under a variety of guises: separation of concerns, structured levels, modular this and that, information hiding, modelling.

A dictionary definition of abstraction (the verb) is: the process of considering (extracting) certain essential properties of objects while omitting other properties that are not relevant (usually inessential details); the act of abstraction or abstracting produces an abstraction (noun) which collectively refers to the set of chosen properties.

From our point of view abstraction does have two important facets which are related but different, namely, extraction (of the essential from the inessential) and idealisation (i.e. the irrelevant details are deviations from the ideal). Often, somewhat loosely, an abstraction may be called a model.

In the following paragraphs I give examples of abstraction applied to computing and more mundane fields.

### Systems Engineering

Systems engineering, in general, is one of the great breakthroughs of the 20th century. Without it, only very clever people, who could carry the plans for the total system (cathedral, television, satellite...) in their heads, could be effective engineers. With systems engineering a bit of clever decomposition can yield a problem that is solvable by teams of mere mortals.

The key concept here is probably that of a *black-box* abstraction; a black-box is completely characterised by: (a) what it expects as inputs; (b) what it produces as outputs; and (c) the relationship between inputs and outputs.

## MULTILEVEL VIEW OF COMPUTING MACHINES

It is impossible and undesirable for engineers or programmers to carry in their minds the hundreds of thousands of transistors, resistors, connections..., and software that make up a computer system. Thus it is necessary to decompose (break-up) the system, into chunks or sub-systems. But we have to be methodical about this: if you break a 2,000,000 component computer into 200,000 sub- systems, you are not much further ahead - where next?

A computer can be viewed as a hierarchy of levels as shown below. At any one time you make up your mind what level concerns you.

### Level 6 Application Level

Here the computer is viewed as a machine which performs a specific function, e.g. a spreadsheet, a word-processor; the user at this level shouldn't have to be concerned with any details of computer science or engineering, just as the average car driver need not be concerned with the internal details of car engines.

### Level 5 High-level Language Level

Here the computer is viewed as a (virtual) machine which obeys the instructions or understands the statements of a high-level language such as C, C++, Java, COBOL, etc. A compiler or interpreter converts these instructions into lower level machine or assembly code.

### Level 4 Assembly Language Level

At this level, we view the computer as being run by a programme (a sequence) of so called assembly level instructions.

Here we see instructions that explicitly move data around between registers, accumulators, programme counters, ports and memory addresses; and instructions that transform or combine their contents (e.g. ADDD, SUBD, LODD). To be effective at this level, the programmer must have a model of the machine - its *architecture*, or, more specifically, its *instruction set architecture (ISA)* that properly expresses: (a) the interconnection of registers to indicate allowable data movements, and (b) the repertoire of transformations and combinations that can be performed in the arithmetic-and-logic unit and elsewhere.

Assembly language is just a symbolic form of the language understood by level 2 below (which are coded as numbers). Assembly language is translated into machine language using an *assembler*.

### Level 3 Operating System Machine Level

At this level, we have operating system software in charge of running the assembly language. In some contexts, this level is absent.

### Level 2 Machine Language Level

Here are the same sort of instructions that we described for the previous level: major difference, they are now coded as numbers, rather than alphanumeric symbols (e.g. 2501 instead of (say) ADDD x). Two points: (a) they are ready for execution in the processor - the Level 1 machine 'understands' them; and, (b) human programmers have great difficulty in understanding them!

### Level 1 Microprogram Level

This level is concerned with the (underlying) engine that implements individual Level 2 instructions by appropriately directing the the components and their interconnections at that level. In some (mostly earlier, but also some modern RISC machines) machines this level does not exist and machine instructions are implemented directly by digital logic.

### Level 0 Digital Logic Level

Here we are at the level of gates and memory cells. The language is made up of 1s and 0s or, at best, binary numbers.

There are certainly levels below level 0 - transistors, p-n junctions, molecules, atoms,...!), but the six above should be enough for us. In fact, we shall be mainly concerned with level 2 and above, though, just for completeness, we will show how some basic components may be built from digital logic *gates*.

At each level, the programmer or engineer or physicist must pay attention to different sorts of object or quantity. At level 5 (high-level language,), the programmer deals with the data types provided by the language. At level 4 you are forced to deal with physical storage locations, registers and the like. And so on, until at level 0 you are concerned with bits (1s and 0s).

The major point is that, the higher the level of abstraction, the more powerful the machine becomes. For example, you want to type a letter on a word-processor. At level 6 you just do it. At level 5 you first have to write a word-processor programmme - allocate a few years or so for that! At level 4 you have to write a compiler so that you can write the word-processor - there isn't much point in trying to write a word-processor in assembler, it'll take so long and be so error prone that the project will never end.

And so on. Down to level 0, where you first have to make a computer from thousands of chips, then write the microcode,..., then write the compiler, the write the word-processor,..., then type the letter.

The difference between working at level 4 (say) and level 2 is like discovering that you can take 100 metre strides, instead of the 1.5 meters of ordinary mortals.

## Chapter 5

# Computer Arithmetic

## FLOATING-POINT UNIT

The Intel Architecture Floating-Point Unit (FPU) provides high-performance floating-point processing capabilities. It supports the real, integer, and BCD-integer data types and the floating-point processing algorithms and exception handling architecture defined in the IEEE 754 and 854 Standards for Floating-Point Arithmetic. The FPU executes instructions from the processor's normal instruction stream and greatly improves the efficiency of Intel Architecture processors in handling the types of high-precision floating-point processing operations commonly found in scientific, engineering, and business applications.

This chapter describes the data types that the FPU operates on, the FPU's execution environment, and the FPU-specific instruction set. Detailed descriptions of the FPU instructions are given in "Instruction Page Key".

## COMPATIBILITY AND EASE OF USE OF THE INTEL ARCHITECTURE FPU

The architecture of the Intel Architecture FPU has evolved in parallel with the architecture of early Intel Architecture processors. The first Intel Math Coprocessors (the Intel 8087, Intel 287, and Intel 387) were companion processors to the Intel 8086/8088, Intel 286, and Intel386 processors, respectively, and were designed to improve and extend the numeric processing capability of the Intel Architecture. The Intel486 DX processor for the first time integrated the CPU and the FPU architectures on one chip. The Pentium processor's FPU offered the same architecture as the Intel486 DX processor's FPU, but with improved performance. The Pentium Pro processor's FPU further extended the floating-point processing capability of Intel Architecture family of processors and added several new instructions to improve processing throughput.

Throughout this evolution, compatibility among the various generations of FPUs and math coprocessors has been maintained. For example, the Pentium Pro processor's FPU is fully compatible with the Pentium and Intel486 DX processors's FPUs.

Each generation of the Intel Architecture FPUs have been explicitly designed to deliver stable, accurate results when programmed using straightforward "pencil and paper" algorithms, bringing the functionality and power of accurate numeric computation into the hands of the general user. The IEEE 754 standard specifically addresses this issue, recognizing the fundamental importance of making numeric computations both easy and safe to use.

For example, some processors can overflow when two single-precision floating-point numbers are multiplied together and then divided by a third, even if the final result is a perfectly valid 32-bit number. The Intel Architecture FPUs deliver the correctly rounded result. Other typical examples of undesirable machine behaviour in straightforward calculations occur when computing financial rate of return, which involves the expression (1 + i)n or when solving for roots of a quadratic equation:

$$\frac{-b \pm \sqrt{b^2 - 4ac}}{2a}$$

If *a* does not equal 0, the formula is numerically unstable when the roots are nearly coincident or when their magnitudes are wildly different. The formula is also vulnerable to spurious over/underflows when the coefficients *a*, *b*, and *c* are all very big or all very tiny. When single-precision (4-byte) floating-point coefficients are given as data and the formula is evaluated in the FPU's normal way, keeping all intermediate results in its stack, the FPU produces impeccable single-precision roots. This happens because, by default and with no effort on the programmer's part, the FPU evaluates all those sub-expressions with so much extra precision and range as to overwhelm almost any threat to numerical integrity.

If double-precision data and results were at issue, a better formula would have to be used, and once again the FPU's default evaluation of that formula would provide substantially enhanced numerical integrity over mere double-precision evaluation.

On most machines, straightforward algorithms will not deliver consistently correct results (and will not indicate when they are incorrect). To obtain correct results on traditional machines under all conditions usually requires sophisticated numerical techniques that go beyond typical programming practice. General application programmers using straightforward algorithms will produce much more reliable programmes using the Intel architectures. This simple fact greatly reduces the software investment required to develop safe, accurate computation-based products.

Beyond traditional numeric support for scientific applications, the Intel architectures have built-in facilities for commercial computing. They can process decimal numbers of up to 18 digits without round-off errors, performing exact arithmetic on integers as large as 264 (or 1018). Exact arithmetic is vital in accounting applications where rounding errors may introduce monetary losses that cannot be reconciled.

The Intel FPU's contain a number of optional numerical facilities that can be invoked by sophisticated users. These advanced features include directed rounding, gradual underflow, and programmed exception-handling facilities.

These automatic exception-handling facilities permit a high degree of flexibility in numeric processing software, without burdening the programmer. While performing numeric calculations, the processor automatically detects exception conditions that can potentially damage a calculation (for example, X ÷ 0 or

$\sqrt{X}$

when X < 0). By default, on-chip exception logic handles these exceptions so that a reasonable result is produced and execution may proceed without programme interruption. Alternatively, the processor can invoke a software exception handler to provide special results whenever various types of exceptions are detected.

## REAL NUMBERS AND FLOATING-POINT FORMATS

This section describes how real numbers are represented in floating-point format in the Intel Architecture FPU. It also introduces terms such as normalized numbers, denormalized numbers, biased exponents, signed zeros, and NaNs. Readers who are already familiar with floating-pcint processing techniques and the IEEE standards may wish to skip this section.

## REAL NUMBER SYSTEM

The real-number system comprises the continuum of real numbers from minus infinity (-·) to plus infinity (+·).

### Binary Real Number System

Because the size and number of registers that any computer can have is limited, only a subset of the real-number continuum can be used in real-number calculations. As shown at the bottom of Figure, the subset of real numbers that a particular FPU supports represents an approximation of the real number system. The range and precision of this real-number subset is determined by the format that the FPU uses to represent real numbers.

Binary Real Number System

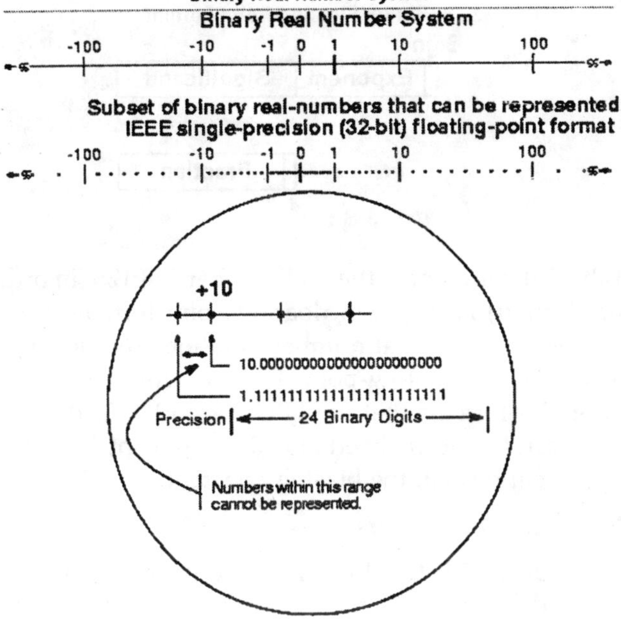


## FLOATING-POINT FORMAT

To increase the speed and efficiency of real-number computations, computers or FPUs typically represent real numbers in a binary floating-point format. In this format, a real number has three parts: a sign, a significand, and an exponent. Figure shows the binary floating-point format that the Intel Architecture FPU uses. This format conforms to the IEEE standard.

The sign is a binary value that indicates whether the number is positive (0) or negative (1). The significand has two parts: a 1-bit binary integer (also referred to as the J-bit) and a binary fraction. The J-bit is often not represented, but instead is an implied value. The exponent is a binary integer that represents the base-2 power that the significand is raised to.

## Binary Floating-Point Format

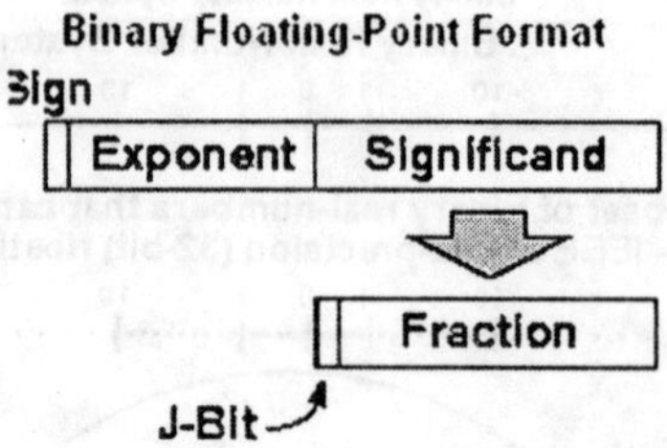


Table 7-1 shows how the real number 178.125 (in ordinary decimal format) is stored in floating-point format. The table lists a progression of real number notations that leads to the single-real, 32-bit floating-point format (which is one of the floating-point formats that the FPU supports). In this format, the significand is normalized and the exponent is biased For the single-real format, the biasing constant is +127.

### Normalized Numbers

In most cases, the FPU represents real numbers in normalized form. This means that except for zero, the significand is always made up of an integer of 1 and the following fraction:

- 1.fff...ff

For values less than 1, leading zeros are eliminated. (For each leading zero eliminated, the exponent is decremented by one.)

**Real Number Notation**

| **Notation** | **Value** | | | |
|---|---|---|---|---|
| Ordinary Decimal | 178.125 | | | |
| Scientific Decimal | $1.78125E_{10}2$ | | | |
| Scientific Binary | $1.0110010001E_{2}111$ | | | |
| Scientific Binary (Biased Exponent) | $1.0110010001E_{2}10000110$ | | | |
| Single-Real Format | Sign | Biased Exponent | Normalized Significand | |
| | 0 | 10000110 10000000000000 | 011001000 | 1. (Implied) |

Representing numbers in normalized form maximizes the number of significant digits that can be accommodated in a significand of a given width. To summarize, a normalized real number consists of a normalized significand that represents a real number between 1 and 2 and an exponent that specifies the number's binary point.

## BIASED EXPONENT

The FPU represents exponents in a biased form. This means that a constant is added to the actual exponent so that the biased exponent is always a positive number. The value of the biasing constant depends on the number of bits available for representing exponents in the floating-point format being used. The biasing constant is chosen so that the smallest normalized number can be reciprocated without overflow.

### Real Number and Non-number Encodings

A variety of real numbers and special values can be encoded in the FPU's floating-point format. These numbers and values are generally divided into the following classes:

- Signed zeros.
- Denormalized finite numbers.
- Normalized finite numbers.
- Signed infinities.
- NaNs.
- Indefinite numbers.

(The term NaN stands for "Not a Number.")

The encodings for these numbers and non-numbers fit into the real number continuum. The encodings shown here are for the IEEE single-precision (32-bit) format, where the term "S" indicates the sign bit, "E" the biased exponent, and "F" the fraction. (The exponent values are given in decimal.)

The FPU can operate on and/or return any of these values, depending on the type of computation being performed. The following sections describe these number and non-number classes.

## SIGNED ZEROS

Zero can be represented as a +0 or a -0 depending on the sign bit. Both encodings are equal in value. The sign of a zero result depends on the operation being performed and the rounding mode being used. Signed zeros have been provided to aid in implementing interval arithmetic. The sign of a zero may indicate the direction from which underflow occurred, or it may indicate the sign of an · that has been reciprocated.

## NORMALIZED AND DENORMALIZED FINITE NUMBERS

Non-zero, finite numbers are divided into two classes: normalized and denormalized. The normalized finite numbers comprise all the non-zero finite values that can be encoded in a normalized real number format between zero and ·. In the single-real format shown in Figure, this group of numbers includes all the numbers with biased exponents ranging from 1 to $254_{10}$ (unbiased, the exponent range is from $-126_{10}$ to $+127_{10}$).

### Real Numbers and NaNs

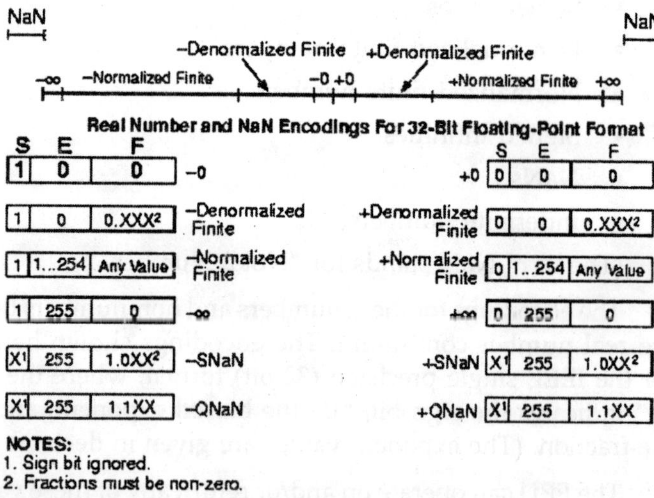


When real numbers become very close to zero, the normalized-number format can no longer be used to represent the numbers. This is because the range of the exponent is not large enough to compensate for shifting the binary point to the right to eliminate leading zeros.

When the biased exponent is zero, smaller numbers can only be represented by making the integer bit (and perhaps other leading bits) of the significand zero. The numbers in this range are called denormalized (or tiny) numbers. The use of leading zeros with denormalized numbers allows smaller numbers to be represented. However, this denormalization causes a loss of precision (the number of significant bits in the fraction is reduced by the leading zeros).

When performing normalized floating-point computations, an FPU normally operates on normalized numbers and produces normalized numbers as results. Denormalized numbers represent an underflow condition.

A denormalized number is computed through a technique called gradual underflow. Table 31-2 gives an example of gradual underflow in the denormalization process. Here the single-real format is being used, so the minimum exponent (unbiased) is $-126_{10}$. The true result in this example requires an exponent of $-129_{10}$ in order to have a normalized number. Since $-129_{10}$ is beyond the allowable exponent range, the result is denormalized by inserting leading zeros until the minimum exponent of $-126_{10}$ is reached.

**Denormalization Process**

| Operation | Sign | Exponent* | Significand |
|---|---|---|---|
| True Result | 0 | -129 | 1.01011100000...00 |
| Denormalize | 0 | -128 | 0.10101110000...00 |
| Denormalize | 0 | -127 | 0.01010111000...00 |
| Denormalize | 0 | -126 | 0.00101011100...00 |
| Denormal Result | 0 | -126 | 0.00101011100...00 |

*NOTE:* * Expressed as an unbiased, decimal number.

In the extreme case, all the significant bits are shifted out to the right by leading zeros, creating a zero result.

The FPU deals with denormal values in the following ways:

- It avoids creating denormals by normalizing numbers whenever possible.
- It provides the floating-point underflow exception to permit programmers to detect cases when denormals are created.
- It provides the floating-point denormal-operand exception to permit procedures or programmes to detect when denormals are being used as source operands for computations.

When a denormal number in single- or double-real format is used as a source operand and the denormal exception is masked, the FPU automatically normalizes the number when it is converted to extended-real format.

## Signed Infinities

The two infinities, +· and -·, represent the maximum positive and negative real numbers, respectively, that can be represented in the floating-point format. Infinity is always represented by a zero significand (fraction and integer bit) and the maximum biased exponent allowed in the specified format (for example, $255_{10}$ for the single-real format).

The signs of infinities are observed, and comparisons are possible. Infinities are always interpreted in the affine sense; that is, -· is less than any finite number and +· is greater than any finite number. Arithmetic on infinities is always exact. Exceptions are generated only when the use of an infinity as a source operand constitutes an invalid operation.

Whereas denormalized numbers represent an underflow condition, the two infinity numbers represent the result of an overflow condition. Here, the normalized result of a computation has a biased exponent greater than the largest allowable exponent for the selected result format.

### NaNs

Since NaNs are non-numbers, they are not part of the real number line. In Figure, the encoding space for NaNs in the FPU floating-point formats is shown above the ends of the real number line. This space includes any value with the maximum allowable biased exponent and a non-zero fraction. (The sign bit is ignored for NaNs.)

The IEEE standard defines two classes of NaN: quiet NaNs (QNaNs) and signaling NaNs (SNaNs). A QNaN is a NaN with the most significant fraction bit set; an SNaN is a NaN with the most significant fraction bit clear. QNaNs are allowed to propagate through most arithmetic operations without signaling an exception. SNaNs generally signal an invalid-operation exception whenever they appear as operands in arithmetic operations. Exceptions are discussed in "Floating-Point Exception Handling".

See "Operating on NaNs", for detailed information on how the FPU handles NaNs.

### Indefinite

For each FPU data type, one unique encoding is reserved for representing the special value indefinite. For example, when operating on real values, the real indefinite value is a QNaN.The FPU produces indefinite values as responses to masked floating-point exceptions.

## FPU ARCHITECTURE

From an abstract, architectural view, the FPU is a coprocessor that operates in parallel with the processor's integer unit. The FPU gets its instructions from the same instruction decoder and sequencer as the integer unit and shares the system bus with the integer unit. Other than these connections, the integer unit and FPU operate independently and in parallel. (The actual microarchitecture of an Intel Architecture processor varies among the various families of processors. For example, the Pentium Pro processor has two integer units and two FPUs; whereas, the Pentium processor has two integer units and one FPU, and the Intel486 processor has one integer unit and one FPU.)

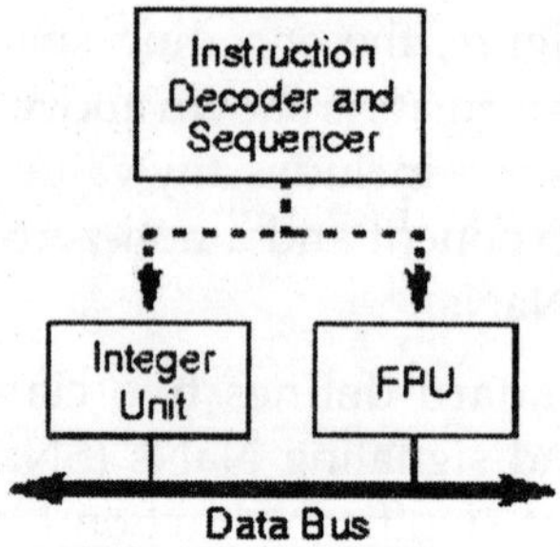


**Fig.** Relationship Between the Integer Unit and the FPU

The instruction execution environment of the FPU consists of 8 data registers (called the FPU data registers) and the following special-purpose registers:

- The status register.
- The control register.
- The tag word register.
- Instruction pointer register.
- Last operand (data pointer) register.
- Opcode register.

These registers are described in the following sections.

## The FPU Data Registers

The FPU data registers consist of eight 80-bit registers. Values are stored in these registers in the extended-real format shown in Figure 31-17. When real, integer, or packed BCD integer values (in any of the formats shown in Figure are loaded from memory into any of the FPU data registers, the values are automatically converted into extended-real format (if they are not already in that format). When computation results are subsequently transferred back into memory from any of the FPU registers, the results can be left in the extended-real format or converted back into one of the other FPU formats (real, integer, or packed BCD integers).

The FPU instructions treat the eight FPU data registers as a register stack.All addressing of the data registers is relative to the register on the top of the stack. The register number of the current top-of-stack register is stored in the TOP (stack TOP) field in the FPU status word. Load operations decrement TOP by one and load a value into the new top-of-stack register, and store operations store the value from the current TOP register in memory and then increment TOP by one. (For the FPU, a load operation is equivalent to a push and a store operation is equivalent to a pop.)

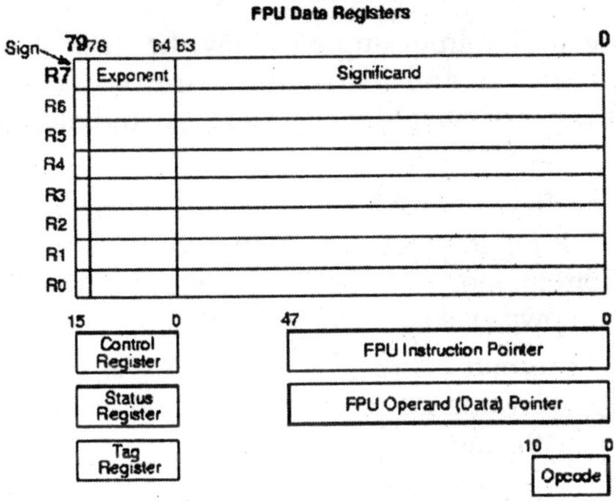


**Fig.** FPU Execution Environment

If a load operation is performed when TOP is at 0, register wraparound occurs and the new value of TOP is set to 7. The floating-point stack-overflow exception indicates when wraparound might cause an unsaved value to be overwritten.

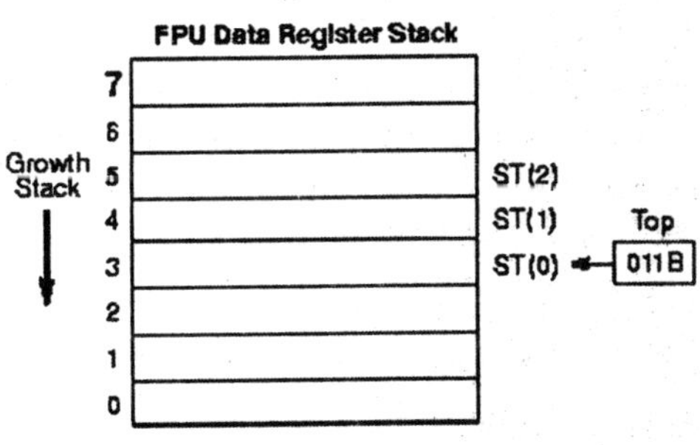


**Fig.** FPU Data Register Stack

Many floating-point instructions have several addressing modes that permit the programmer to implicitly operate on the top of the stack, or to explicitly operate on specific registers relative to the TOP. Assemblers supports these register addressing modes, using the expression ST(0), or simply ST, to represent the current stack top and ST(i) to specify the $i$th register from TOP in the stack ($0 \leq i \leq 7$). For example, if TOP contains 011B (register 3 is the top of the stack), the following instruction would add the contents of two registers in the stack.

Figure shows an example of how the stack structure of the FPU registers and instructions are typically used to perform a series of computations. Here, a two-dimensional dot product is computed, as follows:

1. The first instruction (FLD value1) decrements the stack register pointer (TOP) and loads the value 5.6 from memory into ST(0). The result of this operation is shown in snap-shot (a).
2. The second instruction multiplies the value in ST(0) by the value 2.4 from memory and stores the result in ST(0), shown in snap-shot (b).
3. The third instruction decrements TOP and loads the value 3.8 in ST(0).
4. The fourth instruction multiplies the value in ST(0) by the value 10.3 from memory and stores the result in ST(0), shown in snap-shot (c).
5. The fifth instruction adds the value and the value in ST(1) and stores the result in ST(0), shown in snap-shot (d).

The style of programming demonstrated in this example is supported by the floating-point instruction set. In cases where the stack structure causes computation bottlenecks, the FXCH (exchange FPU register contents) instruction can be used to streamline a computation.

**Parameter Passing With the FPU Register Stack**

Like the general-purpose registers in the processor's integer unit, the contents of the FPU data registers are unaffected by procedure calls, or in other words, the values are maintained across procedure boundaries. A calling procedure can thus use the FPU data registers (as well as the procedure stack) for passing parameter between procedures. The called procedure can reference parameters passed through the register stack using the current stack register pointer (TOP) and the ST(0) and ST(i) nomenclature. It is also common practice for a called procedure to leave a return value or result in register ST(0) when returning execution to the calling procedure or programme.

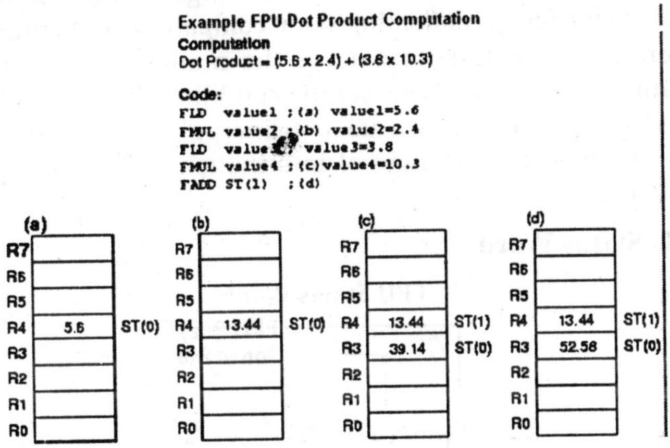


**Figure.** FPU Dot Product Computation

## FPU STATUS REGISTER

The 16-bit FPU status register indicates the current state of the FPU. The flags in the FPU status register include the FPU busy flag, top-of-stack (TOP) pointer, condition code flags, error summary status flag, stack fault flag, and exception flags. The FPU sets the flags in this register to show the results of operations.

The contents of the FPU status register (referred to as the FPU status word) can be stored in memory using the FSTSW/ FNSTSW, FSTENV/FNSTENV, and FSAVE/FNSAVE instructions. It can also be stored in the AX register of the integer unit, using the FSTSW/FNSTSW instructions.

## TOP OF STACK (TOP) POINTER

A pointer to the FPU data register that is currently at the top of the FPU register stack is contained in bits 11 through 13 of the FPU status word. This pointer, which is commonly referred to as TOP (for top-of-stack), is a binary value from 0 to 7. See "The FPU Data Registers", for more information about the TOP pointer.

## CONDITION CODE FLAGS

The four FPU condition code flags (C0 through C3) indicate the results of floating-point comparison and arithmetic operations. Table summarizes the manner in which the floating-point instructions set the condition code flags. These condition code bits are used principally for conditional branching and for storage of information used in exception handling

**FPU Status Word**

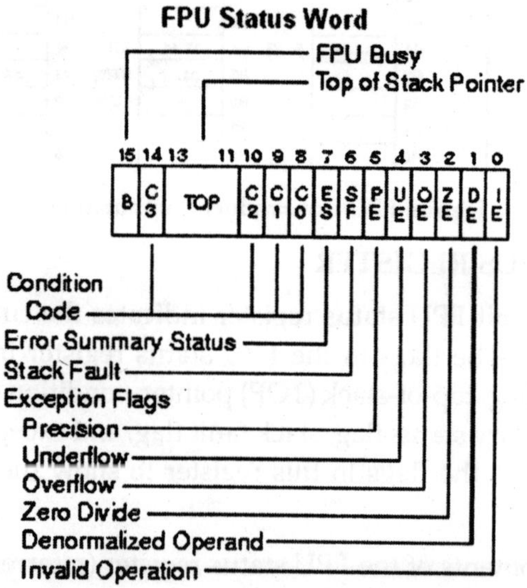


As shown in Table 31-3, the C1 condition code flag is used for a variety of functions. When both the IE and SF flags in the FPU status word are set, indicating a stack overflow or underflow exception (#IS), the C1 flag distinguishes between

overflow (C1=1) and underflow (C1=0). When the PE flag in the status word is set, indicating an inexact (rounded) result, the C1 flag is set to 1 if the last rounding by the instruction was upward. The FXAM instruction sets C1 to the sign of the value being examined.

The FPTAN, FSIN, FCOS, and FSINCOS instructions set the C2 flag to 1 to indicate that the source operand is beyond the allowable range of $\pm 2^{63}$.

Where the state of the condition code flags are listed as undefined in Table 31-3, do not rely on any specific value in these flags.

## FPU Condition Code Interpretation

| FPU Condition Code Interpretation | | | | |
|---|---|---|---|---|
| Instruction | C0 | C3 | C2 | C1 |
| FCOM, FCOMP, FCOMPP, FICOM, FICOMP, FTST, FUCOM, FUCOMP, FUCOMPP | Result of Comparison | | Operands are not Comparable | 0 or #IS |
| FCOMI, FCOMIP, FUCOMI, FUCOMIP | Undefined. (These instructions set the status flags in the EFLAGS register.) | | | #IS |
| FXAM | Operand class | | | Sign |
| FPREM, FPREM1 | Q2 | Q1 | 0=reduction complete 1=reduction incomplete | Q0 or #IS |
| F2XM1, FADD, FADDP, FBSTP, FCMOVcc, FIADD, FDIV, FDIVP, FDIVR, FDIVRP, FIDIV, FIDIVR, FIMUL, FIST, FISTP, FISUB, FISUBR,FMUL, FMULP, FPATAN, FRNDINT, FSCALE, FST, FSTP, FSUB, FSUBP, FSUBR, FSUBRP,FSQRT, FYL2X, FYL2XP1 | Undefined | | | Roundup or #IS |
| FCOS, FSIN, FSINCOS, FPTAN | Undefined | | 1=source operand out of range. | Roundup or #IS (Undefined if C2=1) |
| FABS, FBLD, FCHS, FDECSTP, FILD, FINCSTP, FLD, Load Constants, FSTP (ext. real), FXCH, FXTRACT | Undefined | | | 0 or #IS |
| FLDENV, FRSTOR | Each bit loaded from memory | | | |
| FFREE, FLDCW, FCLEX/FNCLEX, FNOP, FSTCW/FNSTCW, FSTENV/FNSTENV, FSTSW/FNSTSW, | Undefined | | | |
| FINIT/FNINIT, FSAVE/FNSAVE | 0 | 0 | 0 | 0 |

## Exception Flags

The six exception flags (bits 0 through 5) of the status word indicate that one or more floating-point exceptions has been detected since the bits were last cleared. The individual exception flags (IE, DE, ZE, OE, UE, and PE) are described in detail in "Floating-Point Exception Handling". Each of the exception flags can be masked by an exception mask bit in the FPU control word.The exception summary status (ES) flag (bit 7) is set when any of the unmasked exception flags are set. When the ES flag is set, the FPU exception handler is invoked, using one of the techniques described in "Software Exception Handling". (Note that if an exception flag is masked, the FPU will still set the flag if its associated exception occurs, but it will not set the ES flag.)

The exception flags are "sticky" bits, meaning that once set, they remain set until explicitly cleared. They can be cleared by executing the FCLEX/FNCLEX (clear exceptions) instructions, by reinitializing the FPU with the FINIT/FNINIT or FSAVE/FNSAVE instructions, or by overwriting the flags with an FRSTOR or FLDENV instruction.

The B-bit (bit 15) is included for 8087 compatibility only. It reflects the contents of the ES flag.

## STACK FAULT FLAG

The stack fault flag (bit 6 of the FPU status word) indicates that stack overflow or stack underflow has occurred. The FPU explicitly sets the SF flag when it detects a stack overflow or underflow condition, but it does not explicitly clear the flag when it detects an invalid-arithmetic-operand condition. When this flag is set, the condition code flag C1 indicates the nature of the fault: overflow (C1 = 1) and underflow (C1 = 0). The SF flag is a "sticky" flag, meaning that after it is set, the processor does not clear it until it is explicitly instructed to do so (for example, by an FINIT/FNINIT, FCLEX/FNCLEX, or FSAVE/FNSAVE instruction).

## BRANCHING AND CONDITIONAL MOVES ON FPU CONDITION CODES

The Intel Architecture FPU (beginning with the Pentium Pro processor) supports two mechanisms for branching and performing conditional moves according to comparisons of two floating-point values. These mechanism are referred to here as the "old mechanism" and the "new mechanism."

The old mechanism is available in FPU's prior to the Pentium Pro processor and in the Pentium Pro processor. This mechanism uses the floating-point compare instructions (FCOM, FCOMP, FCOMPP, FTST, FUCOMPP, FICOM, and FICOMP) to compare two floating-point values and set the condition code flags (C0 through C3) according to the results. The contents of the condition code flags are then copied into the status flags of the EFLAGS register using a two step process:

1. The FSTSW AX instruction moves the FPU status word into the AX register.

2. The SAHF instruction copies the upper 8 bits of the AX register, which includes the condition code flags, into the lower 8 bits of the EFLAGS register.

When the condition code flags have been loaded into the EFLAGS register, conditional jumps or conditional moves can be performed based on the new settings of the status flags in the EFLAGS register.

## Moving the FPU Condition Codes to the EFLAGS Register

**Moving the FPU Condition Codes to the EFLAGS Register**

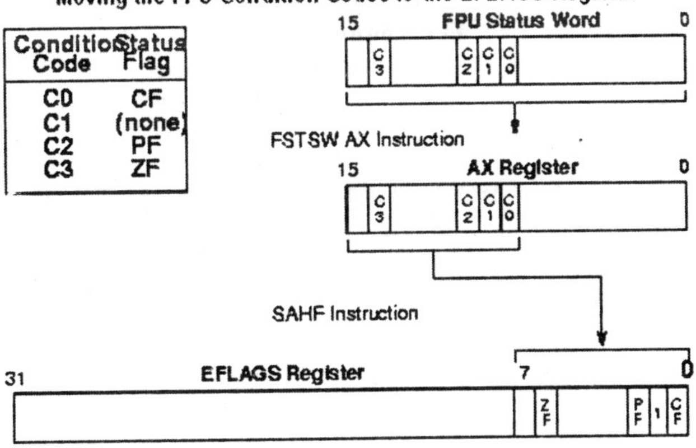


The new mechanism is available only in the Pentium Pro processor. Using this mechanism, the new floating-point compare and set EFLAGS instructions (FCOMI, FCOMIP, FUCOMI, and FUCOMIP) compare two floating-point values and set the ZF, PF, and CF flags in the EFLAGS register directly. A single instruction thus replaces the three instructions required by the old mechanism.

Note also that the FCMOV*cc* instructions (also new in the Pentium Pro processor) allow conditional moves of floating-point values (values in the FPU data registers) based on the setting of the status flags (ZF, PF, and CF) in the EFLAGS register. These instructions eliminate the need for an IF statement to perform conditional moves of floating-point values.

## FPU CONTROL WORD

The 16-bit FPU control word controls the precision of the FPU and rounding method used. It also contains the exception-flag mask bits. The control word is cached in the FPU control register. The contents of this register can be loaded with the FLDCW instruction and stored in memory with the FSTCW/FNSTCW instructions.

When the FPU is initialized with either an FINIT/FNINIT or FSAVE/FNSAVE instruction, the FPU control word is set to 037FH, which masks all floating-point exceptions, sets rounding to nearest, and sets the FPU precision to 64 bits.

### FPU Control Word

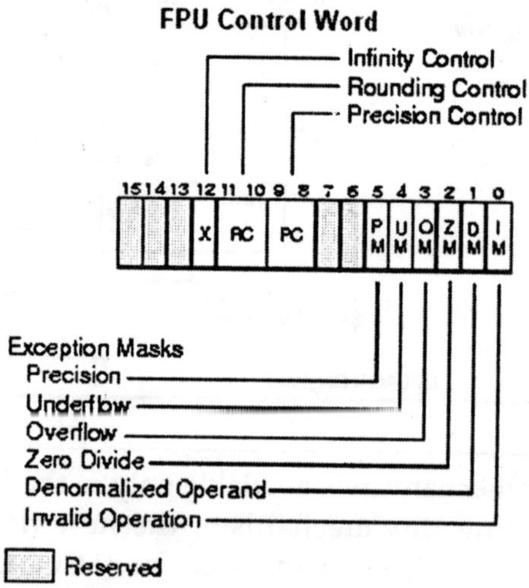


### Exception-Flag Masks

The exception-flag mask bits (bits 0 through 5 of the FPU control word) mask the 6 exception flags in the FPU status word (also bits 0 through 5). When one of these mask bits is set, its corresponding floating-point exception is blocked from being generated.

## Precision Control Field

The precision-control (PC) field (bits 8 and 9 of the FPU control word) determines the precision (64, 53, or 24 bits) of floating-point calculations made by the FPU.The default precision is extended precision, which uses the full 64-bit significand available with the extended-real format of the FPU data registers. This setting is best suited for most applications, because it allows applications to take full advantage of the precision of the extended-real format.

**Precision Control Field (PC)**

| Precision | PC Field |
|---|---|
| Single Precision (24-Bits*) | 00B |
| Reserved | 01B |
| Double Precision (53-Bits*) | 10B |
| Extended Precision (64-Bits) | 11B |

*Includes the implied integer bit.

The double precision and single precision settings, reduce the size of the significand to 53 bits and 24 bits, respectively. These settings are provided to support the IEEE standard and to allow exact replication of calculations which were done using the lower precision data types. Using these settings nullifies the advantages of the extended-real format's 64-bit significand length. When reduced precision is specified, the rounding of the significand value clears the unused bits on the right to zeros.

The precision-control bits only affect the results of the following floating-point instructions: FADD, FADDP, FSUB, FSUBP, FSUBR, FSUBRP, FMUL, FMULP, FDIV, FDIVP, FDIVR, FDIVRP, and FSQRT.

## ROUNDING CONTROL FIELD

The rounding-control (RC) field of the FPU control register (bits 10 and 11) controls how the results of floating-point instructions are rounded. Four rounding modes are supported: round to nearest, round up, round down, and round toward zero. Round to nearest is the default rounding mode and is suitable for most applications. It provides the most accurate and statistically unbiased estimate of the true result.

**Figure.** Rounding Control Field (RC)

| Rounding Mode | RC Field Setting | Description |
|---|---|---|
| Round to nearest (even) | 00B | Rounded result is the closest to the infinitely precise result. If two values are equally close, the result is the even value (that is, the one with the least significant bit of zero). |
| Round down (toward - ·) | 01B | Rounded result is close to but no greater than the infinitely precise result. |
| Round up (toward + ·) | 10B | Rounded result is close to but no less than the infinitely precise result. |
| Round toward zero (Truncate) | 11B | Rounded result is close to but no greater in absolute value than the infinitely precise result. |

The round up and round down modes are termed directed rounding and can be used to implement interval arithmetic. Interval arithmetic is used to determine upper and lower bounds for the true result of a multistep computation, when the intermediate results of the computation are subject to rounding.

The round toward zero mode (sometimes called the "chop" mode) is commonly used when performing integer arithmetic with the FPU.

Whenever possible, the FPU produces an infinitely precise result in the destination format (single, double, or extended real). However, it is often the case that the infinitely precise result of an arithmetic or store operation cannot be encoded exactly in the format of the destination operand.

For example, the following value (*a*) has a 24-bit fraction. The least-significant bit of this fraction (the underlined bit) cannot be encoded exactly in the single-real format (which has only a 23-bit fraction):

(*a*) 1.0001 0000 1000 0011 1001 0111$E_2$ 101

To round this result (*a*), the FPU first selects two representable fractions *b* and *c* that most closely bracket *a* in value ($b < a < c$).

(*b*) 1.0001 0000 1000 0011 1001 011$E_2$ 101

(*c*) 1.0001 0000 1000 0011 1001 100$E_2$ 101

The FPU then sets the result to *b* or to *c* according to the rounding mode selected in the RC field. Rounding introduces an error in a result that is less than one unit in the last place to which the result is rounded.

The rounded result is called the inexact result. When the FPU produces an inexact result, the floating-point precision (inexact) flag (PE) is set in the FPU status word.

When the overflow exception is masked and the infinitely precise result is between the largest positive finite value allowed in a particular format and +·, the FPU rounds the result as shown in Table 31-6.

**Table.** Rounding of Positive Numbers With Masked Overflow

| Rounding Mode | Result |
|---|---|
| Rounding to nearest (even) | + · |
| Rounding toward zero (Truncate) | Maximum, positive finite value |
| Rounding up (toward + ·) | + · |
| Rounding down) (toward - ·) | Maximum, positive finite value |

When the overflow exception is masked and the infinitely precise result is between the largest negative finite value allowed in a particular format and -·, the FPU rounds the result as shown in Table 31-7.

**Table.** Rounding of Negative Numbers With Masked Overflow

| Rounding Mode | Result |
|---|---|
| Rounding to nearest (even) | - · |
| Rounding toward zero (Truncate) | Maximum, negative finite value |
| Rounding up (toward + ·) | Maximum, negative finite value |
| Rounding down) (toward - ·) | - · |

The rounding modes have no effect on comparison operations, operations that produce exact results, or operations that produce NaN results.

## Infinity Control Flag

The infinity control flag (bit 12 of the FPU control word) is provided for compatibility with the Intel 287 Math Coprocessor; it is not meaningful for the Pentium Pro processor FPU or for the Pentium processor FPU, the Intel486 processor FPU, or Intel 387 processor NPX. See "Signed Infinities", for information on how the Intel Architecture FPUs handle infinity values.

## FPU Tag Word

The 16-bit tag word indicates the contents of each the 8 registers in the FPU data-register stack (one 2-bit tag per register). The tag codes indicate whether a register contains a valid number, zero, or a special floating-point number (NaN, infinity, denormal, or unsupported format), or whether it is empty. The FPU tag word is cached in the FPU in the FPU tag word register. When the FPU is initialized with either an FINIT/FNINIT or FSAVE/FNSAVE instruction, the FPU tag word is set to FFFFH, which marks all the FPU data registers as empty.

TAG Values
00 — Valid
01 — Zero
10 — Special: invalid (NaN, unsupported), infinity, or denormal
11 — Empty

**Figure.** FPU Tag Word

Each tag in the FPU tag word corresponds to a physical register (numbers 0 through 7). The current top-of-stack (TOP) pointer stored in the FPU status word can be used to associate tags with registers relative to ST(0).

The FPU uses the tag values to detect stack overflow and underflow conditions. Stack overflow occurs when the TOP pointer is decremented (due to a register load or push operation) to point to a non-empty register. Stack underflow occurs when the TOP pointer is incremented (due to a save or pop operation) to point to an empty register or when an empty register is also referenced as a source operand. A non-empty register is defined as a register containing a zero (01), a valid value (00), or an special (10) value.

Application programmes and exception handlers can use this tag information to check the contents of an FPU data register without performing complex decoding of the actual data in the register. To read the tag register, it must be stored in memory using either the FSTENV/FNSTENV or FSAVE/ FNSAVE instructions. Software cannot directly load or modify the tags in the tag register. The FLDENV and FRSTOR instructions load an image of the tag register into the FPU; however, the FPU uses those tag values only to determine if the data registers are empty (11B) or non-empty (00B, 01B, or 10B). If the tag register image indicates that a data register is empty, the tag in the tag register for that data register is marked empty (11B); if the tag register image indicates that the data register is non-empty, the FPU reads the actual value in the data register and sets the tag for the register accordingly. This action prevents a programme from setting the values in the tag register to incorrectly represent the actual contents of non-empty data registers.

### The FPU Instruction and Operand (Data) Pointers

The FPU stores pointers to the instruction and operand (data) for the last non-control instruction executed in two 48-bit registers: the FPU instruction pointer and FPU operand (data) pointer registers. (This information is saved to provide state information for exception handlers.)

The contents of the FPU instruction and operand pointer registers remain unchanged when any of the control instructions (FINIT/FNINIT, FCLEX/FNCLEX, FLDCW, FSTCW/FNSTCW, FSTSW/FNSTSW, FSTENV/FNSTENV, FLDENV, FSAVE/FNSAVE, FRSTOR, and WAIT/FWAIT) are executed. The contents of the FPU operand register are undefined if the prior non-control instruction did not have a memory operand.

The pointers stored in the FPU instruction and operand pointer registers consist of an offset (stored in bits 0 through 31) and a segment selector (stored in bits 32 through 47).

These registers can be accessed by the FSTENV/FNSTENV, FLDENV, FINIT/FNINIT, FSAVE/FNSAVE and FRSTOR instructions. The FINIT/FNINIT and FSAVE/FNSAVE instructions clear these registers.

For all the Intel Architecture FPUs and NPXs except the 8087, the FPU instruction pointer points to any prefixes that preceded the instruction. For the 8087, the FPU instruction pointer points only to the actual opcode.

**LAST INSTRUCTION OPCODE**

The FPU stores the opcode of the last non-control instruction executed in an 11-bit FPU opcode register. (This information provides state information for exception handlers.) Only the first and second opcode bytes (after all prefixes) are stored in the FPU opcode register. The encoding of these two bytes. Since the upper 5 bits of the first opcode byte are the same for all floating-point opcodes (11011B), only the lower 3 bits of this byte are stored in the opcode register.

**SAVING THE FPU'S STATE**

The FSTENV/FNSTENV and FSAVE/FNSAVE instructions store FPU state information in memory for use by exception handlers and other system and application software. The FSTENV/FNSTENV instruction saves the contents of the status, control, tag, FPU instruction pointer, FPU operand pointer, and opcode registers. The FSAVE/

FNSAVE instruction stores that information plus the contents of the FPU data registers. Note that the FSAVE/FNSAVE instruction also initializes the FPU to default values (just as the FINIT/FNINIT instruction does) after it has saved the original state of the FPU.

**Contents of FPU Opcode Registers**

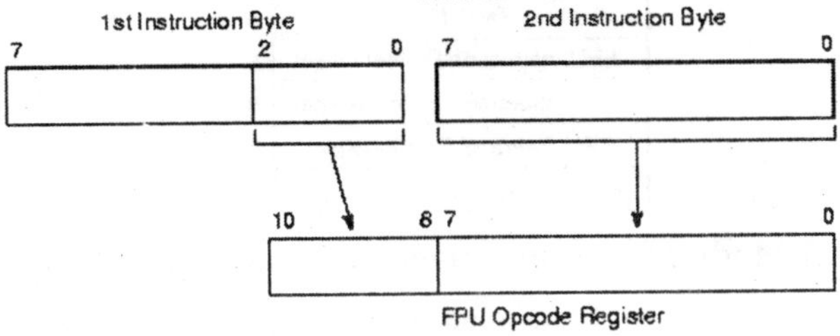


**Protected Mode FPU State Image in Memory, 32-Bit Format**

**32-Bit Protected Mode Format**

| 31 | 16 | 15 0 | |
|---|---|---|---|
| Reserved | | Control Word | 0 |
| Reserved | | Status Word | 4 |
| Reserved | | Tag Word | 8 |
| FPU Instruction Pointer Offset | | | 12 |
| 0 0 0 0 | Opcode 10...00 | FPU Instruction Pointer Selector | 16 |
| FPU Operand Pointer Offset | | | 20 |
| Reserved | | FPU Operand Pointer Selector | 24 |

Reserved

Real Mode FPU State Image in Memory, 32-Bit Format

**32-Bit Real-Address Mode Format**

| 31 | 16 | 15 | 0 | |
|---|---|---|---|---|
| Reserved | | Control Word | | 0 |
| Reserved | | Status Word | | 4 |
| Reserved | | Tag Word | | 8 |
| Reserved | | FPU Instruction Pointer 15...00 | | 12 |
| 0 0 0 0 | FPU Instruction Pointer 31...16 | 0 | Opcode 10...00 | 16 |
| Reserved | | FPU Operand Pointer 15...00 | | 20 |
| 0 0 0 0 | FPU Operand Pointer 31...16 | 0 0 0 0 0 0 0 0 0 0 0 0 | | 24 |

Reserved

## Protected Mode FPU State Image in Memory, 16-Bit Format

**Protected Mode FPU State Image in Memory, 16-Bit Format**

**16-Bit Protected Mode Format**

| 15 … 0 | Offset |
|---|---|
| Control Word | 0 |
| Status Word | 2 |
| Tag Word | 4 |
| FPU Instruction Pointer Offset | 6 |
| FPU Instruction Pointer Selector | 8 |
| FPU Operand Pointer Offset | 10 |
| FPU Operand Pointer Selector | 12 |

## Real Mode FPU State Image in Memory, 16-Bit Format

**Real Mode FPU State Image in Memory, 16-Bit Format**

**16-Bit Real-Address Mode and Virtual-8086 Mode Format**

| 15 | | 0 | Offset |
|---|---|---|---|
| Control Word | | | 0 |
| Status Word | | | 2 |
| Tag Word | | | 4 |
| FPU Instruction Pointer 15...00 | | | 6 |
| IP 19..16 | 0 | Opcode 10...00 | 8 |
| FPU Operand Pointer 15...00 | | | 10 |
| OP 19..16 | 0 | 00000000000 | 12 |

The FLDENV and FRSTOR instructions allow FPU state information to be loaded from memory into the FPU. Here, the FLDENV instruction loads only the status, control, tag, FPU instruction pointer, FPU operand pointer, and opcode registers, and the FRSTOR instruction loads all the FPU registers, including the FPU stack registers.

## FLOATING-POINT DATA TYPES AND FORMATS

The Intel Architecture FPU recognizes and operates on seven data types, divided into three groups: reals, integers, and packed BCD integers. Figure shows the data formats for each of the FPU data types. Table gives the length, precision, and approximate normalized range that can be represented of each FPU data type. Denormal values are also supported in each of the real types, as required by IEEE Std. 854.

With the exception of the 80-bit extended-real format, all of these data types exist in memory only. When they are loaded into FPU data registers, they are converted into extended-real format and operated on in that format.

## Floating-Point Unit Data Type Formats

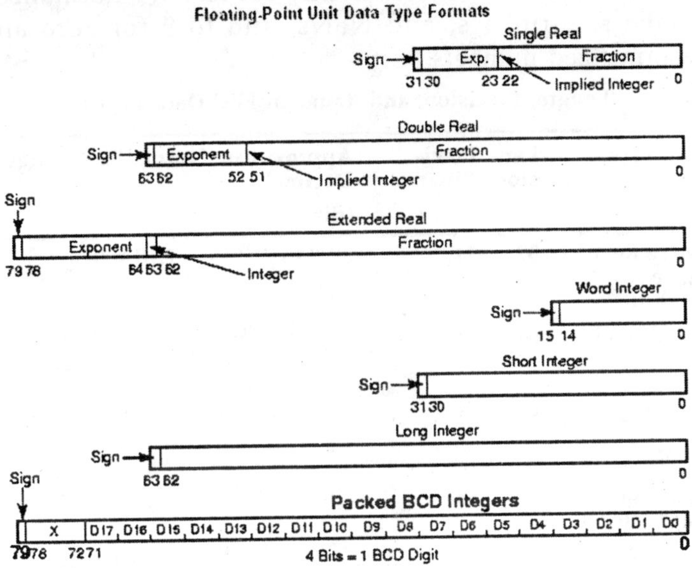


When stored in memory, the least significant byte of an FPU data-type value is stored at the initial address specified for the value. Successive bytes from the value are then stored in successively higher addresses in memory. The floating-point instructions load and store memory operands using only the initial address of the operand.

### REAL NUMBERS

The FPU's three real data types (single-real, double-real, and extended-real) correspond directly to the single-precision, double-precision, and double-extended-precision formats in the IEEE standard. The extended-precision format is the format used by the data registers in the FPU. Table 31-8 gives the precision and range of these data types and Figure gives the formats.

For the single-real and double-real formats, only the fraction part of the significand is encoded. The integer is assumed to be 1 for all numbers except 0 and denormalized finite numbers. For the extended-real format, the integer is contained in bit 63, and the most-significant fraction bit is bit 62. Here, the integer is explicitly set to 1 for normalized numbers, infinities, and NaNs, and to 0 for zero and denormalized numbers.

**Length, Precision, and Range of FPU Data Types**

| Data Type gth | Len- sion | Preci- Binary | Approximate Normalized Range Decimal (Bits) | |
|---|---|---|---|---|
| Binary Real Single real 3.40 ¥ $10^{38}$ | 32 | 24 | $2^{-126}$ to $2^{127}$ | 1.18 ¥ 10 38 to |
| Double real $10^{308}$ | 64 | 53 | $2^{-1022}$ to $2^{1023}$ | 2.23 ¥ $10^{-308}$ to 1.79 ¥ |
| Extended real $10^{4932}$ | 80 | 64 | $2^{-16382}$ to $2^{16383}$ | 3.37 ¥ $10^{-4932}$ to 1.18 ¥ |
| Binary Integer Word integer | 16 | 15 | $-2^{15}$ to $2^{15} - 1$ | -32,768 to 32,767 |
| Short integer | 32 | 31 | $-2^{31}$ to $2^{31} - 1$ | -2.14 ¥ $10^{9}$ to 2.14 ¥ $10^{9}$ |
| Long integer $10^{18}$ | 64 | 63 | $-2^{63}$ to $2^{63} - 1$ | -9.22 ¥ $10^{18}$ to 9.22 ¥ |
| Packed BCD Integers | 80 | 18 (dec-imaldigits) | Not Pertinent | $(-10^{18} + 1)$ to $(10^{18} - 1)$ |

The exponent of each real data type is encoded in biased format. The biasing constant is 127 for the single-real format, 1023 for the double-real format, and 16,383 for the extended-real format.

Table 31-9 shows the encodings for all the classes of real numbers (that is, zero, denormalized-finite, normalized-finite, and ·) and NaNs for each of the three real data-types. It also gives the format for the real indefinite value.

When storing real values in memory, single-real values are stored in 4 consecutive bytes in memory; double-real values are stored in 8 consecutive bytes; and extended-real values are stored in 10 consecutive bytes.

**Table:** Real Number and NaN Encodings

| Class | | Sign | Biased Exponent | Significand Integer[1] | Fraction |
|---|---|---|---|---|---|
| | +· | 0 | 11..11 | 1 | 00..00 |
| | +Normals | 0 | 11..10 | 1 | 11..11 |
| | | . | . | . | . |
| | | 0 | 00..01 | 1 | 00..00 |
| Positive | +Denormals | 0 | 00..00 | 0 | 11.11 |
| | | . | . | . | . |
| | | 0 | 00..00 | 0 | 00..01 |
| | +Zero | 0 | 00..00 | 0 | 00..00 |
| | -Zero | 1 | 00..00 | 0 | 00..00 |
| | -Denormals | 1 | 00..00 | 0 | 00..01 |
| | | . | . | . | . |
| | | 1 | 00..00 | 0 | 11..11 |
| Negative | -Normals | 1 | 00..01 | 1 | 00..00 |
| | | . | . | . | . |
| | | 1 | 11..10 | 1 | 11..11 |
| | -· | 1 | 11..11 | 1 | 00..00 |
| | SNaN | X | 11..11 | 1 | 0X..XX[2] |
| NaNs | QNaN | X | 11..11 | 1 | 1X..XX |
| | Real Indefinite (QNaN) | 1 | 11..11 | 1 | 10..00 |
| | Single-Real: | | ←8 Bits → | | ←23 Bits → |
| | Double-Real: | | ←11 Bits → | | ←52 Bits → |
| | Extended-Real | | ←15 Bits → | | ←63 Bits → |

As a general rule, values should be stored in memory in double-real format. This format provides sufficient range and precision to return correct results with a minimum of programmer attention. The single-real format is appropriate for applications that are constrained by memory; however, it provides less precision and a greater chance of overflow. The single-real format is also useful for debugging algorithms, because rounding problems will manifest themselves more quickly in this format. The extended-real format is normally reserved for holding intermediate results in the FPU registers and constants. Its extra length is designed to shield final results from the effects of rounding and overflow/underflow in intermediate calculations. However, when an application requires the maximum range and precision of the FPU (for data storage, computations, and results), values can be stored in memory in extended-real format.

The real indefinite value is a QNaN encoding that is stored by several floating-point instructions in response to a masked floating-point invalid-operation exception.

Integer bit is implied and not stored for single-real and double-real formats. The fraction for SNaN encodings must be non-zero.

## BINARY INTEGERS

The FPU's three binary integer data types (word, short, and long) have identical formats, except for length. Table 31-8 gives the precision and range of these data types and Figure gives the formats. Table gives the encodings of the three binary integer types.

**Figure.** Binary Integer Encodings

| Class | Sign | Magnitude | |
|---|---|---|---|
| Positive | Largest | 0 | 11..11 |
| | | . | . |
| | | . | . |
| | | . | . |
| | Smallest | 0 | 00..01 |
| Zero | 0 | 00..00 | |
| Negative | Smallest | 1 | 11..11 |
| | | . | . |
| | | . | . |
| | | . | . |
| | | . | . |
| | Largest | 1 | 00..00 |
| Integer Indefinite | 1 | 00..00 | |
| | | Word Integer: | 15 bits |
| | | Short Integer: | 31 Bits 63 Bits |
| | | Long Integer: | |

The most significant bit of each format is the sign bit (0 for positive and 1 for negative). Negative values are represented in standard two's complement notation. The quantity zero is represented with all bits (including the sign bit) set to zero. Note that the FPU's word-integer data type is identical to the word-integer data type used by the processor's integer unit and the short-integer format is identical to the integer unit's doubleword-integer data type.

Word-integer values are stored in 2 consecutive bytes in memory; short-integer values are stored in 4 consecutive bytes; and long-integer values are stored in 8 consecutive bytes. When loaded into the FPU's data registers, all the binary integers are exactly representable in the extended-real format.

The binary integer encoding 100..00B represents either of two things, depending on the circumstances of its use:

- The largest negative number supported by the format ($-2^{15}$, $-2^{31}$, or $-2^{63}$).
- The integer indefinite value.

If this encoding is used as a source operand (as in an integer load or integer arithmetic instruction), the FPU interprets it as the largest negative number representable in the format being used. If the FPU detects an invalid operation when storing an integer value in memory with an FIST/FISTP instruction and the invalid-operation exception is masked, the FPU stores the integer indefinite encoding in the destination operand as a masked response to the exception. In situations where the origin of a value with this encoding may be ambiguous, the invalid-operation exception flag can be examined to see if the value was produced as a response to an exception.

If the integer indefinite is stored in memory and is later loaded back into an FPU data register, it is interpreted as the largest negative number supported by the format.

## DECIMAL INTEGERS

Decimal integers are stored in a 10-byte, packed BCD format. Table 31-8 gives the precision and range of this data type and Figure shows the format. In this format, the first 9 bytes hold 18 BCD digits, 2 digits per byte The least-significant digit is contained in the lower half-byte of byte 0 and the most-significant digit is contained in the upper half-byte of byte 9. The most significant bit of byte 10 contains the sign bit (0 = positive and 1 = negative). (Bits 0 through 6 of byte 10 are don't care bits.) Negative decimal integers are not stored in two's complement form; they are distinguished from positive decimal integers only by the sign bit.

Table 31-11 gives the possible encodings of value in the decimal integer data type.

The decimal integer format exists in memory only. When a decimal integer is loaded in a data register in the FPU, it is automatically converted to the extended-real format. All decimal integers are exactly representable in extended-real format.

The packed decimal indefinite encoding is stored by the FBSTP instruction in response to a masked floating-point invalid-operation exception. Attempting to load this value with the FBLD instruction produces an undefined result.

## UNSUPPORTED EXTENDED-REAL ENCODINGS

The extended-real format permits many encodings that do not fall into any of the categories shown in Table 31-9. Table 31-12 shows these unsupported encodings. Some of these encodings were supported by the Intel 287 math coprocessor; however, most of them are not supported by the Intel 387 math coprocessor, or the internal FPUs in the Intel486, Pentium, or Pentium Pro processors. These encodings are no longer supported due to changes made in the final version of IEEE Std. 754 that eliminated these encodings.

The categories of encodings formerly known as pseudo-NaNs, pseudo-infinities, and un-normal numbers are not supported. The Intel 387 math coprocessor and the internal FPUs in the Intel486, Pentium, and Pentium Pro processors generate the invalid-operation exception when they are encountered as operands.

The encodings formerly known as pseudo-denormal numbers are not generated by the Intel 387 math coprocessor and the internal FPUs in the Intel486, Pentium, and Pentium Pro processors; however, they are used correctly when encountered as operands. The exponent is treated as if it were 00..01B and the mantissa is unchanged. The denormal exception is generated.

**Figure.** Packed Decimal Integer Encodings

| Class | | Sign | Biased Exponent | Significand | |
|---|---|---|---|---|---|
| | | | | Integer | Fraction |
| | Quiet | 0 | 11..11 | 0 | 11..11 |
| | | 0 | 11..11 | | 10..00 |
| Positive Pseudo-NaNs | Signaling | 0 | 11..11 | 0 | 01..11 |
| | | 0 | 11..11 | | 00..01 |
| | Pseudo-infinity | 0 | 11..11 | 0 | 00..00 |
| | Unnormals | 0 | 11..10 | 0 | 11..11 |
| | | 0 | 00..01 | | 00..00 |
| Positive Reals | Pseudo-denormals | 0 | 00..00 | 1 | 11..11 |
| | | 0 | 00..00 | | 00..00 |
| | Pseudo-denormals | 1 | 00..00 | 1 | 11..11 |
| | | 1 | 00..00 | | 00..00 |
| Negative Reals | Unnormals | 1 | 11..10 | 0 | 11..01 |
| | | 1 | 00..01 | | 00..00 |
| | Pseudo-infinity | 1 | 11..11 | 0 | 00..00 |
| Negative Pseudo-NaNs | Signaling | 1 | 11..11 | 0 | 01..11 |
| | | 1 | 11..11 | | 00..01 |
| | Quiet | 1 | 11..11 | 0 | 11..11 |
| | | 1 | 11..11 | | 10..00 |
| | | | ←15 bits → | | ←63 bits → |

**NOTE:** * UUUU means bit values are undefined and may contain any value.

## FPU INSTRUCTION SET

The floating-point instructions that the Intel Architecture FPU supports can be grouped into six functional categories:

- Data transfer instructions
- Basic arithmetic instructions

- Comparison instructions
- Transcendental instructions
- Load constant instructions
- FPU control instructions

The following section briefly describes the instructions in each category. Detailed descriptions of the floating-point instructions are given in "Instruction Page Key".

**Unsupported Extended-Real Encodings**

| Class | | Sign | Biased Exponent | Significand Integer | Significand Fraction |
|---|---|---|---|---|---|
| | Quiet | 0 | 11..11 | 0 | 11..11 |
| | | | . | | . |
| | | 0 | 11..11 | | 10..00 |
| Positive Pseudo-NaNs | Signaling | 0 | 11..11 | 0 | 01..11 |
| | | . | . | | . |
| | | 0 | 11..11 | | 00..01 |
| | Pseudo-infinity | 0 | 11..11 | 0 | 00..00 |
| | Unnormals | 0 | 11..10 | 0 | 11..11 |
| | | | . | | . |
| Positive Reals | | 0 | 00..01 | | 00..00 |
| | Pseudo-denormals | 0 | 00..00 | 1 | 11..11 |
| | | | | | . |
| | | 0 | 00..00 | | 00..00 |
| | Pseudo-denormals | 1 | 00..00 | 1 | 11..11 |
| | | . | . | | . |
| | | 1 | 00..00 | | 00..00 |
| Negative Reals | Unnormals | 1 | 11..10 | 0 | 11..01 |
| | | . | . | | . |
| | | 1 | 00..01 | | 00..00 |
| | Pseudo-infinity | 1 | 11..11 | 0 | 00..00 |
| Negative Pseudo-NaNs | Signaling | 1 | 11..11 | 0 | 01..11 |
| | | . | . | | . |
| | | 1 | 11..11 | | 00..01 |
| | Quiet | 1 | 11..11 | 0 | 11..11 |
| | | . | . | | . |
| | | 1 | 11..11 | | 10..00 |
| | | | ←15 bits→ | | ←63 bits→ |

## Escape (ESC) Instructions

All of the instructions in the FPU instruction set fall into a class of instructions known as escape (ESC) instructions. All of these instructions have a common opcode format, which is slightly different from the format used by the integer and operating-system instructions.

## FPU Instruction Operands

Most floating-point instructions require one or two operands, which are located on the FPU data-register stack or in memory. (None of the floating-point instructions accept immediate operands.)

When an operand is located in a data register, it is referenced relative to the ST(0) register (the register at the top of the register stack), rather than by a physical register number. Often the ST(0) register is an implied operand.

Operands in memory can be referenced using the same operand addressing methods available for the integer and system instructions.

## Data Transfer Instructions

The data transfer instructions perform the following operations:

- Load real, integer, or packed BCD operands from memory into the ST(0) register.
- Store the value in the ST(0) register in memory in real, integer, or packed BCD format.
- Move values between registers in the FPU register stack.

## Data Transfer Instructions

| Real | | Integer | | Packed Decimal | |
|---|---|---|---|---|---|
| FLD | Load Real | FILD | Load Integer | FBLD | Load Packed Decimal |
| FST | Store Real | FIST | Store Integer | | |
| FSTP | Store Real and Pop | FISTP | Store Integer and Pop | FBSTP | Store Packed Decimal and Pop |
| FXCH | Exchange Register Contents | | | | |
| FCMOV*cc* | Conditional Move | | | | |

Operands are normally stored in the FPU data registers in extended-real format (see "Precision Control Field"). The FLD (load real) instruction pushes a real operand from memory onto the top of the FPU data-register stack. If the operand is in single- or double-real format, it is automatically converted to extended-real format. This instruction can also be used to push the value in a selected FPU data register onto the top of the register stack.

The FILD (load integer) instruction converts an integer operand in memory into extended-real format and pushes the value onto the top of the register stack. The FBLD (load packed decimal) instruction performs the same load operation for a packed BCD operand in memory.

The FST (store real) and FIST (store integer) instructions store the value in register ST(0) in memory in the destination format (real or integer, respectively). Again, the format conversion is carried out automatically.

The FSTP (store real and pop), FISTP (store integer and pop), and FBSTP (store packed decimal and pop) instructions store the value in the ST(0) registers into memory in the destination format (real, integer, or packed BCD), then performs a pop operation on the register stack. A pop operation causes the ST(0) register to be marked empty and the stack pointer (TOP) in the FPU control work to be incremented by 1. The FSTP instruction can also be used to copy the value in the ST(0) register to another FPU register [ST(i)].

The FXCH (exchange register contents) instruction exchanges the value in a selected register in the stack [ST(i)] with the value in ST(0).

The FCMOV*cc* (conditional move) instructions move the value in a selected register in the stack [ST(i)] to register ST(0). These instructions move the value only if the conditions specified with a condition code (*cc*) are satisfied. The conditions being tested with the FCMOV*cc* instructions are represented by the status flags in the EFLAGS register. The condition code mnemonics are appended to the letters "FCMOV" to form the mnemonic for a FCMOV*cc* instruction.

**Table: Floating-Point Conditional Move Instructions**

| Instruction Mnemonic | Status Flag States | Condition Description |
|---|---|---|
| FCMOVB | CF=1 | Below |
| FCMOVNB | CF=0 | Not below |
| FCMOVE | ZF=1 | Equal |
| FCMOVNE | ZF=0 | Not equal |
| FCMOVBE | (CF or ZF)=1 | Below or equal |
| FCMOVNBE | (CF or ZF)=0 | Not below nor equal |
| FCMOVU | PF=1 | Unordered |
| FCMOVNU | PF=0 | Not unordered |

Like the CMOV*cc* instructions, the FCMOV*cc* instructions are useful for optimizing small IF constructions. They also help eliminate branching overhead for IF operations and the possibility of branch mispredictions by the processor.

## Load Constant Instructions

The following instructions push commonly used constants onto the top [ST(0)] of the FPU register stack:

| FLDZ | Load +0.0 |
|---|---|
| FLD1 | Load +1.0 |
| FLDPI | Load |
| FLDL2T | Load $\log_2 10$ |
| FLDL2E | Load $\log_2 e$ |
| FLDLG2 | Load $\log_{10} 2$ |
| FLDLN2 | Load $\log_e 2$ |

The constant values have full extended-real precision (64 bits) and are accurate to approximately 19 decimal digits. They are stored internally in a format more precise than extended real. When loading the constant, the FPU rounds the more precise internal constant according to the RC (rounding control) field of the FPU control word. See "Pi", for information on the constant.

## BASIC ARITHMETIC INSTRUCTIONS

The following floating-point instructions perform basic arithmetic operations on real numbers. Where applicable, these instructions match IEEE Standard 754:

| | |
|---|---|
| FADD/FADDP | Add real |
| FIADD | Add integer to real |
| FSUB/FSUBP | Subtract real |
| FISUB | Subtract integer from real |
| FSUBR/FSUBRP | Reverse subtract real |
| FISUBR | Reverse subtract real from integer |
| FMUL/FMULP | Multiply real |
| FIMUL | Multiply integer by real |
| FDIV/FDIVP | Divide real |
| FIDIV | Divide real by integer |
| FDIVR/FDIVRP | Reverse divide |
| FIDIVR | Reverse divide integer by real |
| FABS | Absolute value |
| FCHS | Change sign |
| FSQRT | Square root |
| FPREM | Partial remainder |
| FPREM1 | IEEE partial remainder |
| FRNDINT | Round to integral value |
| FXTRACT | Extract exponent and significand |

The add, subtract, multiply and divide instructions operate on the following types of operands:

- Two FPU register values.
- A register value and a real or integer value in memory.

Operands in memory can be in single-real, double-real, short-integer, or word-integer format. They are converted to extended-real format automatically.

Reverse versions of the subtract and divide instructions are provided to foster efficient coding. For example, the FSUB instruction subtracts the value in a specified FPU register [ST(i)] from the value in register ST(0); whereas, the FSUBR instruction subtracts the value in ST(0) from the value in ST(i). The results of both operations are stored in register ST(0). These instructions eliminate the need to exchange values between register ST(0) and another FPU register to perform a subtraction or division.

The pop versions of the add, subtract, multiply and divide instructions pop the FPU register stack following the arithmetic operation.

The FPREM instruction computes the remainder from the division of two operands in the manner used by the Intel 8087 and Intel 287 math coprocessors; the FPREM1 instructions computes the remainder is the manner specified in the IEEE specification.

The FSQRT instruction computes the square root of the source operand.

The FRNDINT instructions rounds a real value to its nearest integer value, according to the current rounding mode specified in the RC field of the FPU control word. This instruction performs a function similar to the FIST/FISTP instructions, except that the result is saved in a real format.

The FABS, FCHS, and FXTRACT instructions perform convenient arithmetic operations. The FABS instruction produces the absolute value of the source operand. The FCHS instruction changes the sign of the source operand. The FXTRACT instruction separates the source operand into its exponent and fraction and stores each value in a register in real format.

Comparison of real values differ from comparison of integers because real values have four (rather than three) mutually exclusive relationships: less than, equal, greater than, and unordered.

The unordered relationship is true when at least one of the two values being compared is a NaN or in an undefined format. This additional relationship is required because, by definition, NaNs are not numbers, so they cannot have less than, equal, or greater than relationships with other real values.

The FCOM, FCOMP, and FCOMPP instructions compare the value in register ST(0) with a real source operand and set the condition code flags (C0, C2, and C3) in the FPU status word according to the results. If an unordered condition is detected (one or both of the values is a NaN or in an undefined format), a floating-point invalid-operation exception is generated.

The pop versions of the instruction pop the FPU register stack once or twice after the comparison operation is complete.

The FUCOM, FUCOMP, and FUCOMPP instructions operate the same as the FCOM, FCOMP, and FCOMPP instructions. The only difference is that with the FUCOM, FUCOMP, and FUCOMPP instructions, if an unordered condition is detected because one or both of the operands is a QNaN, the floating-point invalid-operation exception is not generated.

**Table:** Setting of FPU Condition Code Flags for Real Number Comparisons

| Condition | C3 | C2 | C0 |
|---|---|---|---|
| ST(0) > Source Operand | 0 | 0 | 0 |
| ST(0) < Source Operand | 0 | 0 | 1 |
| ST(0) = Source Operand | 1 | 0 | 0 |
| Unordered | 1 | 1 | 1 |

The FICOM and FICOMP instructions also operate the same as the FCOM and FCOMP instructions, except that the source operand is an integer value in memory. The integer value is automatically converted into an extended real value prior to making the comparison. The FICOMP instruction pops the FPU register stack following the comparison operation.

The FTST instruction performs the same operation as the FCOM instruction, except that the value in register ST(0) is always compared with the value 0.0.

The FCOMI and FCOMIP instructions are new in the Intel Pentium Pro processor. They perform the same comparison as the FCOM and FCOMP instructions, except that they set the status flags (ZF, PF, and CF) in the EFLAGS register to indicate the results of the comparison instead of the FPU condition code flags. The FCOMI and FCOMIP instructions allow condition branch instructions (J*cc*) to be executed directly from the results of their comparison.

**Table:** Setting of EFLAGS Status Flags for Real Number Comparisons

| Comparison Results | ZF | PF | CF |
|---|---|---|---|
| ST0 > ST(*i*) | 0 | 0 | 0 |
| ST0 < ST(*i*) | 0 | 0 | 1 |
| ST0 = ST(*i*) | 1 | 0 | 0 |
| Unordered | 1 | 1 | 1 |

The FUCOMI and FUCOMIP instructions operate the same as the FCOMI and FCOMIP instructions, except that they do not generate a floating-point invalid-operation exception if the unordered condition is the result of one or both of the operands being a QNaN. The FCOMIP and FUCOMIP instructions pop the FPU register stack following the comparison operation.

It also sets the C1 flag to indicate the sign of the value.

### Branching on the FPU Condition Codes

The processor does not offer any control-flow instructions that branch on the setting of the condition code flags (C0, C2, and C3) in the FPU status word. To branch on the state of these flags, the FPU status word must first be moved to the AX register in the integer unit. The FSTSW AX (store status word) instruction can be used for this purpose. When these flags are in the AX register, the TEST instruction can be used to control conditional branching as follows:

1. Check for an unordered result. Use the TEST instruction to compare the contents of the AX register with the constant 0400H. This operation will clear the ZF flag in the EFLAGS register if the condition code flags indicate an unordered result; otherwise,

the ZF flag will be set. The JNZ instruction can then be used to transfer control (if necessary) to a procedure for handling unordered operands.

**Table:** TEST Instruction Constants for Conditional Branching

| Order | Constant | Branch |
|---|---|---|
| ST(0) > Source Operand | 4500H | JZ |
| ST(0) < Source Operand | 0100H | JNZ |
| ST(0) = Source Operand | 4000H | JNZ |
| Unordered | 0400H | JNZ |

2. Check ordered comparison result. Use the constants given in Table 31-17 in the TEST instruction to test for a less than, equal to, or greater than result, then use the corresponding conditional branch instruction to transfer programme control to the appropriate procedure or section of code.

If a programme or procedure has been thoroughly tested and it incorporates periodic checks for QNaN results, then it is not necessary to check for the unordered result every time a comparison is made.

See "Branching and Conditional Moves on FPU Condition Codes", for another technique for branching on FPU condition codes.

Some non-comparison FPU instructions update the condition code flags in the FPU status word. To ensure that the status word is not altered inadvertently, store it immediately following a comparison operation.

## TRIGONOMETRIC INSTRUCTIONS

The following instructions perform four common trigonometric functions:

| FSIN | Sine |
|---|---|
| FCOS | Cosine |
| FSINCOS | Sine and cosine |
| FPTAN | Tangent |
| FPATAN | Arctangent |

These instructions operate on the top one or two registers of the FPU register stack and they return their results to the stack. The source operands must be given in radians.

The FSINCOS instruction returns both the sine and the cosine of a source operand value. It operates faster than executing the FSIN and FCOS instructions in succession.

The FPATAN instruction computes the arctangent of ST(1) divided by ST(0). It is useful for converting rectangular coordinates to polar coordinates.

**Pi**

When the argument (source operand) of a trigonometric function is within the range of the function, the argument is automatically reduced by the appropriate multiple of $2\pi$ through the same reduction mechanism used by the FPREM and FPREM1 instructions. The internal value of that the Intel Architecture FPU uses for argument reduction and other computations is as follows:

$\pi == 0.f * 2^2$

where:

f = C90FDAA2 2168C234 C

(The spaces in the fraction above indicate 32-bit boundaries.)

This internal $\pi$ value has a 66-bit mantissa, which is 2 bits more than is allowed in the significand of an extended-real value. (Since 66 bits is not an even number of hexadecimal digits, two additional zeros have been added to the value so that it can be represented in hexadecimal format. The least-significant hexadecimal digit (C) is thus 1100B, where the two least-significant bits represent bits 67 and 68 of the mantissa.)

This value of $\pi$ has been chosen to guarantee no loss of significance in a source operand, provided the operand is within the specified range for the instruction.

If the results of computations that explicitly use $\pi$ are to be used in the FSIN, FCOS, FSINCOS, or FPTAN instructions, the full 66-bit fraction of π should be used. This insures that the results are consistent with the argument-reduction algorithms that these instructions use. Using a rounded version of π can cause inaccuracies in result values, which if propagated through several calculations, might result in meaningless results.

A common method of representing the full 66-bit fraction of π is to separate the value into two numbers (high π and low π) that when added together give the value for π shown earlier in this section with the full 66-bit fraction:

$\pi = \text{high } \pi + \text{low } \pi$

For example, the following two values (given in scientific notation with the fraction in hexadecimal and the exponent in decimal) represent the 33 most-significant and the 33 least-significant bits of the fraction:

high π (unnormalized) = $0.\text{C90FDAA20} \times 2^{+2}$

low π (unnormalized) = $0.\text{42D184698} \times 2^{-31}$

These values encoded in standard IEEE double-real format are as follows:

high π = 400921FB 54400000

low π = 3DE0B461 1A600000

(Note that in the IEEE double-real format, the exponents are biased (by 1023) and the fractions are normalized.)

Similar versions of π can also be written in extended-real format.

When using this two-part π value in an algorithm, parallel computations should be performed on each part, with the results kept separate. When all the computations are complete, the two results can be added together to form the final result.

The complications of maintaining a consistent value of π for argument reduction can be avoided, either by applying the trigonometric functions only to arguments within the range of the automatic reduction mechanism, or by performing all argument reductions (down to a magnitude less than $\pi/4$) explicitly in software.

## LOGARITHMIC, EXPONENTIAL, AND SCALE

The following instructions provide two different logarithmic functions, an exponential function, and a scale function.

| | |
|---|---|
| FYL2X | Compute log ($y*\log_2 x$) |
| FYL2XP1 | Compute log epsilon ($y * \log_2(x + 1)$) |
| F2XM1 | Compute exponential ($2^x - 1$) |
| FSCALE | Scale |

The FYL2X and FYL2XP1 instructions perform two different base 2 logarithmic operations. The FYL2X instruction computes the log of ($y * \log_2 x$). This operation permits the calculation of the log of any base using the following equation:

$$\log_b x = (1/\log_2 b) * \log_2 x$$

The FYL2XP1 instruction computes the log epsilon of ($y * \log_2 (x + 1)$). This operation provides optimum accuracy for values of epsilon ($\varepsilon$) that are close to 0.

The F2XM1 instruction computes the exponential ($2^x - 1$). This instruction only operates on source values in the range -1.0 to +1.0.

The FSCALE instruction multiplies the source operand by a power of 2.

## TRANSCENDENTAL INSTRUCTION ACCURACY

The algorithms that the Pentium and Pentium Pro processors use for the transcendental instructions (FSIN, FCOS, FSINCOS, FPTAN, FPATAN, F2XM1, FYL2X, and FYL2XP1) allow a higher level of accuracy than was possible in earlier Intel Architecture math coprocessors and FPUs. The accuracy of these instructions is measured in terms of units in the last place (ulp). For a given argument $x$, let $f(x)$ and $F(x)$ be the correct and computed (approximate) function values, respectively. The error in ulps is defined to be:

$$error = \left| \frac{f(x) - F(x)}{2^{k-63}} \right|$$

where $k$ is an integer such that

$$1 \leq 2^{-k} f(x) < 2$$

With the Pentium and Pentium Pro processors, the worst case error on transcendental functions is less than 1 ulp when rounding to the nearest-even and less than 1.5 ulps when rounding in other modes. The functions are guaranteed to be monotonic, with respect to the input operands, throughout the domain supported by the instruction.

With the Intel486 processor and Intel 387 math coprocessor, the worst-case, transcendental-function error is typically 3 or 3.5 ulps, but is sometimes as large as 4.5 ulps.

## FPU CONTROL INSTRUCTIONS

The following instructions control the state and modes of operation of the FPU. They also allow the status of the FPU to be examined:

FINIT/FNINIT Initialize FPU

FLDCW Load FPU control word

FSTCW/FNSTCW Store FPU control word

FSTSW/FNSTSW Store FPU status word

FCLEX/FNCLEX Clear FPU exception flags

FLDENV Load FPU environment

FSTENV/FNSTENV Store FPU environment

FRSTOR Restore FPU state

FSAVE/FNSAVE Save FPU state

FINCSTP Increment FPU register stack pointer

FDECSTP Decrement FPU register stack pointer

FFREE Free FPU register

FNOP No operation

WAIT/FWAIT Check for and handle pending unmasked FPU exceptions

The FINIT/FNINIT instructions initialize the FPU and its internal registers to default values.

The FLDCW instructions loads the FPU control word register with a value from memory. The FSTCW/FNSTCW and FSTSW/FNSTSW instructions store the FPU control and status words, respectively, in memory (or for an FSTSW/FNSTSW instruction in a general-purpose register).

The FSTENV/FNSTENV and FSAVE/FNSAVE instructions save the FPU environment and state, respectively, in memory. The FPU environment includes all the FPU's control and status registers; the FPU state includes the FPU environment and the data registers in the FPU register stack. (The FSAVE/FNSAVE instruction also initializes the FPU to default values, like the FINIT/FNINIT instruction, after it saves the original state of the FPU.)

The FLDENV and FRSTOR instructions load the FPU environment and state, respectively, from memory into the FPU. These instructions are commonly used when switching tasks or contexts.

The WAIT/FWAIT instructions are synchronization instructions. (They are actually mnemonics for the same opcode.) These instructions check the FPU status word for pending unmasked FPU exceptions. If any pending unmasked FPU exceptions are found, they are handled before the processor resumes execution of the instructions (integer, floating-point, or system instruction) in the instruction stream. The WAIT/FWAIT instructions are provided to allow synchronization of instruction execution between the FPU and the processor's integer unit. See "Floating-Point Exception Synchronization" for more information on the use of the WAIT/FWAIT instructions.

## WAITING VS. NON-WAITING INSTRUCTIONS

All of the floating-point instructions except a few special control instructions perform a wait operation (similar to the

WAIT/FWAIT instructions), to check for and handle pending unmasked FPU exceptions, before they perform their primary operation (such as adding two real numbers). These instructions are called waiting instructions. Some of the FPU control instructions, such as FSTSW/FNSTSW, have both a waiting and a non-waiting versions. The waiting version (with the "F" prefix) executes a wait operation before it performs its primary operation; whereas, the non-waiting version (with the "FN" prefix) ignores pending unmasked exceptions. Non-waiting instructions allow software to save the current FPU state without first handling pending exceptions or to reset or reinitialize the FPU without regard for pending exceptions.

**Note:** When operating a Pentium or Intel486 processor in MS-DOS compatibility mode, it is possible (under unusual circumstances) for a non-waiting instruction to be interrupted prior to being executed to handle a pending FPU exception. The circumstances where this can happen and the resulting action of the processor are described in "No-Wait FPU Instructions Can Get FPU Interrupt in Window". When operating a Pentium Pro processor in MS-DOS compatibility mode, non-waiting instructions can not be interrupted in this way.

### Unsupported FPU Instructions

The Intel 8087 instructions FENI and FDISI and the Intel 287 math coprocessor instruction FSETPM perform no function in the Intel 387 math coprocessor, or the Intel486, Pentium, or Pentium Pro processors. If these opcodes are detected in the instruction stream, the FPU performs no specific operation and no internal FPU states are affected.

### Operating on NaNs

As was described in "NaNs", the FPU supports two types of NaNs: SNaNs and QNaNs. An SNaN is any NaN value with its most-significant fraction bit set to 0 and at least one other fraction bit set to 1. (If all the fraction bits are set to 0, the value is an ·.) A QNaN is any NaN value with the most-significant fraction bit set to 1. The sign bit of a NaN is not interpreted.

As a general rule, when a QNaN is used in one or more arithmetic floating-point instructions, it is allowed to propagate through a computation. An SNaN on the other hand causes a floating-point invalid-operation exception to be signaled. SNaNs are typically used to trap or invoke an exception handler. They must be inserted by software; that is, the FPU never generates an SNaN as a result.

The floating-point invalid-operation exception has a flag and a mask bit associated with it in the FPU status and control registers, respectively (see "Floating-Point Exception Handling"). The mask bit determines how the FPU handles an SNaN value. If the floating-point invalid-operation mask bit is set, the SNaN is converted to a QNaN by setting the most-significant fraction bit of the value to 1. The result is then stored in the destination operand and the floating-point invalid-operation flag is set. If the invalid-operation mask is clear, a floating-point invalid-operation fault is signaled and no result is stored in the destination operand.

When a real operation or exception delivers a QNaN result, the value of the result depends on the source operands, as shown in Table.

Except for the rules given at the beginning of this section for encoding SNaNs and QNaNs, software is free to use the bits in the significand of a NaN for any purpose. Both SNaNs and QNaNs can be encoded to carry and store data, such as diagnostic information.

### Rules for Generating QNaNs

| Source Operands | QNaN Result |
|---|---|
| An SNaN and a QNaN. | The QNaN source operand. |
| Two SNaNs. | The SNaN with the larger significand converted into a QNaN. |
| Two QNaNs. | The QNaN with the larger significand. |
| An SNaN and a real value. | The SNaN converted into a QNaN. |
| A QNaN and a real value. | The QNaN source operand. |
| Neither source operand | The default QNaN *real indefinite*. |

is a NaN and a floating-point invalid-operation exception is signaled.

## Uses for Signaling NANs

By unmasking the invalid operation exception, the programmer can use signaling NaNs to trap to the exception handler. The generality of this approach and the large number of NaN values that are available provide the sophisticated programmer with a tool that can be applied to a variety of special situations.

For example, a compiler can use signaling NaNs as references to uninitialized (real) array elements. The compiler can preinitialize each array element with a signaling NaN whose significand contained the index (relative position) of the element. Then, if an application programme attempts to access an element that it had not initialized, it can use the NaN placed there by the compiler. If the invalid operation exception is unmasked, an interrupt will occur, and the exception handler will be invoked. The exception handler can determine which element has been accessed, since the operand address field of the exception pointers will point to the NaN, and the NaN will contain the index number of the array element.

## Uses for Quiet NANs

Quiet NaNs are often used to speed up debugging. In its early testing phase, a programme often contains multiple errors. An exception handler can be written to save diagnostic information in memory whenever it was invoked. After storing the diagnostic data, it can supply a quiet NaN as the result of the erroneous instruction, and that NaN can point to its associated diagnostic area in memory. The programme will then continue, creating a different NaN for each error. When the programme ends, the NaN results can be used to access the diagnostic data saved at the time the errors occurred. Many errors can thus be diagnosed and corrected in one test run.

In embedded applications which use computed results in further computations, an undetected QNaN can invalidate all subsequent results. Such applications should therefore periodically check for QNaNs and provide a recovery mechanism to be used if a QNaN result is detected.

## FLOATING-POINT EXCEPTION HANDLING

The FPU detects six classes of exception conditions while executing floating-point instructions:

- Invalid operation
  - o Stack overflow or underflow
  - o Invalid arithmetic operation
- Divide-by-zero
- Denormalized operand
- Numeric overflow
- Numeric underflow
- Inexact result (precision)

The nomenclature of "#" symbol followed by one or two letters is used in this manual to indicate exception conditions. It is merely a short-hand form and is not related to assembler mnemonics.

Each of the six exception classes has a corresponding flag bit in the FPU status word and a mask bit in the FPU control word. In addition, the exception summary (ES) flag in the status word indicates when any of the exceptions has been detected, and the stack fault (SF) flag (also in the status word) distinguishes between the two types of invalid-operation exceptions.

When the FPU detects a floating-point exception, it sets the appropriate flags in the FPU status word, then takes one of two possible courses of action:

- Handles the exception automatically, producing a predefined (and often times usable result), while allowing programme execution to continue undisturbed.

- Invokes a software exception handler to handle the exception.

The following sections describe how the FPU handles exceptions (either automatically or by calling a software exception handler), how the FPU detects the various floating-point exceptions, and the automatic (masked) response to the floating-point exceptions.

## ARITHMETIC VS. NON-ARITHMETIC INSTRUCTIONS

When dealing with floating-point exceptions, it is useful to distinguish between arithmetic instructions and non-arithmetic instructions. Non-arithmetic instructions have no operands or do not make substantial changes to their operands. Arithmetic instructions do make significant changes to their operands; in particular, they make changes that could result in a floating-point exception being signaled. Table 31-19 lists the non-arithmetic and arithmetic instructions. It should be noted that some non-arithmetic instructions can signal a floating-point stack (fault) exception, but this exception is not the result of an operation on an operand.

### Automatic Exception Handling

If the FPU detects an exception condition for a masked exception (an exception with its mask bit set), it sets the exception flag for the exception and delivers a predefined (default) response and continues executing instructions. The masked (default) responses to exceptions have been chosen to deliver a reasonable result for each exception condition and are generally satisfactory for most floating-point applications. By masking or unmasking specific floating-point exceptions in the FPU control word, programmers can delegate responsibility for most exceptions to the FPU and reserve the most severe exception conditions for software exception handlers.

Because the exception flags are "sticky," they provide a cumulative record of the exceptions that have occurred since they were last cleared. A programmer can thus mask all exceptions, run a calculation, and then inspect the exception flags to see if any exceptions were detected during the calculation.

**Table.** Arithmetic and Non-arithmetic Instructions (Sheet 1 of 2)

| **Non-arithmetic Instructions** | **Arithmetic Instructions** |
|---|---|
| FABS | F2XM1 |
| FCHS | FADD/FADDP |
| FCLEX | FBLD |
| FDECSTP | FBSTP |
| FFREE | FCOM/FCOMP/FCOMPP |
| FINCSTP | FCOS |
| FINIT/FNINIT | FDIV/FDIVP/FDIVR/FDIVRP |
| FLD (register-to-register) | FIADD |
| FLD (extended format from memory) | FICOM/FICOMP |
| FLD constant | FIDIV/FIDIVR |
| FLDCW | FILD |
| FLDENV | FIMUL |
| FNOP | FIST/FISTP |
| FRSTOR | FISUB/FISUBR |
| FSAVE/FNSAVE | FLD (conversion) |
| FST/FSTP (register-to-register) | FMUL/FMULP |
| FSTP (extended format to memory) | FPATAN |
| FSTCW/FNSTCW | FPREM/FPREM1 |
| FSTENV/FNSTENV | FPTAN |
| FSTSW/FNSTSW | FRNDINT |
| WAIT/FWAIT | FSCALE |
| FXAM | FSIN |
| FXCH | FSINCOS |
| | FSQRT |
| | FST/FSTP (conversion) |

| | |
|---|---|
| | FSUB/FSUBP/FSUBR/FSUBRP |
| | FTST |
| | FUCOM/FUCOMP/FUCOMPP |
| | FXTRACT |
| | FYL2X/FYL2XP1 |

Note that when exceptions are masked, the FPU may detect multiple exceptions in a single instruction, because it continues executing the instruction after performing its masked response. For example, the FPU can detect a denormalized operand, perform its masked response to this exception, and then detect numeric underflow.

## SOFTWARE EXCEPTION HANDLING

### Native Mode

The native mode for handling floating-point exceptions is selected by setting the NE flag in control register CR0 to 1. In this mode, if the FPU detects an exception condition while executing a floating-point instruction and the exception is unmasked (the mask bit for the exception is cleared), the FPU sets the flag for the exception and the ES flag in the FPU status word. It then invokes the software exception handler through the floating-point-error exception (#MF, vector 16), immediately before execution of any of the following instructions in the processor's instruction stream:

- The next floating-point instruction, unless it is one of the non-waiting instructions (FNINIT, FNCLEX, FNSTSW, FNSTCW, FNSTENV, and FNSAVE).
- The next WAIT/FWAIT instruction.
- The next MMX instruction.

If the next floating-point instruction in the instruction stream is a non-waiting instruction, the FPU executes the instruction without invoking the software exception handler.

### MS-DOS* Compatibility Mode

If the NE flag in control register CR0 is set to 0, the MS-DOS compatibility mode for handling floating-point exceptions is selected. In this mode, the software exception handler for floating-point exceptions is invoked externally using the processor's FERR#, INTR, and IGNNE# pins. This method of reporting floating-point errors and invoking an exception handler is provided to support the floating-point exception handling mechanism used in PC systems that are running the MS-DOS or Windows* 95 operating system.

The MS-DOS compatibility mode is typically used as follows to invoke the floating-point exception handler:

1. If the FPU detects an unmasked floating-point exception, it sets the flag for the exception and the ES flag in the FPU status word.
2. If the IGNNE# pin is deasserted, the FPU then asserts the FERR# pin either immediately, or else delayed (deferred) until just before the execution of the next waiting floating-point instruction or MMX™ instruction. Whether the FERR# pin is asserted immediately or delayed depends on the type of processor, the instruction, and the type of exception.
3. If a preceding floating-point instruction has set the exception flag for an unmasked FPU exception, the processor freezes just before executing the next WAIT instruction, waiting floating-point instruction, or MMX instruction. Whether the FERR# pin was asserted at the preceding floating-point instruction or is just now being asserted, the freezing of the processor assures that the FPU exception handler will be invoked before the new floatingpoint (or MMX) instruction gets executed.
4. The FERR# pin is connected through external hardware to IRQ13 of a cascaded, programmable interrupt controller (PIC). When the FERR# pin is asserted, the PIC is programmed to generate an interrupt 75H.
5. The PIC asserts the INTR pin on the processor to signal the interrupt 75H.

6. The BIOS for the PC system handles the interrupt 75H by branching to the interrupt 2 (NMI) interrupt handler.
7. The interrupt 2 handler determines if the interrupt is the result of an NMI interrupt or a floating-point exception.
8. If a floating-point exception is detected, the interrupt 2 handler branches to the floating-point exception handler.

If the IGNNE# pin is asserted, the processor ignores floating-point error conditions. This pin is provided to inhibit floating-point exceptions from being generated while the floating-point exception handler is servicing a previously signaled floating-point exception.

"Guidelines for Writing FPU Exception Handlers", describes the MS-DOS compatibility mode in much greater detail.

## Typical Floating-Point Exception Handler Actions

After the floating-point exception handler is invoked, the processor handles the exception in the same manner that it handles non-FPU exceptions. (The floating-point exception handler is normally part of the operating system or executive software.) A typical action of the exception handler is to store FPU state information in memory (with the FSTENV/ FNSTENV or FSAVE/FNSAVE instructions) so that it can evaluate the exception and formulate an appropriate response (see "Saving the FPU's State"). Other typical exception handler actions include:

- Examining stored FPU state information (control, status, and tag words, and FPU instruction and operand pointers) to determine the nature of the error.
- Correcting the condition that caused the error.
- Clearing the exception bits in the status word.

- Returning to the interrupted programme and resuming normal execution.

If the faulting floating-point instruction is followed by one or more non-floating-point instructions, it may not be useful to re-execute the faulting instruction. See "Floating-Point Exception Synchronization", for more information on synchronizing floating-point exceptions.

In cases where the handler needs to restart programme execution with the faulting instruction, the IRET instruction cannot be used directly. The reason for this is that because the exception is not generated until the next floating-point or WAIT/FWAIT instruction following the faulting floating-point instruction, the return instruction pointer on the stack may not point to the faulting instruction. To restart programme execution at the faulting instruction, the exception handler must obtain a pointer to the instruction from the saved FPU state information, load it into the return instruction pointer location on the stack, and then execute the IRET instruction.

In lieu of writing recovery procedures, the exception handler can do the following:

- Increment an exception counter for later display or printing.
- Print or display diagnostic information (such as, the FPU environment and registers).
- Halt further programme execution.

See "FPU Exception Handling Examples", for general examples of floating-point exception handlers and for specific examples of how to write a floating-point exception handler when using the MS-DOS compatibility mode.

## FLOATING-POINT EXCEPTION CONDITIONS

### Invalid Operation Exception

The floating-point invalid-operation exception occurs in response to two general types of operations:

- Stack overflow or underflow (#IS).
- Invalid arithmetic operand (#IA).

The flag for this exception (IE) is bit 0 of the FPU status word, and the mask bit (IM) is bit 0 of the FPU control word. The stack fault flag (SF) of the FPU status word indicates the type of operation caused the exception. When the SF flag is set to 1, a stack operation has resulted in stack overflow or underflow; when the flag is cleared to 0, an arithmetic instruction has encountered an invalid operand. Note that the FPU explicitly sets the SF flag when it detects a stack overflow or underflow condition, but it does not explicitly clear the flag when it detects an invalid-arithmetic-operand condition. As a result, the state of the SF flag can be 1 following an invalid-arithmetic-operation exception, if it was not cleared from the last time a stack overflow or underflow condition occurred. See "Stack Fault Flag", for more information about the SF flag.

**Stack Overflow or Underflow Exception (#IS)**

The FPU tag word keeps track of the contents of the registers in the FPU register stack.It then uses this information to detect two different types of stack faults:

- Stack overflow-an instruction attempts to write a value into a non-empty FPU register
- Stack underflow-an instruction attempts to read a value from an empty FPU register.

When the FPU detects stack overflow or underflow, it sets the IE flag (bit 0) and the SF flag (bit 6) in the FPU status word to 1. It then sets condition-code flag C1 (bit 9) in the FPU status word to 1 if stack overflow occurred or to 0 if stack underflow occurred.

If the invalid-operation exception is masked, the FPU then returns the real, integer, or BCD-integer indefinite value to the destination operand, depending on the instruction being executed. This value overwrites the destination register or memory location specified by the instruction.

If the invalid-operation exception is not masked, a software exception handler is invoked (see "Software Exception Handling") and the top-of-stack pointer (TOP) and source operands remain unchanged.

The term stack overflow comes from the condition where the a programme has pushed eight values onto the FPU register stack and the next value pushed on the stack causes a stack wraparound to a register that already contains a value. The term stack underflow refers to the opposite condition from stack overflow. Here, a programme has popped eight values from the FPU register stack and the next value popped from the stack causes stack wraparound to an empty register.

## INVALID ARITHMETIC OPERAND EXCEPTION (#IA)

The FPU is able to detect a variety of invalid arithmetic operations that can be coded in a programme. These operations generally indicate a programming error, such as dividing · by ·. Table 31-20 lists the invalid arithmetic operations that the FPU detects. This group includes the invalid operations defined in IEEE Std. 854.

When the FPU detects an invalid arithmetic operand, it sets the IE flag (bit 0) in the FPU status word to 1. If the invalid-operation exception is masked, the FPU then returns an indefinite value to the destination operand or sets the floating-point condition codes, as shown in Table 31-20. If the invalid-operation exception is not masked, a software exception handler is invoked and the top-of-stack pointer (TOP) and source operands remain unchanged.

## DIVIDE-BY-ZERO EXCEPTION (#Z)

The FPU reports a floating-point zero-divide exception whenever an instruction attempts to divide a finite non-zero operand by 0. The flag (ZE) for this exception is bit 2 of the FPU status word, and the mask bit (ZM) is bit 2 of the FPU control word. The FDIV, FDIVP, FDIVR, FDIVRP, FIDIV, and FIDIVR instructions and the other instructions that perform division internally (FYL2X and FXTRACT) can report the divide-by-zero exception.

When a divide-by-zero exception occurs and the exception is masked, the FPU sets the ZE flag and returns the values shown in Table 7-21. If the divide-by-zero exception is not masked, the ZE flag is set, a software exception handler is invoked, and the top-of-stack pointer (TOP) and source operands remain unchanged.

**Table:** Divide-By-Zero Conditions and the Masked Responses to Them

| Condition | Masked Response |
|---|---|
| Divide or reverse divide operation with a 0 divisor. | Returns an · signed with the exclusive OR of the sign of the two operands to the destination operand. |
| FYL2X instruction. | Returns an · signed with the opposite sign of the non-zero operand to the destination operand. |
| FXTRACT instruction. | ST(1) is set to - ; ST(0) is set to 0 with the same sign as the source operand. |

## Denormal Operand Exception (#D)

The FPU signals the denormal-operand exception under the following conditions:

- If an arithmetic instruction attempts to operate on a denormal operand (see "Normalized and Denormalized Finite Numbers").
- If an attempt is made to load a denormal single- or double-real value into an FPU register. (If the denormal value being loaded is an extended-real value, the denormal-operand exception is not reported.)

The flag (DE) for this exception is bit 1 of the FPU status word, and the mask bit (DM) is bit 1 of the FPU control word.

When a denormal-operand exception occurs and the exception is masked, the FPU sets the DE flag, then proceeds with the instruction. The denormal operand in single- or double-real format is automatically normalized when converted to the extended-real format. Operating on denormal numbers will produce results at least as good as, and often better than, what can be obtained when denormal numbers are flushed to zero. In fact, subsequent operations will benefit from the additional precision of the internal extended-real format. Most programmers mask this exception so that a computation may proceed, then analyse any loss of accuracy when the final result is delivered.

When a denormal-operand exception occurs and the exception is not masked, the DE flag is set and a software exception handler is invoked (see "Software Exception Handling"). The top-of-stack pointer (TOP) and source operands remain unchanged. When denormal operands have reduced significance due to loss of low-order bits, it may be advisable to not operate on them. Precluding denormal operands from computations can be accomplished by an exception handler that responds to unmasked denormal-operand exceptions.

### Numeric Overflow Exception (#O)

The FPU reports a floating-point numeric overflow exception (#O) whenever the rounded result of an arithmetic instruction exceeds the largest allowable finite value that will fit into the real format of the destination operand. For example, if the destination format is extended-real (80 bits), overflow occurs when the rounded result falls outside the unbiased range of $-1.0 * 2^{16384}$ to $1.0 * 2^{16384}$ (exclusive). Numeric overflow can occur on arithmetic operations where the result is stored in an FPU data register. It can also occur on store-real operations (with the FST and FSTP instructions), where a within-range value in a data register is stored in memory in a single- or double-real format. The overflow threshold range for the single-real format is $-1.0 * 2^{128}$ to $1.0 * 2^{128}$; the range for the double-real format is $-1.0 * 2^{1024}$ to $1.0 * 2^{1024}$.

The numeric overflow exception cannot occur when overflow occurs when storing values in an integer or BCD integer format. Instead, the invalid-arithmetic-operand exception is signaled.

The flag (OE) for the numeric-overflow exception is bit 3 of the FPU status word, and the mask bit (OM) is bit 3 of the FPU control word.

When a numeric-overflow exception occurs and the exception is masked, the FPU sets the OE flag and returns one of the values shown in Table 31-22. The value returned depends on the current rounding mode of the FPU (see "Rounding Control Field")..

**Table.** Masked Responses to Numeric Overflow

| Rounding Mode | Sign of True Result | Result |
|---|---|---|
| To nearest | + | +· |
| | - | -· |
| Toward -· | + | Largest finite positive number |
| | - | -· |
| Toward +· | + | +· |
| | - | Largest finite negative number |
| Toward zero | + | Largest finite positive number |
| | - | Largest finite negative number |

The action that the FPU takes when numeric overflow occurs and the numeric-overflow exception is not masked, depends on whether the instruction is supposed to store the result in memory or on the register stack.

If the destination is a memory location, the OE flag is set and a software exception handler is invoked (see "Software Exception Handling"). The top-of-stack pointer (TOP) and source and destination operands remain unchanged.

If the destination is the register stack, the exponent of the rounded result is divided by $2^{24576}$ and the result is stored along with the significand in the destination operand. Condition code bit C1 in the FPU status word (called in this situation the "round-up bit") is set if the significand was rounded upward and cleared if the result was rounded toward 0. After the result is stored, the OE flag is set and a software exception handler is invoked.

The scaling bias value 24,576 is equal to 3 .* $2^{13}$. Biasing the exponent by 24,576 normally translates the number as nearly as possible to the middle of the extended-real exponent range so that, if desired, it can be used in subsequent scaled operations with less risk of causing further exceptions.

When using the FSCALE instruction, massive overflow can occur, where the result is too large to be represented, even with a bias-adjusted exponent. Here, if overflow occurs again, after the result has been biased, a properly signed · is stored in the destination operand.

### Numeric Underflow Exception (#U)

The FPU reports a floating-point numeric underflow exception (#U) whenever the rounded result of an arithmetic instruction is "tiny" (that is, less than the smallest possible normalized, finite value that will fit into the real format of the destination operand). For example, if the destination format is extended-real (80 bits), underflow occurs when the rounded result falls in the unbiased range of $-1.0 * 2^{-16382}$ to $1.0 * 2^{-16382}$ (exclusive). Like numeric overflow, numeric underflow can occur on arithmetic operations where the result is stored in an FPU data register. It can also occur on store-real operations (with the FST and FSTP instructions), where a within-range value in a data register is stored in memory in a single- or double-real format. The underflow threshold range for the single-real format is $-1.0 * 2^{-126}$ to $1.0 * 2^{-126}$; the range for the double-real format is $-1.0 * 2^{-1022}$ to $1.0 * 2^{-1022}$. (The numeric underflow exception cannot occur when storing values in an integer or BCD integer format.)

The flag (UE) for the numeric-underflow exception is bit 4 of the FPU status word, and the mask bit (UM) is bit 4 of the FPU control word.

When a numeric-underflow exception occurs and the exception is masked, the FPU denormalizes the result (see "Normalized and Denormalized Finite Numbers"). If the denormalized result is exact, the FPU stores the result in the destination operand, without setting the UE flag. If the denormal result is inexact, the FPU sets the UE flag, then goes on to handle the inexact-result exception condition (see "Inexact-Result (Precision) Exception (#P)"). It is important to note that if numeric-underflow is masked, a numeric-underflow exception is signaled only if the denormalized result is inexact. If the denormalized result is exact, no flags are set and no exceptions are signaled.

The action that the FPU takes when numeric underflow occurs and the numeric-underflow exception is not masked, depends on whether the instruction is supposed to store the result in memory or on the register stack.

If the destination is a memory location, the UE flag is set and a software exception handler is invoked (see "Software Exception Handling"). The top-of-stack pointer (TOP) and source and destination operands remain unchanged.

If the destination is the register stack, the exponent of the rounded result is multiplied by $2^{24576}$ and the product is stored along with the significand in the destination operand. Condition code bit C1 in the FPU the status register (acting here as a "round-up bit") is set if the significand was rounded upward and cleared if the result was rounded toward 0. After the result is stored, the UE flag is set and a software exception handler is invoked.

The scaling bias value 24,576 is the same as is used for the overflow exception and has the same effect, which is to translate the result as nearly as possible to the middle of the extended-real exponent range.

When using the FSCALE instruction, massive underflow can occur, where the result is too tiny to be represented, even with a bias-adjusted exponent. Here, if underflow occurs again, after the result has been biased, a properly signed 0 is stored in the destination operand.

**Inexact-Result (Precision) Exception (#P)**

The inexact-result exception (also called the precision exception) occurs if the result of an operation is not exactly representable in the destination format. For example, the fraction 1/3 cannot be precisely represented in binary form. This exception occurs frequently and indicates that some (normally acceptable) accuracy has been lost. The exception is supported for applications that need to perform exact arithmetic only. Because the rounded result is generally satisfactory for most applications, this exception is commonly masked. Note that the transcendental instructions [FSIN, FCOS, FSINCOS, FPTAN, FPATAN, F2XM1, FYL2X, and FYL2XP1] by nature produce inexact results.

The inexact-result exception flag (PE) is bit 5 of the FPU status word, and the mask bit (PM) is bit 5 of the FPU control word.

If the inexact-result exception is masked when an inexact-result condition occurs and a numeric overflow or underflow condition has not occurred, the FPU sets the PE flag and stores the rounded result in the destination operand. The current rounding mode determines the method used to round the result (see "Rounding Control Field"). The C1 (round-up) bit in the FPU status word indicates whether the inexact result was rounded up (C1 is set) or "not rounded up" (C1 is cleared). In the "not rounded up" case, the least-significant bits of the inexact result are truncated so that the result fits in the destination format.

If the inexact-result exception is not masked when an inexact result occurs and numeric overflow or underflow has not occurred, the FPU performs the same operation described in the previous paragraph and, in addition, invokes a software exception handler (see "Software Exception Handling").

If an inexact result occurs in conjunction with numeric overflow or underflow, one of the following operations is carried out:

- If an inexact result occurs along with masked overflow or underflow, the OE or UE flag and the PE flag are set and the result is stored as described for the overflow or underflow exceptions (see "Numeric Overflow Exception (#O)" or "Numeric

Underflow Exception (#U)"). If the inexact-result exception is unmasked, the FPU also invokes the software exception handler.

- If an inexact result occurs along with unmasked overflow or underflow and the destination operand is a register, the OE or UE flag and the PE flag are set, the result is stored as described for the overflow or underflow exceptions, and the software exception handler is invoked.
- If an inexact result occurs along with unmasked overflow or underflow and the destination operand is a memory location, the inexact-result condition is ignored.

## EXCEPTION PRIORITY

The processor handles exceptions according to a predetermined precedence. When an instruction generates two or more exception conditions, the exception precedence sometimes results in the higher-priority exception being handled and the lower-priority exceptions being ignored. For example, dividing an SNaN by zero can potentially signal an invalid-arithmetic-operand exception (due to the SNaN operand) and a divide-by-zero exception. Here, if both exceptions are masked, the FPU handles the higher-priority exception only (the invalid-arithmetic-operand exception), returning a real indefinite to the destination. Alternately, a denormal-operand or inexact-result exception can accompany a numeric underflow or overflow exception, with both exceptions being handled.

The precedence for floating-point exceptions is as follows:

1. Invalid-operation exception, subdivided as follows:
   a. Stack underflow.
   b. Stack overflow.
   c. Operand of unsupported format.
   d. SNaN operand.

2. QNaN operand. Though this is not an exception, the handling of a QNaN operand has precedence over lower-priority exceptions. For example, a QNaN divided by zero results in a QNaN, not a zero-divide exception.
3. Any other invalid-operation exception not mentioned above or a divide-by-zero exception.
4. Denormal-operand exception. If masked, then instruction execution continues, and a lower-priority exception can occur as well.
5. Numeric overflow and underflow exceptions in conjunction with the inexact-result exception.
6. Inexact-result exception.

Invalid operation, zero divide, and denormal operand exceptions are detected before a floating-point operation begins, whereas overflow, underflow, and precision errors are not detected until a true result has been computed. When a pre-operation exception is detected, the FPU register stack and memory have not yet been updated, and appear as if the offending instructions has not been executed. When a post-operation exception is detected, the register stack and memory may be updated with a result (depending on the nature of the error).

## FLOATING-POINT EXCEPTION SYNCHRONIZATION

Because the integer unit and FPU are separate execution units, it is possible for the processor to execute floating-point, integer, and system instructions concurrently. No special programming techniques are required to gain the advantages of concurrent execution. (Floating-point instructions are placed in the instruction stream along with the integer and system instructions.) However, concurrent execution can cause problems for floating-point exception handlers.

This problem is related to the way the FPU signals the existence of unmasked floating-point exceptions. (Special exception synchronization is not required for masked floating-point exceptions, because the FPU always returns a masked result to the destination operand.)

When a floating-point exception is unmasked and the exception condition occurs, the FPU stops further execution of the floating-point instruction and signals the exception event. On the next occurrence of a floating-point instruction or a WAIT/FWAIT instruction in the instruction stream, the processor checks the ES flag in the FPU status word for pending floating-point exceptions. It floating-point exceptions are pending, the FPU makes an implicit call (traps) to the floating-point software exception handler. The exception handler can then execute recovery procedures for selected or all floating-point exceptions.

Synchronization problems occur in the time frame between when the exception is signaled and when it is actually handled. Because of concurrent execution, integer or system instructions can be executed during this time frame. It is thus possible for the source or destination operands for a floating-point instruction that faulted to be overwritten in memory, making it impossible for the exception handler to analyse or recover from the exception.

To solve this problem, an exception synchronizing instruction (either a floating-point instruction or a WAIT/ FWAIT instruction) can be placed immediately after any floating-point instruction that might present a situation where state information pertaining to a floating-point exception might be lost or corrupted. Floating-point instructions that store data in memory are prime candidates for synchronization. For example, the following three lines of code have the potential for exception synchronization problems:

FILD COUNT; Floating-point instruction

INC COUNT; Integer instruction

FSQRT; Subsequent floating-point instruction

In this example, the INC instruction modifies the result

of a floating-point instruction (FILD). If an exception is signaled during the execution of the FILD instruction, the result stored in the COUNT memory location might be overwritten before the exception handler is called.

Rearranging the instructions, as follows, so that the FSQRT instruction follows the FILD instruction, synchronizes the exception handling and eliminates the possibility of the exception being handled incorrectly.

FILD COUNT; Floating-point instruction

FSQRT; Subsequent floating-point instruction synchronizes

; any exceptions generated by the FILD instruction.

INC COUNT; Integer instruction

The FSQRT instruction does not require any synchronization, because the results of this instruction are stored in the FPU data registers and will remain there, undisturbed, until the next floating-point or WAIT/FWAIT instruction is executed. To absolutely insure that any exceptions emanating from the FSQRT instruction are handled (for example, prior to a procedure call), a WAIT instruction can be placed directly after the FSQRT instruction.

Note that some floating-point instructions (non-waiting instructions) do not check for pending unmasked exceptions (see "FPU Control Instructions"). They include the FNINIT, FNSTENV, FNSAVE, FNSTSW, FNSTCW, and FNCLEX instructions. When an FNINIT, FNSTENV, FNSAVE, or FNCLEX instruction is executed, all pending exceptions are essentially lost (either the FPU status register is cleared or all exceptions are masked). The FNSTSW and FNSTCW instructions do not check for pending interrupts, but they do not modify the FPU status and control registers. A subsequent "waiting" floating-point instruction can then handle any pending exceptions.

## Floating-Point Exceptions Summary

Table lists the floating-point instruction mnemonics in alphabetical order. For each mnemonic, it summarizes the exceptions that the instruction may cause. "Floating-Point Exception Conditions", for a detailed discussion of the floating-point exceptions. The following codes indicate the floating-point exceptions:

| | |
|---|---|
| #IS | Invalid-operation exception for stack underflow or stack overflow. |
| #IA | Invalid-operation exception for invalid arithmetic operands and unsupported formats. |
| #D | Denormal-operand exception. |
| #Z | Divide-by-zero exception. |
| #O | Numeric-overflow exception. |
| #U | Numeric-underflow exception. |
| #P | Inexact-result (precision) exception. |

## Chapter 6

# Devices

### BINARY TO BCD CONVERTER

1. Shift the binary number left one bit.
2. If 8 shifts have taken place, the BCD number is in the *Hundreds, Tens,* and *Units* column.
3. If the binary value in any of the BCD columns is 5 or greater, add 3 to that value in that BCD column.

4. Go to 1.

| Operation | Hundreds | Tens | Units | Binary | |
|---|---|---|---|---|---|
| HEX | | | | F | F |
| Start | | | | 1111 | 1111 |

**Example: Convert hex E to BCD**

| Operation | Tens | Units | Binary |
|---|---|---|---|
| HEX | | | E |
| Start | | | 1 1 1 0 |
| Shift 1 | | 1 | 1 1 0 |
| Shift 2 | | 1 1 | 1 0 |
| Shift 3 | | 1 1 1 | 0 |
| Add 3 | | 1 0 1 0 | 0 |
| Shift 4 | 1 | 0 1 0 0 | |
| BCD | 1 | 4 | |

## Example: Convert hex FF to BCD

| Operation | Hundreds | Tens | Units | Binary | |
|---|---|---|---|---|---|
| HEX | | | | F | F |
| Start | | | | 1 1 1 1 | 1 1 1 1 |
| Shift 1 | | | 1 | 1 1 1 1 | 1 1 1 |
| Shift 2 | | | 1 1 | 1 1 1 1 | 1 1 |
| Shift 3 | | | 1 1 1 | 1 1 1 1 | 1 |
| Add 3 | | | 1 0 1 0 | 1 1 1 1 | 1 |
| Shift 4 | | 1 | 0 1 0 1 | 1 1 1 1 | |
| Add 3 | | 1 | 1 0 0 0 | 1 1 1 1 | |
| Shift 5 | | 1 1 | 0 0 0 1 | 1 1 1 | |
| Shift 6 | | 1 1 0 | 0 0 1 1 | 1 1 | |
| Add 3 | | 1 0 0 1 | 0 0 1 1 | 1 1 | |
| Shift 7 | 1 | 0 0 1 0 | 0 1 1 1 | 1 | |
| Add 3 | 1 | 0 0 1 0 | 1 0 1 0 | 1 | |
| Shift 8 | 1 0 | 0 1 0 1 | 0 1 0 1 | | |
| BCD | 2 | 5 | 5 | | |

## Truth table for Add-3 Module

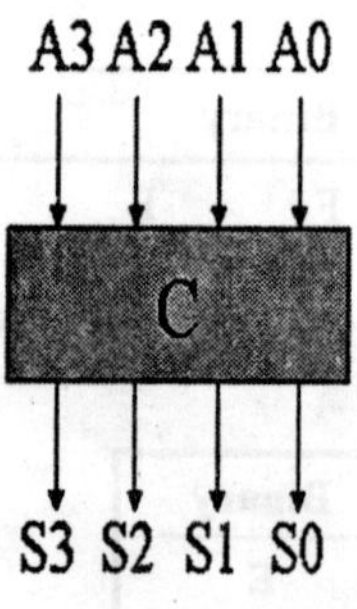


| A3 | A2 | A1 | A0 | S3 | S2 | S1 | S0 |
|---|---|---|---|---|---|---|---|
| 0 | 0 | 0 | 0 | 0 | 0 | 0 | 0 |
| 0 | 0 | 0 | 1 | 0 | 0 | 0 | 1 |
| 0 | 0 | 1 | 0 | 0 | 0 | 1 | 0 |
| 0 | 0 | 1 | 1 | 0 | 0 | 1 | 1 |
| 0 | 1 | 0 | 0 | 0 | 1 | 0 | 0 |
| 0 | 1 | 0 | 1 | 1 | 0 | 0 | 0 |
| 0 | 1 | 1 | 0 | 1 | 0 | 0 | 1 |
| 0 | 1 | 1 | 1 | 1 | 0 | 1 | 0 |
| 1 | 0 | 0 | 0 | 1 | 0 | 1 | 1 |
| 1 | 0 | 0 | 1 | 1 | 1 | 0 | 0 |
| 1 | 0 | 1 | 0 | X | X | X | X |
| 1 | 0 | 1 | 1 | X | X | X | X |
| 1 | 1 | 0 | 0 | X | X | X | X |
| 1 | 1 | 0 | 1 | X | X | X | X |
| 1 | 1 | 1 | 0 | X | X | X | X |
| 1 | 1 | 1 | 1 | X | X | X | X |

Here is a Verilog module for this truth table.

## BINARY-TO-BCD CONVERTER MODULE

Here is a structural Verilog module corresponding to the logic diagram.

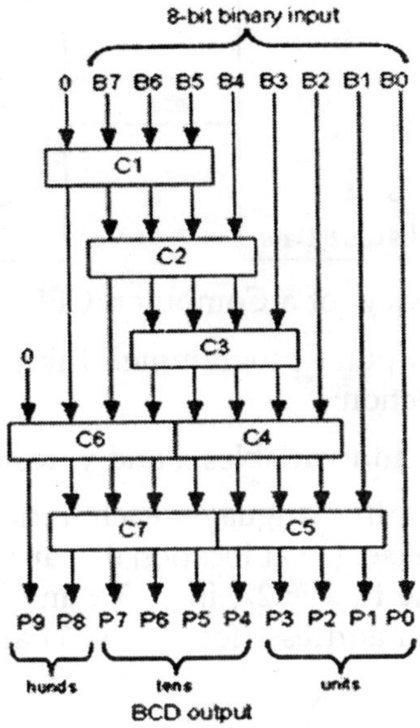


## SCOPE

These notes provide an introduction to the architecture and organisation of digital computers. These are course notes for the module CSC 722 Computer Architecture, part of the course MSc/PgDip in Computer Science and Applications, School of Computer Science, The Queen's University of Belfast.

## OVERVIEW

A very simple model of a computer is shown in Figure. At its simplest, the Central Processing Unit (CPU) is a glorified calculator, the memory stores the results of calculations - it is a set of labelled cells - the label is called the address, each cell contains a number - data. The bus is simply a pipeline along which data and addresses can flow.

Both data and addresses are stored as numbers, though data numbers may be *interpreted* otherwise, e.g. as text characters.

As well as containing data, the memory also contains the programme - in the form of numeric instructions. Ultimately, everything is reduced to numbers.

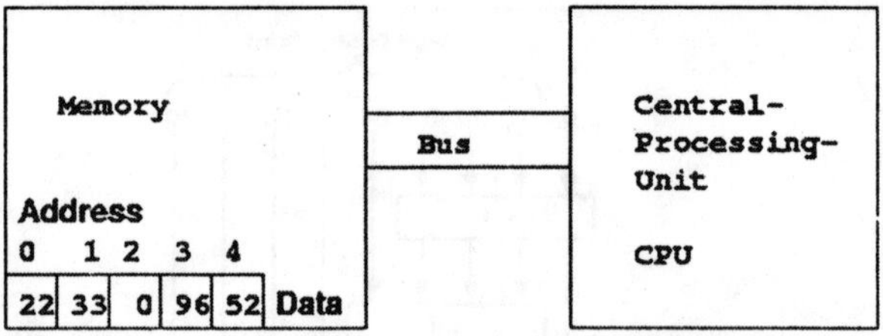


**Figure:** Overview of a Computer: CPU and Memory

What is a computer programme? Take, for example, the C/C++/Java instruction:

z = x + y; /* add variables x and y, result in z*/

In a programming language, each variable is associated with a memory cell: e.g. x at location 0, y at 1, z at 2; therefore in Figure the value in x is 22, in y, 33, and in z, 0. Note the difference between address (for y, it is 1) and data or value (for y it is 33).

### Java - interpreted?

The fact that Java is *interpreted,* rather than compiled, makes it a little different. Nonetheless, what we say about general computer organisation remains valid. To execute the instruction, the CPU may need to execute a number of sub-instructions (machine instructions), e.g.

P1.

Read the contents of memory cell corresponding to x.

P2.

Read the contents of memory cell corresponding to y.

P3.

Do the addition,

P4.

Write the result in the memory cell corresponding to z.

*Four* or *five* machine instructions per high-level language instruction is typical.

Although we usually talk of just bus, there are three parts to a normal bus: the data-bus, the address-bus, and the control part. The bus operates as follows, take P2 above: first the address (1) is put on the address-bus, then control asserts read-memory, some time later the contents of address 1 (33) is put on the data-bus.

Some detail is missing:

- Control of the CPU, e.g. stepping it through P1...P4.
- Where do the machine instructions P1...P4 come from?

The answer to these is that the machine instructions are just another form of data, and the controller in the CPU must fetch them from memory, and execute them; thus, there are two sorts of data flowing along the bus - actual numeric values, and machine instructions; the controller is in a continuous cycle:

- Fetch P1.
- Execute P1.
- Fetch P2...Execute P2.
- ...and keep on until it reaches a halt instruction.

This is the famous fetch-execute cycle.

In the remainder, I will fill in some more detail - going from an overview to increasing detail; the idea is that you stop when the detail gets too much.

# Chapter 7

# MS Word

## PART I

### INTRODUCTION

This unit seeks to introduce you to MS Word. You will learn about MS Word menus and its commands, basic information required to create, save, print, open and modify documents. These documents can be letters, faxes, emails, resumes, reports, brochures, newsletters, web pages and advertisements. You will also learn to work with the standard toolbar and the formatting toolbar.

### Objectives

After studying this unit, you should be able to

- Identify the MS Word screen layout and its components,
- Identify the various menus and their functions,
- Understand the standard toolbar and its options, and
- Understand the formatting toolbar and its options.

## ABOUT MS WORD

Windows and MS Office are Microsoft's two most popular programmes. One is an operating system and the other a bundle suite comprising MS Word (word processor), MS Excel (spreadsheet), MS Power Point (graphics presentation programme), MS Access (relational database), MS Outlook, MS Publisher and MS FrontPage. Together, these two flagship programmes have a worldwide vice-like grip and a near monopoly over the personal computer packaged software market. Not only are they the most preferred and widely used programmes in this segment, they have become a benchmark against which all other products are evaluated. If all this sounds like an ad-copy of Microsoft's Office, it was not meant to be. From your (and our) point of view, this simply means that once having learnt and mastered these packages, in spite of a high rate of technological obsolescence in the computer industry, the skills acquired would never go waste. No matter where you work and what you do, MS Office and specially MS Word, MS Power Point and MS Excel would be of great use to computer users.

Microsoft Word is a full-featured word processing programme, which can be used for any work involving creating and managing text. You can use it from the simplest to the most complex of word processing applications. Using Word, you can write letters and reports, prepare bills and invoices, prepare office stationery –letter heads, envelopes, forms, etc., design brochures, pamphlets, newsletters, magazines, etc.

In short, you would find it extremely difficult to think of a word processing feature not available in Microsoft Word. For most tasks, Word offers several ways of doing the same thing. It is left to the user to find which one is preferable to him. Since covering all the different methods for doing the same task would require a book running into thousand pages, we have taken the liberty to illustrate the methods(s) we considered most user-friendly. As you gain more proficiency in using Word you will yourself discover other methods of doing your tasks.

## STARTING MS WORD

To start Word click once on the Start button, choose All Programmes and click once on Microsoft Word.

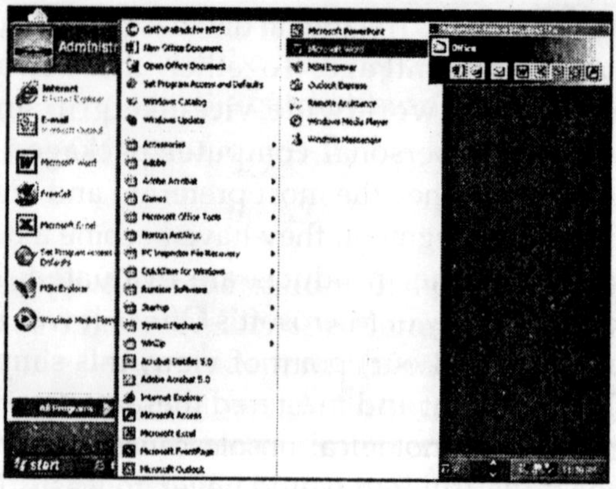

On starting Word you would see a Word main screen with the Tip of the Day (unless somebody had instructed not to do so, in the last session). These tips are Word's way of teaching you new tricks and techniques while you work. Most of these tips are quite informative and some are even entertaining.

Read the tip, if you have the time and the inclination, then click once on OK button in the dialogue box to start working on the document.

## MS WORD SCREEN LAYOUT

Parts of a Word Window is described below:

### Title Bar

This tells you which application package is currently running and which document is currently open.

### Menu Bar

This is the traditional Windows style drop-down menu. When you point to any menu title and click once with the mouse, the menu will open, displaying all the commands available under this menu title. Clicking on the desired command would tell Word to execute that command. Some commands have ellipses (...) in front of them. These commands have further sub commands. Commands appearing dimmed cannot be executed unless the prerequisite functions required by that command have been performed, e.g. you cannot use the Copy or Cut command from Edit menu unless you have selected a piece of text first. Many commands also have a keyboard shortcut specified against their names.

### Standard Toolbar

Toolbars contain buttons, drop-down menus and other controls that help you to quickly alter that appearance and arrangement of documents by executing a variety of Word commands. Toolbars are very helpful and convenient in quickly executing commands without having to go through the menus. The standard toolbar contains icons for basic functions like opening files, saving files, printing files, cut, copy, paste etc.

### Formatting Toolbar

This contains icons for changing the look of your text (called "formatting" in computer jargon); for example, there are icons for changing fonts, styles, font sizes, text alignment etc.

### Ruler

The ruler lets you make changes in margins and indents, and helps in creating document as per required dimensions.

### Scroll Tools

It helps you to travel within your document. You can go anywhere, up and down, right and left in your document mainly by two ways: Using the horizontal and vertical scroll bars with the help of the mouse; or using the keyboard to press PgUp, PgDn, Home, End and arrow keys.

## Status Bar

Also called the Status Area, it is normally the last line on your screen. This gives the following information about your work:

- Current page
- Section number

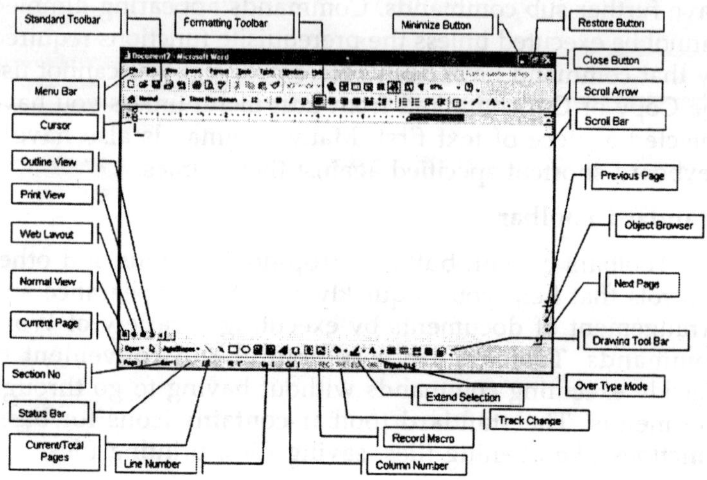


- Current/Total pages in the document
- Current cursor position (where the cursor is presently located)
- Current line number Record macro – whether macro recording is on or not
- Track Revision – whether revisions have been made or not
- Extend Selection
- Over type Mode – whether you are in Insert mode or Overwrite mode
- Help for WordPerfect users – whether on or not.

## Cursor

Also called the Insertion Pointer, it denotes the place where text, graphics or any other item would be placed when you type, overwrite or insert it. This looks like a tall, skinny toothpick and keeps blinking so that you can locate it easily.

### Mouse Pointer

When your mouse pointer looks like an I-beam you should be able to move it freely about the screen. This is used for either placing the cursor at the desired place (take the mouse pointer there and click) or choosing any command either from the menu or from toolbars. The mouse pointer changes shape when in the process of doing certain tasks and at this time the cursor disappears.

## CREATING DOCUMENTS

Word always starts by opening an untitled "normal" document so that you can begin from scratch. This "normal" document is based upon all the default values (another name for predefined settings) provided by Word, i.e. standard page size, standard margins, font type and size etc. You can change these settings and create your own customised documents based upon new settings. You can also save your new settings in a specific kind of file, called a Template file, which will help you to quickly create documents based upon these customised settings. You can create your own letter-heads; fax sheets, invoices, memos etc. as templates so as to save substantial work and printing costs. Since these templates are like ready-made, pre-printed forms, all you have to do is fill in the blanks, very similar to filling in paper forms manually. Templates have been covered in more detail later.

### How to Type in Word

Once Word has been started, you can immediately start typing. When you press character keys on the keyboard, you can see the corresponding characters appear in the Word window. Use the spacebar when you want to separate characters and words from each other. Use the Tab key when you want to move the cursor or text from one Tab stop to another, and also when you want to create a blank longer than one space between words.

### Insert and Overtype Modes

Word normally uses the insert mode. In this mode, Word does not overtype the existing text but pushes it forward. By pressing the **Ins** key, you can switch to overtype mode. In this mode, the new text replaces the old text after the cursor. To switch between Overtype/Insert modes, press the Insert key. In the Insert mode, when you place the cursor in the middle of two words and start typing, the new text is inserted between the two words and all the text below this line is automatically adjusted. In the overtype mode, when you place the cursor in the middle of two words and start typing, the new text overwrites the previous text.

## VISUALIZING AND PLANNING FOR A NEW DOCUMENT

Just like you visualize an entire building before it is constructed (the blueprint), it is a good habit to think about the overall look and contents of the document before you actually start creating it. Word gives you onscreen clues about how your printed document would look like before it is actually printed.

If you provide some basic information such as paper size and orientation (portrait or landscape, i.e. lengthwise or widthwise printing respectively), Word would display, while you are creating the document, simple information like margins, page endings, line endings, the relative size and placement of text and graphics and so on. Therefore, it is always a good idea to start by specifying the page size, printer, margins etc. before entering text.

## TYPING TEXT

Typing text in word is similar to typing it on a normal typewriter, except for three major differences (there are over a million minor differences!). Unless you want to start a new paragraph don't press the 'Enter' key. The moment you reach the end of the right margin of your page, word automatically places the cursor at the beginning of the next line. This feature is called word wrap and it does away with the irritating necessity of either having to yank a lever (like in a typewriter) at the end of each line or pressing Enter after every line. While typing, when you reach the end of a line Word automatically figures out whether the next word that you are typing can fit within the current line, if not, the next word is automatically placed in the next new line. This means that you don't have to bother about left or right margins while typing. Simply go ahead and keep on typing, word would take care of these things automatically.

Do not bother if you make mistakes while typing. Thanks to Word's editing features, you can always go back anywhere in your document and correct the mistakes, make alterations, additions or deletions. Not only this, Word's spelling programme would help you to rectify all spelling mistakes. Do not bother about how your text looks – in form of size, looks or placement. Again, Word's advanced formatting features would help you later, to really beautify your work. Normally, it is faster to type "Plain vanilla" text first, finish entry and then bother about formatting the document ("formatting" includes specifying font type, font size, font attributes like bold, italics, underline, colour, placement etc.). However, as explained earlier, page setup details should ideally be specified right in the beginning before typing the text.

## SOME 'DON'TS'

(a) Don't use the spacebar to indent paragraphs. Instead, use the tab key for the indent control in Word's ruler (the top handle on the left hand side).

(b) Don't use spacebar to centre or otherwise position text. Use the left, right and centre alignment buttons from formatting bar instead.

(c) Don't use spacebar to create columns. Use Word's table or column command instead.

(d) Don't hit enter key repeatedly for starting the matter on new page. Use insert page break command instead.

## MS WORD MENUS

The **Menu bar** located below the title bar consists of a drop down menu and the sub menu along with the keyboard shortcut commands against their names. For executing most tasks, the user has three options.

(a) Choose the desired command from the Menu option provided by either using the mouse or using cursor movement keys, or

(b) Press the appropriate shortcut keys and combination from the keyboard, or

(c) Click once on the relevant Icon from the displayed toolbar.

Although there is no right or wrong approach, most users find the third option the simplest and the fastest.

This section deals with the various menu options available in MS Word.

## File Menu

New

Creates a new blank document based on the default template.

***Open***

Opens an existing document or a template.

***Close***

Closes the active document without exiting Ms Word and prompts you to save any unsaved changes.

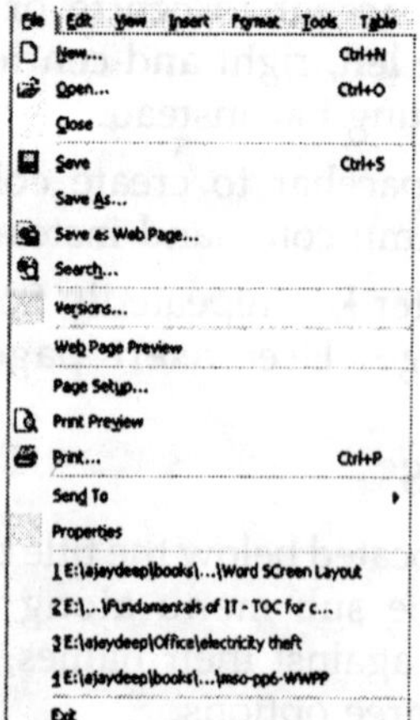

### *Save*

Saves the active document with the same file name, format and in the current location.

### *Save As*

Saves the active document with the different file name or format and location, as desired.

### *Save as Web Page*

Saves the current document as a Web Page in the form of an Internet file.

### *Search*

Finds files, web pages and outlook items based on the search criteria you enter.

### *Versions*

Saves and manages multiple versions of the document in a single file.

### *Web Page Preview*

Shows your active document as a web page in your browser.

### *Page Setup*

Allows you to set the margins, orientation, paper size and source, and other layout options for your document.

### *Print Preview*

Shows you the preview of your document, exactly the way it will look on the paper.

### *Print*

Allows you to print and define the print settings of your current document to the defined printer.

### *Send To*

Sends the active document as an email or a fax to the desired recipient.

***Properties***

Displays the properties of the current document, i.e. the creation date, the title, author, number of paragraphs, lines, words, characters, pages etc. in the file.

***Exit***

Closes the MS Word Software after prompting you to save any unsaved documents.

**Edit Menu**

***Undo Last Commands***

Reverses the last command.

***Replace Last Commands***

Restores the last command again once you undo it.

***Cut***

Removes a word, line or a block, as selected and places it in the special memory called the clip board, from where it can be retrieved.

***Copy***

Copies the cut word, line or a block and places it on the office clipboard.

***Office Clipboard***

Is a special place in the computer's memory from where cut or copied word, line or block can be retrieved.

***Paste***

Inserts the cut or copied selection at the defined point and replaces any active selection.

***Paste Special***

Inserts the cut or copied selection at the defined point and replaces any active selection in the specified format.

***Paste as Hyperlink***

Defines the inserted cut or copied selections as a link to another document.

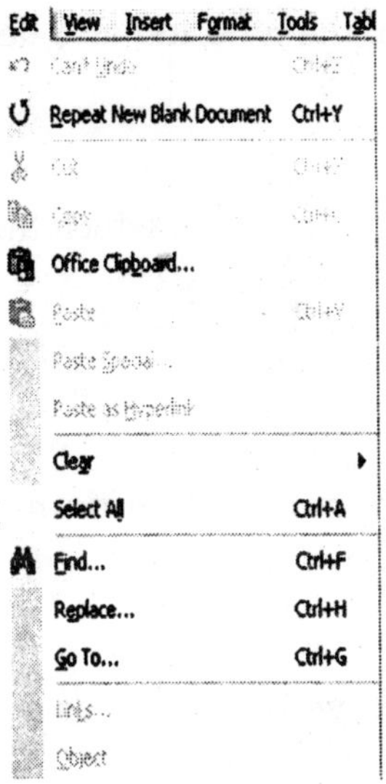


### *Clear*

Directly removes the selected character, word, line or a block without putting it on the clipboard.

### *Select All*

Selects all the contents of the active document including the text and graphics.

### *Find*

Searches for a specified character, word within the active document.

### *Replace*

Searches for and replaces a specified character or a word in the active document.

### *Go To*

Moves the cursor to the desired page, section line, bookmark, comment etc.

### *Links*

Displays or changes information for each link in the current document including the name and location of the source file, the item, the type and also define the updating of the link.

### *Objects*

Activates the application in which the selected object was created so that you can modify it.

## View Menu

### *Normal*

Shows the document in the normal view. This is the default document view.

### *Web Layout*

Shows your active document as a webpage, as it will appear in the web browser.

### *Print Layout*

Shows your active document as it will appear on paper after printing.

### *Outline*

Shows your active window so that you can examine and work with the structure of your file in the classic outline form.

### *Task Pane*

Window which pops out on the right side of the document screen and has the options to choose from the recently opened documents, new documents, WebPages or emails, the clip board menu, basic search menu, inserting clip arts, style and formatting of your document and mail merge etc.

### *Toolbars*

Give you the option to display the required tool bar in form of buttons, menus or a combination of both, making the commands available to you at a single click. The most important Toolbar is the Menu bar, which is permanently on the top of the screen. The rest of the tool bars like Standard toolbar, Formatting toolbar, Drawing toolbar and the Picture toolbar can be added or removed from the screen as and when desired.

### *Ruler*

Allows you to keep a track of the margins and tabs. When this option is activated, you can see the horizontal and the vertical ruler along with the marking in inches and the tab marks.

### *Show Paragraph Marks*

Shows the end of the paragraph with a special character which is non printable.

### *Gridlines*

Shows the checkered marks on the work area of the current document once you enable the option.

### *Document Map*

Shows the structure of the current document in the left hand side pane.

### *Header and Footer*

Defines a common text, picture or both which has to appear on the top (header) and bottom (footer) of every page. These can be page numbers, dates, references, company logo etc.

### *Footnotes*

Defines comments, or provide references that appear at the end of each page in a document.

***Markup***

Marks the comments, and tracks and defines all the changes done in the document.

***Full Screen***

Once this option is activated, the entire menu and tool bars are hidden and you can view the document on the whole screen without any rulers, startup bar and tool bars etc.

***Zoom***

With this option you can reduce or enlarge the view of your document. Zoom options include zoom to page widths, text width, whole page etc.

*Insert Menu*

***Break***

Inserts page break, column break, and text wrapping break or section breaks.

***Page Numbers***

Inserts page numbers in your document on every page that is automatically updated when you add or delete a page.

***Date and Time***

Inserts the current date and time which is automatically updated when you open or print the document.

***Auto Text***

Stores text or graphics you need to frequently use.

***Field***

Inserts a field at the insertion point. Use fields to insert a variety of

up-to-date information.

***Symbol***

Inserts special characters and symbols from the installed fonts in your list.

***Comment***

Inserts a comment at the desired insertion point.

### *Reference*

Inserts a reference, which can be a footnote, caption, cross-reference or an index table, at the desired insertion point.

### *Web Component*

Inserts a component for use on the webpage, such as lines, bars for the navigation and lists views of document libraries.

### *Picture*

Inserts pictures from clip art, word art, charts and diagrams, auto shapes from the libraries, scanners cameras or other documents.

### *Diagram*

Inserts diagrams in the form of organization charts, cycle, radial, Venn and target diagrams.

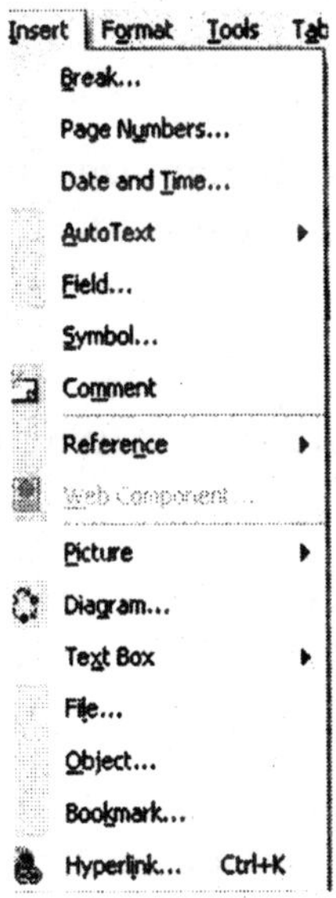


### *Text Box*

Inserts a box where you can click and type text in a horizontal or a vertical fashion in an active window at the desired insertion point in your active document.

### *File*

Inserts a file or a part of your file at the desired insertion point in the active document.

### *Object*

Inserts an object such as image, media clip, presentation, table, chart, slide, picture, video, sound etc.

### *Bookmark*

Creates a bookmark which you can use to mark selected points in your active document.

### *Hyperlink*

Inserts a link through which you can directly connect to a location in the current document, webpage, or a file created in a different programme.

## Format Menu

### *Font*

Changes the font style, font size, font effect, text effect and character spacing for the selected text.

### *Paragraph*

Changes the paragraph indents and spacing, line and page break and other paragraph formatting options.

### *Bullets and Numbering*

Adds or modifies the bullets or numbers in the selected paragraphs.

### *Borders and Shading*

Applies shading in the selected paragraph and creates borders around the selected area in different styles and colours.

### *Columns*

Changes the number of columns along with the column width and spacing in the document or a section of the document.

### *Tabs*

Defines the position and alignment of the tabs and determines the type of leader character for each tab stop.

### *Drop Cap*

A drop cap is traditionally the first letter in the paragraph and it appears in the left margin or dropped from the base line of the first line in the paragraph. The drop cap formats a letter or word or the selected text with a large initial or dropped capital letter.

### *Text Direction*

Changes the orientation of desired/selected text from horizontal to vertical in a table cell.

### *Change Case*

Changes the sentence case; upper, lower case, toggle case etc. for the desired/selected text.

### *Fit Text*

Changes the width for the selected text so that it fits horizontally.

### *Asian Layout*

Changes the layout of the selected text, i.e. the phonetic guide, enclosed characters, horizontal or vertical, combined characters, or enclose two lines in one.

### *Backgrounds*

Fills colours, effects printed watermarks from selected picture and adds it as a background to the document.

### *Theme*

Applies a new or different design to a document, webpage, email, or data access page.

### *Frames*

Creates a table of content by using the heading of your page and formats it on the left frame of the page.

### *Auto Format*

Analyses the content of the active document and then automatically formats it.

### *Style and Formatting*

Displays the style and formatting task pane, where you can re-apply formatting easily, create styles, and select all the text with the same formatting.

### *Reveal Formatting*

Finds the text with similar formatting and then can also compare it with another selection.

### *Object*

Formats the line, colour, fill and pattern size, position and other properties of the selected objects.

## Tools Menu

### *Spelling and Grammar*

Checks the writing style, spellings and grammar of the active document and suggests the possible corrections.

### *Language*

Provides an option to choose a language for the selected text in the document that contains more than one language.

### *Word Count*

Shows the exact number of characters, words, lines and paragraph in the active document.

### *Auto Summarize*

Displays a summary of the sentences which are most relevant to the theme.

### *Speech*

It has the inbuilt speech recognition software, which converts your speech into text. It also sets up the speech recognition software to select menus, toolbars and dialogue item boxes.

### *Track Changes*

It marks and keeps a track of changes in your current document, by the reviewer's name.

### *Compare and Merge Document*

You can compare your document with any other document with the option to merge the two. The changes can be displayed as markup in a new document or any of the old documents.

### *Protect Document*

It gives you an option to protect your document or part of your online form except as specified. It also gives you the option to protect it with a password so that only privileged users can make changes to the document, mark revisions, or fill in the online form.

### *Online Collaboration*

Starts a spontaneous online net meeting by sending an invitation to other participants, who are also online using Microsoft Net meeting on their computers. It also has the feature of scheduling an online meeting by using names from the address book of your email programme, and displays the discussions toolbar, where you can insert a new discussion.

### *Letters and Mailings*

It has the letter wizard feature which quickly helps you create letters. The Mail merge wizard helps you create form, letters, mailing labels, envelops, catalogs and different types of mail merge documents that have the same or different address, and send the same body text to different users, without having to type the letter again and again.

### *Tools on the Web*

Connects you to the Microsoft Office tools available online for further information and integrated e-services of Microsoft.

### *Macro*

Is a series of actions, which you can record for repetitive execution. With the Macro dialog box you can edit, run or delete. You can also record a new macro in the visual basic editor.

*Templates and Add-ins*

Attaches a different template to the active document, with an option to load add-in programmes and update document styles.

*Auto Correct Options*

Sets the option to automatically correct text for any typing error as you type, and also stores and reuses frequently used text.

*Customise*

Gives you an option to customise the toolbar buttons, menu commands and shortcut key assignments including the icon size, font and the menu animation etc.

*Options*

Provides you an option to customise the Microsoft Office Program's default settings, such as the screen appearance, printing, editing, spell check, file location, typography, track changes etc.

**Tables Menu**

*Draw Table*

Gives you the option to draw customised tables in your active document. You can also have nested tables.

*Insert*

Allows you to insert tables, rows, columns or cells in the selected table.

*Delete*

Allows you to delete tables, rows, columns or cells in the selected table.

*Select*

Allows you to select tables, rows, columns or cells.

### *Merge Cells*

Combines the contents of the selected adjacent cell into a single cell.

### *Split Cells*

Splits a single cell into multiple cells, i.e. you can increase the number of rows or columns.

### *Split Table*

Divides a table into two separate tables and inserts a paragraph mark above the row that contains the insertion point.

### *Table Auto Format*

Automatically formats the table with a predefined format including the borders and shading of the table. It also resizes the table to fit the contents of the table cells.

### *Auto Fit*

Gives you the option to automatically fit the contents in the table or fit the table in the window, or define the table width or distribute the rows and columns evenly.

### *Heading Rows Repeat*

If your table spans more than one page, you can designate a particular row to be the table heading that is repeated on every subsequent page.

### *Convert*

Gives an option to convert the selected text into a table or converts a selected table into text.

### *Sort*

Arranges the data in the required order, i.e. ascending or descending, based upon the criteria, i.e. the column on which you want to sort.

### *Formula*

Gives you the option to perform mathematical calculations on numbers.

### *Hide Gridlines*

Gives you the option to show or hide the table gridlines. Gridlines are dotted lines on your table, which help to see which cell you are working in. Gridlines are not printable. In case you want to print the gridlines, you can use the borders and shadings command from the format menu.

### *Table Properties*

Sets various options to format the table, i.e. options like table size, alignment, text wrapping etc.

## Windows Menu

### *New Window*

Opens a new window with exactly the same contents making it easier for you to view different parts of the file at the same time.

### *Arrange All*

Displays all the open files in separate windows on the screen making it easier for you to cut-copy-paste between files.

### *Split*

Splits the active window into panes or removes the split from an already split window.

### *Currently Open Files*

These are the list of currently open files. It also tick marks and shows the file you are currently working within the active window.

## Help Menu

### *Microsoft Word Help*

Launches the MS Office Assistant, which provides help and tips to accomplish your tasks.

### *Hide the Office Assistant*

Displays or hides the office assistant from the active screen.

### *What's This*

Provides help on the topic clicked on.

### *Office on the Web*

Connects to Microsoft's website, where you can get help and updated information on office programmes.

### *Active Product*

Launches the activation wizard so that you can activate or update your copy of Microsoft Office.

### *WordPerfect Help*

Helps you learn the MS Word equivalent for WordPerfect for DOS commands and key combinations.

### *Detect and Repair*

Automatically finds and fixes all the errors in Microsoft Office.

### *About Microsoft Word*

Displays the basic information about your computer and operating system along with the version details, copyright, legal and licensing notices, the user name, organization name and the software serial number.

## STANDARD TOOLBAR

The standard toolbar contains buttons, with the help of which you can execute commands, quickly without going through the menus. With the standard toolbar you can create, open, save and print your documents. With the help of the standard toolbar icons, you can send your documents as e-mails; insert tables, objects, pictures, charts, diagrams in your document.

### New

To create a new document based on the default template.

(1) Choose New from the File menu.

(2) Click on Blank Document in the New Document menu on the right panel.

## Open

To open an existing document or a template.

(1) Choose Open from the File menu;

(2) Choose the directory where your document is saved;

(3) Type in your file name here;

(4) Click once on Open; and

(5) Double click on the file name.

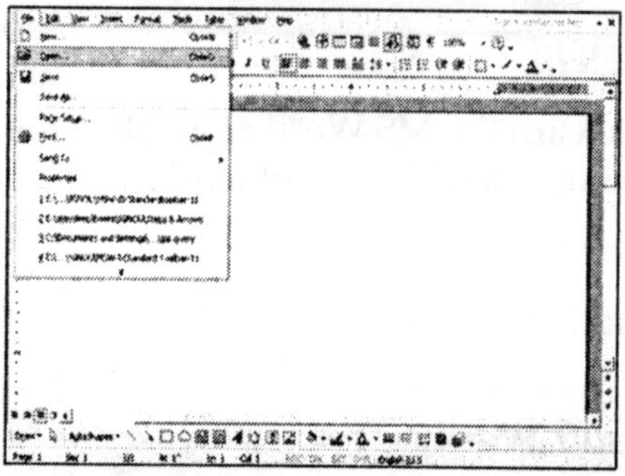

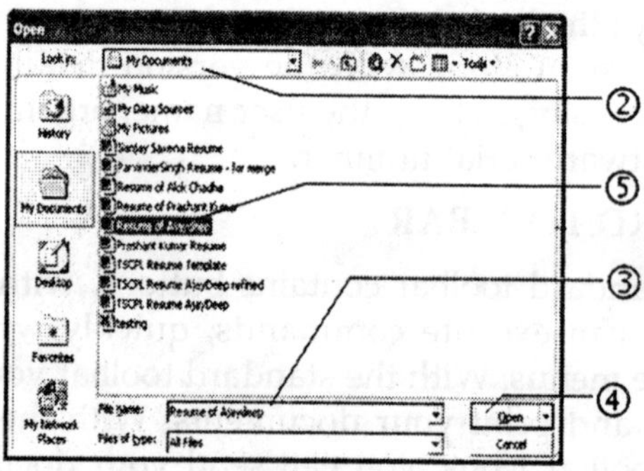


## Save

To save the active document or template.

(1) Choose Save command from the File menu.

## Save As

To save the active file with a different filename or in a different location.

(1) Choose Save As command from the File menu;

(2) Choose the directory where you want to save the document;

(3) Type in the file name you want to save the file as; and

(4) Click once on Save.

## Page Setup

To modify the page setup

(1) Choose Page Setup from the File menu; and

(2) Click on OK once you have defined your page settings.

Page Setup allows you to set options like Paper margins, Paper settings, Page Layout and Document Grid. These options are provided through the following three tabbed sub-menus.

- Margins You can set the margins here.
- Paper You can change the paper size or source here.
- Layout You can change the paper layout here.

## Margins

(a) Click here to define the Top, Bottom, Left, Right, Gutter and Gutter Position.

(b) Click on the desired Orientation, i.e. Landscape or Portrait.

(c) Click here to set options for multiple pages.

(d) Click here to define the portion of the document you want to apply these settings to.

(e) Click here to get the default settings.

## Paper

(a) Click here to define the paper size or define the custom size here.

(b) Click here to define the printer tray you want to print the first page from and the rest of the pages can be defined in the subsequent column.

(c) Click here to define the portion of the document you wish to apply these settings to.

(d) Click here to define the print options.

(e) Click here to get the default settings.

**Layout**

(a) Click here to define the beginning of the new section.

(b) Click here to define the header and footer pages.

(c) Click here to define the distance between the edge of the page and top of the header/footer.

(d) Click here to define the vertical alignment of the page.

(e) Click here to define the portion of the document you wish to apply these settings on.

(f) Click here to add or remove the line numbers from the portion of document currently selected in the apply to option.

(g) Click here to apply the borders around each document.

(h) Click here to get the default settings.

**Print**

To print the document or the template.

(1) Click on the Print option from the File menu;

(2) Select the Printer name here; and

(3) Click on OK after you have defined all the settings

   (a) Click here to change the printing options for the selected printer.

   (b) Click here to find the network printer based on the printer name, model etc.

   (c) Click here to print your document in a file instead of a printer.

   (d) Click here to define the number of copies you want to print.

(e) Click here to print multiple copies on a single sheet of paper.

(f) Click here to print multiple papers on single sheet.

(g) Click here to scale the paper size.

(h) Click here to define the printing options.

(iClick here to select the page or the page range you want to print.

(j) Choose the document or the part of document you want to print.

**Print Preview**

It shows a preview of the document as it will be printed on paper.

(1) Click on the Print Preview option in the file menu.

(a) This will show how your page will look on paper (when printed).

**Spell Check**

Checks the grammar of your document and also identifies any spelling mistakes within the current document.

(1) Click on the Spelling and Grammar option in the Tools Menu.

(a) This displays a dialogue window, that displays spelling mistakes in red and grammatical errors in green. You can choose from the following options to check your document.

(b) Ignore leaves the highlighted spelling mistake or grammatical error unchanged and finds the next error.

(c) Ignore All leaves all instances of the error unchanged throughout the document continuing with the spell/grammar check.

(d) Add to Directory option adds the highlighted word in the Not in the Dictionary option in the custom dictionary.

(e) Change accepts the current selection in the suggestion box. You can also edit the text and then click change.

(f) Change All changes all instances of the word not in the dictionary or capitalization box to the word in the suggestion box. You can also edit the text in the suggestion box and then click on Change All.

(g) Auto Correct adds the spelling error and its correction in the auto correct list so that it will automatically correct errors as you type it.

(h) Choose the directory language from here.

(i) Options defines the spelling and grammar checking details.

(j) Click here to undo the last change.

**Cut-Paste**

The **Cut** command cuts the selection and puts it on the clipboard, whereas the **Paste** command inserts the clipboard contents at the insertion point.

(1) Select the portion of the document you want to remove. Drag your mouse pointer on the selection and press the right mouse button. Choose the Cut option from the drop down menu.

(2) Place the cursor on the insertion point and press the right mouse button. Choose the Paste option.

(a) You will notice the selected text has been moved from the original place to the new specified location.

**Copy-Paste**

The **Copy** command copies the selection and adds it on the clipboard, whereas the **Paste** command inserts the clipboard contents at the insertion point.

(1) Select the portion of the document you want to copy. Drag your mouse pointer on the selection and press the right mouse button. Choose the Copy option.

(2) Place the cursor on the insertion point and press the right mouse button. Choose the Paste option.

  (a) You will notice the selected text has been moved from the original place to the new specified location.

**Undo-Redo**

Undo reverses certain commands and Redo reverses the action of undo command.

(1) Click on Undo or Redo buttons to perform the desired task.

**Tables**

Inserts tables in your active document and also customises your table according to your requirement. You can also create nested tables.

(1) Click on the Draw Table option from the Table menu.

(2) Click here to draw a table.

(3) Click on the Insertion point and drag your mouse.

(4) Once you release the mouse you will find your table. You can similarly add more rows and/or columns.

  (a) You will see the Tables and Borders toolbar. You can use the toolbar options to create your tables and format your table borders.

**Zoom**

Enlarges or reduces the display of your active document between 10 and

400 percent.

(1) Click here to enlarge or reduce the display of your active window, according to your requirement.

  (a) What the Standard toolbar is used for?

  (b) What is the difference between 'Save' and 'Save As'?

  (c) What is the difference between 'Cut' and 'Copy' commands?

(d) What are the three most commonly used commands while printing any document?

## FORMATTING TOOLBAR

The formatting toolbar contains buttons, drop-down menus and other controls, which help you to format and align your document, like changing font style, size, colour, text alignment, bulleting and numbering etc. These buttons help you quickly execute commands without having to go through menus.

### Font

Highlight the text you want to format

(1) Click on the Font option in the Format Menu of the Standard Toolbar. A dialogue box is displayed where you can choose options to format your text.

(a) Choose the Font from the scroll down arrow.

(b) Choose the Font Style from the scroll down arrow.

(c) Choose the Font size here, i.e. bold, italics or underline.

(d) Choose the Font Colour here.

(e) Click here to get the predefined default font formatting.

(2) Click on OK once after you have selected your formatting settings.

### Bullets

To add or remove bullets from the selected paragraph or text.

(1) Choose the Bullets and Numbering option from the Format menu.

(2) Click on the Bulleted option from the pop up menu.

(3) Choose your desired Bullet style.

(4) Click once on OK.

## Numbering

To add or remove bullets and/or numbering from the selected paragraph or text.

(1) Choose the Bullets and Numbering option from the Format menu.

(2) Click on the Numbered option (or Bullets in case you wish to add bullets to your text) from the pop up menu.

(3) Choose your desired Number style.

(4) Click once on OK.

## Left-Right-Centre Alignment, Justify

(1) Select the text you want to align.

(2) Click on the Left Align button on the Formatting toolbar if you wish to align the text on the left side of the page.

(3) Click on the Right Align button on the Formatting toolbar if you wish to align the text on the right side of the page.

(4) Click on the Centre Align button on the Formatting toolbar if you wish to align the text in the centre of the page.

(5) Click on the Justify button on the Formatting toolbar if you wish to align the text with both the margins of your page.

(a) You can see your text aligned to the left of your page.

(b) You can see your text aligned in the centre of your page.

(c) You can see your text aligned to the right of your page.

(d) You can see your text aligned with both the margins of your page.

## Line Spacing

It changes the space between the lines of your text.

(1) Select the text by highlighting it.

(2) Click on the Line Spacing button on the Formatting toolbar and select the desired spacing from the drop-down menu.

(a) You will get your desired line spacing for the selected text.

**Right Indenting**

It indents the paragraph to the next Tab.

(1) Place the cursor at the beginning of the paragraph you want to indent.

(2) Click on the Increase Indent button on the Formatting toolbar.

(a) You can see your paragraph has moved to the next tab.

Left Indenting

Indents the paragraph to the previous Tab.

(1) Place the cursor at the beginning of the paragraph you wish to indent.

(2) Click on the Decrease Indent button on the Formatting Toolbar.

(a) You can see your paragraph has moved to the Previous tab.

**Highlighter**

Highlighter marks the text so that it is highlighted and stands out from the surrounding text.

(1) Select the text you wish to highlight.

(2) Click on the Highlighter button on the Formatting toolbar and select the desired colour.

(3) The selected text is highlighted in the selected colour.

(a) For what purpose the Formatting toolbar is used?

(b) What are the four possible text alignments?

(c) What is the difference between bullets and numbered list?

## SUMMARY

In this unit, you have studied about MS Word, the full featured, easy to use word processor. You have also studied the various menu options and commonly used toolbars – Standard and Formatting.

### Menu Options

- File menu displays the commands to open a new or an existing file, saves and closes the file, prints and defines the page settings. It also has an option to display the file properties along with a list of the four most recently used files.
- Edit menu displays the commands to edit or format your text, find or find and replace a particular word or a line. It also has an option to cut-copy-paste a part or a paragraph.
- View menu displays the commands to select the toolbars to be displayed each time you open the word window, to hide or show the task pane, gridlines, header and footer, paragraph marks etc.
- Insert menu displays the commands to insert page breaks, section breaks. It also displays the options to insert pictures, diagrams, text boxes, files, objects, bookmarks and hyperlinks.
- Format menu allows you to format your text/ paragraph by changing text fonts, adding bullets or numbering, borders and shading, tabs, columns etc.
- Tool menu displays the commands to check for spelling mistakes and grammatical errors, languages, fix broken text, compare and merge documents, track changes etc.
- Table menu displays the commands to draw, modify and format tables. It also has options to define the formulas for calculations in the tables.
- Windows menu displays the option to create a new window, splits an existing window or arranges all

the open windows. It also displays the currently open files.

- Help displays the commands to launch the MS Word help, hides or shows the office assistant.

**Toolbars**

The Standard Toolbar

With standard tool bar, you can perform the following tasks:

- New creates a new document.
- Open opens an existing document.
- Save saves your document for future use.
- E-mail sends your document as an e-mail through MS Outlook.
- Print prints your document on paper.
- Print Preview allows you to see your document as it will look when printed.
- Spell Check checks spellings and grammar of your current document.
- Cut moves the selected part of the document onto the clipboard.
- Copy moves the selected text to another place.
- Paste copies the cut or copied text selection to the insertion point.
- Undo reverses the last command.
- Redo reverses the action of the last command.
- Tables inserts customised tables in your document.

***The Formatting Toolbar***

The formatting toolbar helps you perform the following tasks:

- Font style, Size and Colour change the font style, size and colour.

- Bulleting applies bullets to the selected text.
- Numbering applies numbering to your selected lines/ paragraph.
- Alignment aligns your paragraph (Left, Right, Centre, and Justify).
- Line Spacing defines the distance between your lines.
- Right Indenting indents your selected paragraph to the right.
- Left Indenting indents your selected paragraph to the left.
- Highlighter highlights the selected text in the colour selected.

## PART II

## INTRODUCTION

Microsoft Word is a full-featured word processing programme, which can be used for any work involving creating and managing text. You can use it from the simplest to the most complex word processing applications. Using Word, you can write letters and reports, prepare bills and invoices, prepare office stationery – letter heads, envelopes, forms etc., design brochures, pamphlets, newsletters, magazines etc.

In this unit, you will learn how to create, save, close, open and print a simple document. You will also learn how to create a document using MS Word templates. We shall also learn creating and modifying tables and various formatting commands like changing fonts, font size, text colour and alignment of the text.

### Objectives

After studying this unit, you should be able to

- Create, save, open and print your document,
- Save your document as a web page,
- Create tables and modify them,

- Insert tables, pictures, diagrams, charts and objects in your document,
- Define your page setup and printing options,
- Align and format your document,
- Create bullets and numbered lists,
- Format your document; define the font style, font size, font colour etc., and
- Check your document for spelling mistakes and grammatical errors.

## CREATING A SIMPLE DOCUMENT

Word always starts by opening an untitled "normal" document, so that you can begin from scratch. This "normal" document is based upon all the default values (another name for pre-defined settings) provided by Word, i.e. standard page size, standard margins, font type and size etc. You can change these settings and create your own customised documents based upon new settings. You can also save your new settings in a specific kind of file, called a Template file, which will help you to quickly create documents, based upon these customised settings. You can create your own letterheads; fax sheets, invoices, memos etc. as templates so as to save substantial work and printing costs. Since these templates are like ready-made, pre-printed forms, all you have to do is fill in the blanks, very similar to filling in paper forms manually. Templates have been covered in more detailed later.

## TYPES OF COMPUTER INFECTION

When you go through or rather listen the news, you hear about many different forms of electronic infection. The most common are:

### *Viruses*

Computer viruses are called viruses, because they share some of the traits of biological viruses. A computer virus passes from computer to computer, like a biological virus passes from person to person.

A virus is a small piece of software, that piggybacks on real programmes. Once it is running, it is then able to infect other programmes or documents. For example, a virus might attach itself to a programme such as a spreadsheet programme. Each time the spreadsheet programme runs, the virus runs too, and it has the chance to reproduce (by attaching to other programmes) or wreak havoc.

### *E-mail Viruses*

An e-mail virus moves around in e-mail messages, and usually replicates itself by automatically mailing itself to dozens of people in the victim's

e-mail address book.

### *Worms*

A worm is a small piece of software that uses computer networks and security holes to replicate itself. A copy of the worm scans the network for another machine that has a specific security hole. It copies itself to the new machine using the security hole, and then starts replicating from there, as well.

### *Trojan Horses*

A Trojan horse is simply a computer programme. The programme claims to do one thing (it may claim to be a game) but instead does damage when you run it (it may erase the data stored in your hard disk). Trojan horses have no way to replicate automatically.

## ANTI-VIRUS SOFTWARE

In order to combat the menace of viruses, specialized companies have developed special purpose software typically called "*anti-virus software*" to help the users to detect, remove, and prevent further invasion of viruses.

Some of the commonly used anti-virus packages are:

(a) Norton Antivirus (b) McAfee Antivirus

(c) Escan (d) Trend Micro

(e) AVG

## Starting MS Word

To start Microsoft Word

(a) Click once on the Start button, choose All Programmes and click once on Microsoft Word; or

(b) Directly click on the Word icon from the Office Shortcut Bar on the Desktop; or

(c) Click on the Microsoft Word icon on the recently used programmes list above the Programmes Menu.

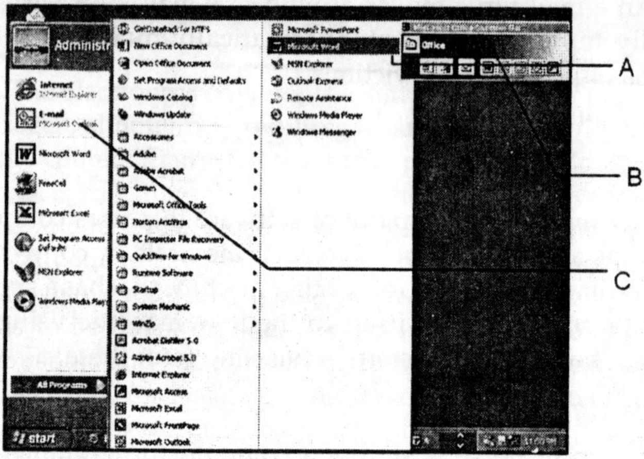


## Opening a New Document

(1) Click on New from the File menu to create a new template; and

(2) Click on Blank Document in the New Document option on the right panel.

## Entering Text

(1) Click here and start typing in your text.

   (A) Don't worry about the formatting of the text. Keep on typing your text without pressing enter key. Once you need to start a new paragraph press the enter key.

## Changing the Font Style

(1) Highlight the heading by clicking the left mouse button from the starting of the text you want to change the font, and drag it till the end of the text.

(2) Click on the Font Box of the formatting toolbar. Click once on the pull down arrow symbol and a list of the available fonts will drop down. Browse the list with the mouse and click on the desired font, i.e. Garamond in this case.

   (a) Once you click on the desired font, the drop down list will disappear and the desired font will be applied on the selected text.

**Changing the Font Size**

(1) Highlight the text as explained earlier; and

(2) Click on the Font Size Box of the formatting toolbar. Click once on the down arrow symbol and a list of the available font sizes will drop down. Browse the list with the mouse and click on the desired Font Size, i.e. 16 in this case.

   (a) Once you click on the desired font size, the drop down list will go and the desired font size will be applied on the selected text.

**Changing the Font Colour**

(1) Highlight the text as explained earlier; and

(2) Click on the Font Colour Box of the formatting toolbar. Click once on the pull down arrow symbol and a list of the available font colours will drop down. Browse the list with the mouse and click on the desired Font Colour, i.e. blue grey in this case.

   (a) Once you click on the desired font colour, the drop down list will go and the desired font colour will be applied on the selected text.

**Changing Text Attribute**

Applying the Bold Attribute

(1) Highlight the text as explained earlier; and

(2) Click once on the Bold Button of the formatting toolbar.

(a) Once you click on the Bold button, you can see your text attribute to be bold.

(b) Similarly, you can apply the bold attribute to the sub headings also.

**Underlining the Text**

(1) Highlight the text as explained earlier; and

(2) Click once on the Underline Button of the formatting toolbar.

- Once you click on the Underline button, you can see your selected text has been underlined.

**Italicizing the Text**

(1) Highlight the text as explained earlier; and

(2) Click once on the Italic Button of the formatting toolbar.

- Once you click on the Italic button, you can see that the attribute of your text has been changed to Italics.

**Bullets**

(1) Highlight the text as explained earlier;

(2) Click once on the Bullets and Numbering option from the format menu;

(3) Click on the Bullet style you wish to use from the options on the pop up screen; and

(4) Click on OK once.

- Once you click on the OK button you can see your text has been bulleted.

**Numbering the Text**

(1) Highlight the text as explained earlier;

(2) Click once on the Bullets and Numbering option from the format menu;

(3) Click on the Number style you wish to use from the options on the pop up screen; and

(4) Click on OK once.

- Once you click on the OK button, you can see your text is numbered.

## Aligning the Text

Centreing the Text

(1) Highlight the text as explained earlier; and

(2) Click on the Centre icon once on the formatting toolbar.

- Once you click on the Centre button you can see your heading in the centre of the page.

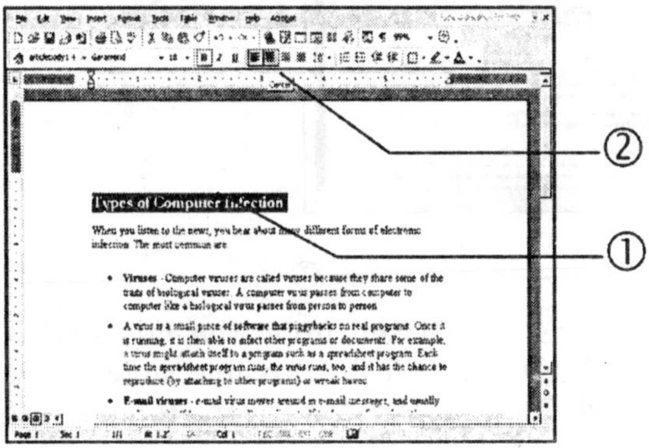


## Justifying the Text

(1) Highlight the text as explained earlier; and

(2) Click on the Justify icon once on the formatting toolbar.

- Once you click on the Justify button, you can see that your paragraph has been justified to both the horizontal edges of the page.

## Spelling and Grammar Check

(1) Place the cursor right in the beginning of the document to ensure that the complete document is checked for spelling and grammatical errors. (Although even if you will place the cursor anywhere in the middle, Spelling check feature will prompt you and start from the beginning);

(2) Choose Spelling and Grammar command from the Tools menu;

(3) Once you click on the Spelling and Grammar command, the spell check dialog box appears. The spell check dialog box gives you the following options. Click on the options you want to use.

Click on OK once.

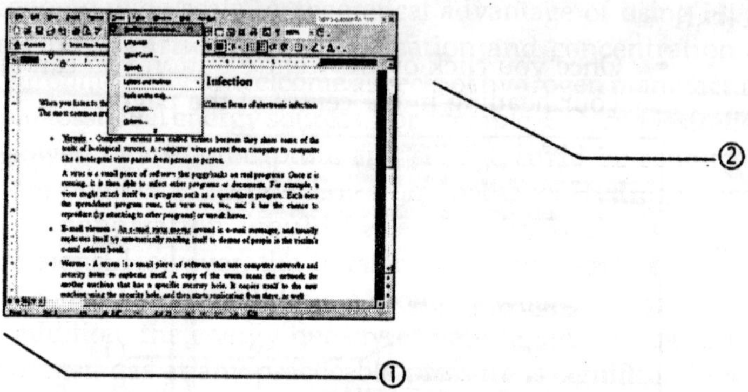


Suggestions Based upon the misspelled words, Word would give you all the possible suggestions for the correct word. In case you don't want to choose from the suggestions, you can simply type the correct word and click once on the change button.

Ignore Though this word is not found in the dictionary, leave it unchanged.

| Ignore All | Ignore this word for all subsequent occurrences. |
|---|---|
| Change | Change this word with the specified suggestion. |
| Change all | Change this word for all subsequent occurrences, with the suggestion specified. |
| Add | Add this word to the dictionary. |
| Auto-Correct | Add the suggested corrections to Auto-Correct. |
| Options | For changing Spell Checks default settings. |

| | |
|---|---|
| Undo Last | Cancel for the previous replacement. |
| Cancel | Terminate Spell Check and return to the document. |

## Print Preview

(1) Choose Print Preview command from File menu.

- This is how your document will look like on print. Click on the Print option if you don't have to make any changes and print the document or click on the Close option and make the relevant changes.

## Print

(1) Choose Print command from the File menu;

(2) Choose your printer from the list;

(3) Click here to choose All. This would print all of the pages of the current document; and

(4) Click on OK button to print.

## Saving the Document

(1) Choose Save command from the File menu;

(2) Type the file name by which you wish to save your file; and

(3) Click on the Save button.

## Closing the Document

(1) Choose Close command from the File menu.

## Opening the Document

(1) Choose Open command from the File menu;

(2) Specify the correct directory path where you have saved your file;

(3) Choose the file by clicking it once; and

(4) Click once on the Open button to open the selected file.

## Exiting MS Word

Choose Exit command from File command menu to end your MS Word session.

## CREATING A DOCUMENT THROUGH TEMPLATE

Every Microsoft Word document is based on a *template.* A template determines the basic attributes for a document such as default font, font size, page margins, page size, page orientation etc. The two basic types of templates are *global templates* and *document templates*. Global templates, including the *Normal template* (on which all new documents are based by default), contain settings that are available to all documents. Document templates, such as the memo or fax template (accessed by selecting the New Document dialog box from the

File → New command), contain settings that are available only to documents based on these templates. For example, if you create a memo using the memo template, the memo can use the settings from both the memo template as well as the settings in any global template.

Word provides a variety of pre-defined document templates. You can also *create your own document templates* such as templates for your company's letter head, fax form, invoice etc.

We shall now work on an exercise involving *Creating an Inter Office Memo* created using MS Word's Elegant Memo template.

### INTEROFFICE MEMO

Date: 12/25/2005

To: All TSCPL Members

Cc: The Managing Directors

From: ajaydeep

RE: New Year Party

All TSCPL staff members along with their family members are cordially invited to the New Years Party at 10:00 PM on 31st Dec at Maharaja Hall, The Radisson Hotel, New Delhi.

Dress Code is Smart Casuals.

AjayDeep Singh
Office/Chief Admin Officer

**Selecting a Template**

(1) Start MS Word;

(2) Click on the New Blank Document from the file menu;

(3) Click on the General Templates option from the New form Template option on the right panel;

(4) Choose Memo Wizard in the Memo option from the Template popup menu; and

(5) Click once on the OK Button.

**STARTING A TEMPLATE AND SELECTING THE TEMPLATE STYLE**

(1) Click once on the Next button to start the Memo wizard Template;

(2) Click once on the Elegant Style radio button to select it; and

(3) Click once on Next to continue.

**HEADER AND THE HEADER ITEMS**

(1) Click on the Yes Radio button and type in the text here, if you want to include a title;

(2) Click once on the Next button;

(3) Click on the header items you want to include in the memo and type in the item here; and

(4) Click once on the Next button.

**RECIPIENT'S NAMES AND THE CLOSING ITEMS**

(1) Type in the Recipients address here and click on the To radio button;

(2) Type in the Second Recipients address here and click on the Cc radio Button;

(3) Click on the option here to have as separate page for your distribution list;

(4) Click once on the Next button;

(5) Tick and type in the closing items you would like to include in the memo; and

(6) Click once on the Next button.

## HEADER AND FOOTER

(1) Tick the header you want to include in your memo;

(2) Tick the footer you want to include in your memo;

(3) Click once on the Next button; and

(4) Click once on the Finish Button.

MS Word provides an easy to use Table Menu, through which you can create very sophisticated tables in a matter of minutes. These tables once created can be easily modified to insert, delete, merge or split, existing rows and columns. Let us follow the instructions, given below, to create the invoice sample given in Exercise 4.3.

It may be kept in mind that although you can create tables of any kind using MS Word, in case these tables involve lot of figure and calculations it is better to use MS Excel rather than MS Word, since MS Excel has been specifically designed for this purpose.

## CREATING ROWS AND COLUMNS

(1) Type in your text and place the cursor on the point where you want to insert the Table;

(2) Click on the Table sub menu in the Insert Option from the Table Menu;

(3) Type here the Number of columns desired;

(4) Type here the number of rows desired; and

(5) Click on OK once.

- You get your desired Table box once you release the mouse button.

### Inserting Rows and Columns

(1) Click once on the Rows above option in the Insert option of the Table.

- You will find a row inserted above your column.

(2) Click once on the Columns to the Left option in the Insert option of the Table Menu.

- You will find a column inserted to the left of your table. Similarly, you can add in more rows and

**Merging Cells**

(a) Now you can type in your text in the cells. You need to merge the last row of the table so as to fit in the amount in words.

(1) Highlight the cell you want to merge; and

(2) Click on the Merge Cell Option from the Table Menu.

(b) Your cells of the last rows have merged to one cell and now you can type in your text.

(c) Your final table is ready to use now. You can now type and format the rest of your text as explained earlier to complete your exercise.

Now, you can type in the rest of your text and complete your exercise.

(a) What is a Template?

(b) List and define the types of templates.

(c) What is the difference between a normal document and a normal template?

## Chapter 8

# Internet and E-mailing

### INTRODUCTION

This unit familiarizes you with the basics of Internet. It also highlights the key usages that the Internet is put to, the various options available to connect to the Internet, the common terms associated with the Internet and facilities available on the Internet. It also details how you could set up your own e-mail account for sending and receiving mails and use the Internet chat facility to keep in touch with your friends anywhere in the world.

### OBJECTIVES

After studying this unit, you should be able to

- Identify the key usages of the Internet,
- Understand the various options available for Internet connectivity along with their merits and limitations,
- Identify the Internet protocol used for transmitting and receiving data over the Internet,
- Understand the common terminology used in context with the Internet,
- Use the search facility to search for, virtually, any information available on the Internet,
- Create and use your e-mail account to send and receive messages, and
- Use the Internet chat to communicate with people in other cities and countries.

## INTERNET BASICS

In the past, computers were stand-alone systems. Transferring information from one computer to another required media like a floppy disk or tape. Resources like the CD-ROM drive and peripherals like printers and scanners could not be shared across computers.

Interconnecting the computers or networking came as a welcome solution resulting in a cost-effective way to share equipment across all connected computers thereby helping people work collectively.

A network can be as simple as linking two computers or may consist of hundreds and thousands of different types of computers and peripherals, connected directly or indirectly.

The Internet is simply a series of computers, linked to one another around the world, communicating almost instantaneously with one another. It comprises tens and thousands of computer networks (a single network may consist of all the computers of an office linked to each other. A larger network may be connecting all the computers within a university premises) communicating with each other like a big net or web! It can be termed as a 'network of networks'. These computer networks are physically linked with one another through telephone, radio, cable lines, satellite, or even fiber optic.

The Internet has literally put a world of information at ones fingertips.

The Internet is the best thing that could have happened to us.

Computer Networks are available in different types:

### Local Area Network (LAN)

LAN connects two or more communication devices (like computers and printers) over a relatively short distance. LANs usually work within an office premises, a factory or a campus where communication devices are connected through a cable, within a distance of 2000 feet. Most LAN networks are shared medium networks, where the workstations shares and waits for its turn to use a resource such as printer, plotter etc.

Newer terms like WLAN and Bluetooth Technology are also associated with LAN today.

**Wireless Local Area Network (WLAN)**

Wireless local area network provides LAN connectivity within a small geographic area, normally within 150 meters, and is typically used where cabling is either not possible or would be very cumbersome, for instance, you may wish to provide LAN connectivity in an open air restaurant!

**Bluetooth Technology**

Bluetooth technology is a wireless medium for sharing information across computers and other electronic devices like mobile phones, Personal Digital Assistants (PDAs) etc., using low power radio frequency.

**Wide Area Network (WAN)**

WAN networks span larger areas than a single building or a campus. They are long-haul networks covering wide geographical areas and often require multiple communication connections like leased lines, satellites and microwave radio links to interconnect various LANs. LANs are usually measured in feet, while WANs are measured in miles.

**Metropolitan Area Networks (MAN)**

A group of LANs connected through a high-speed, seamless interconnection, within a 'metropolitan' area, is termed as a Metropolitan Area Network (MAN). The word 'metropolitan' does not necessarily mean a 'city' but can be any area that is spread out, but is treated as one entity, e.g. a company having its two buildings on the opposite sides of the road.

MAN connects users with computer resources in a geographic area that is larger than that covered by a LAN but smaller than the area covered by a WAN.

A recent trend includes installations of wireless MANs.

## KEY USAGES

The key usages that the Internet is put to include:

### Online Shopping

Online shopping is one of the biggest uses of the Net. Internet has helped in removing all barriers of distance and nationality. Logging onto a web portal, you can buy products and services from across the globe and pay for the same using your international credit/debit cards. All without ever having to step away from your office or home computer!

Online shopping has evolved from simple purchase and sale transactions to sophisticated online bidding and auctioning. From purchasing of gum chewed by Britney Spears to buying a state-of-art car, can all be done using web portals like eBay.com, Bazee.com, etc.

### Internet Telephony and Chatting

Till a few years ago chatting on the Internet was one of the fastest growing uses of the World Wide Web. In a typical chat session, two or more individuals (from anywhere in the world) would log in to a chat room and converse with each other by typing. The typed message was instantaneously relayed on the computers of the chat room individuals. Because of its ease of use and anonymity, this was a greatly favoured medium among students, businessmen and housewives alike.

Some years ago some smart geeks figured out that Internet grid does not care what you send over it. Whether it is data, voice or video its all the same for the Net pipe. So, it is no wonder that you can now call up any phone number in the world through a computer based Internet line at a fraction of a cost of a normal landline call. Improvements in connectivity speed and proliferation of broadband has ensured that the voice and picture quality of Internet telephony is not only as good, but sometimes even better than that of conventional phones.

It is just a matter of time when all calls will be local calls!

### Distance Education

Because of its non-intrusive and flexible mechanism, the Internet provides a perfect medium for knowledge sharing and information dissemination. As with other things, Internet has removed the geographical barriers such that a professor delivering a lecture in California can be heard and seen in real-time in Hyderabad. Students, especially those who are working, need not now be physically present in a classroom. You can now pursue specialized higher studies in the comfort of your own office or home – all you need is a simple desktop and a reliable internet connection.

### Sharing Music and Books

**Napster.com** pioneered the concept of sharing music between music lovers. Although Napster.com is now no longer a free music site, there are hundreds of other web clones with slight variations, who offer free download of music.

The publishing industry has also realised the immense potential of e-books (electronic books). No printing costs, no distribution costs, and no stocking costs! Simply convert your paperback book into an electronic one (most commonly an Adobe Acrobat file) and let web browsers download this by making online payment at considerably reduced rates.

### Banking

The banking industry was the first one to use IT in a major way to automate operations and save costs. It was banks who pioneered the concept of ATMs which made the paradigm shift of outsourcing bank-office work back to the clients. In an ATM, the bank customer himself/herself feeds in his account details instead of a bank clerk, thereby saving the bank considerable time and money. This concept became the cornerstone for the BPO industry especially the ITES (IT Enabled Services). Internet provides the next logical step towards taking the bank to the doorstep of the customer. You can now view your account details, transfer money, make requests for cheque books and drafts, get information on new products and services, all by accessing the bank's website.

### Travel

The travel industry has been another major gainer from the Internet boom. Whether it is the hotels, motels or inns, airlines, train companies, taxi or car rental companies all of these have gained tremendously, by offering their services through websites. The customers, on the other hand, have also greatly benefitted because they can now compare rates, make online bookings, avail rock-bottom discounts, make last minute iternary changes, and pay online without having to run around multiple offices. This convenience has not only made travel more comfortable, but because of easy access of information and bookings, expanded the travel market substantially, by reaching out to people who would not have traveled so often otherwise.

### Bill Payments

Thanks to the government sector also for realizing the benefits of IT, it is now possible to make online payments of public utilities like electricity, phones, water etc. by using credit cards as a payment medium. Private sector companies were anyway ahead in the race and so you can virtually buy almost anything on the Net by making online payments.

## INTERNET CONNECTIVITY OPTIONS

There are various options available to connect to the Internet. The commonly used ones are explained below.

### Dial-Up

Dial-up provides connecting a device to a network using modem over the public telephone network. Dial-up access is really just like a phone connection, except that instead of two individuals on the two ends you have computer devices. Since the dial-up uses the regular telephone lines, the quality of connection is not always good. In the past, the maximum data transfer rate over a dial-up connection was limited to 56 kbps (56,000 bits per second). Newer technologies are providing better transfer rates.

## Integrated Services Digital Network (ISDN)

ISDN, as the name suggests, is a digital communications line. It allows for transmission of data, voice, video and graphics, at very high speeds, over standard communication lines. ISDN lines can carry large amounts of data, while providing a single common interface to access digital communication services required for varying devices, while keeping it transparent to the end user. Owing to these features, ISDN applications have revolutionized the way businesses communicate. ISDN is not restricted to public telephone networks, but can use packet switched networks, CATV networks, telex etc.

## Digital Subscriber Lines (DSL)

A DSL connection is a very high-speed connection that uses the same wires as a regular telephone line. Many local companies, in addition to their regular phone services, also provide Internet services (DSLs). DSLs are, therefore, available in some (not all) areas where regular phone services are available. A DSL connection has a much higher speed of connection than a regular dial-up connection (56 kbps) and the connection can be left open, while you use your phone line for voice calls!

The reliability and monthly rates for a DSL connection are comparable to that of the cable network service, but the connection speed is slower.

## Leased Line

An alternative way to connect two computers is through a leased line. It is like a 'private circuit' between the two machines. A leased line can best be understood as a permanent dedicated communication link between two points and is reserved, exclusively for the leased line purchaser.

A leased line can be a twisted pair, coax cable, or (more recently) a fibre optic cable. Leased lines have varying data transfer rates, going up to a speed of 1.544 Mbps. Using multiplexing techniques, these transfer rates can be divided between voice and data.

Large companies having high Internet usage, usually go in for leased lines since it is a more cost effective solution than the traditional one like ISDN.

### Cable Internet Services

Now-a-day, in addition to the traditional cable services, most of the cable TV companies also provide Internet services. These services come at reasonable monthly rates, are reliable and have high download transmission and upload rates. You could contact your local cable provider to get more information on services provided by them.

### Internet Protocols

'Protocol' defines a set of rules or code of behaviour. In the context of networking, protocol defines a 'language' of conventions and rules that specify how the data will be packaged, sent and acknowledged.

Before we dwell more into the internet protocols, let us first discuss addressing.

The Internet consists of a large number of computers connected with each other and hence there is need of a proper addressing system. Each computer within this network (called a host) must be uniquely identifiable. This is done by attaching a number and a name to it.

### IP Address

The Internet Protocol (IP) address is an unique number that defines the location of your computer, such that it is an identifiable machine within all the computers connected to the Internet. This is a 32-bit number and is divided into four octets. For readability purposes, humans represent these IP addresses in a decimal notation that use periods to separate each octet. For example, the IP address

00001010 00000000 00000000 00000010

in decimal notation separated with periods is represented as 10.0.0.2.

Since each byte is 8 bits in length, in each octet in an IP address ranges in value from a minimum of 0 to a maximum of 255. Thus, the full range of IP addresses is from 0.0.0.0 through 255.255.255.255 which is total of 4,294,967,296 possible IP addresses.

## Domain Naming System (DNS)

In a network, computers and devices can be grouped together and can be administered as a unit with common rules and procedures, sharing a common name. Such a group is referred to as a Domain.

Domain Naming System (or Service), commonly known as the DNS, is an Internet service that translates domain names to or from IP addresses, which is the actual basis of addressing on the Internet. Some examples of domain names include Microsoft.com, Yahoo.com etc. The last three letters of the address provides information about the kind of organization to which the address belongs.

**Table: Commonly Used Abbreviations in Domain Names**

| Abbreviation | What It Represents |
|---|---|
| Com | Commercial organization |
| org | Non-profit organizations |
| net | Networking organizations |
| gov | Government agencies |
| edu | Educational institutions |
| in | Indian organization |

## Communication Protocol

When different computers, peripherals and devices are connected in a network they need to follow a set of standard rules for transmitting and receiving data to avoid data collision. These set of rules and conventions are called Protocols. The Internet uses a set of communication protocols called the Transmission Control Protocol/Internet Protocol (TCP/IP). This protocol enables information to be transferred between dissimilar computers and is, therefore, said to bind the Internet.

Technically speaking, Transmission Control Protocol (TCP) and Internet Protocol (IP) are two distinct network protocols. They are so commonly used together that TCP/IP has become a standard terminology to refer to either or both of the protocols.

### *TCP*

When two computers wish to communicate with each other reliably, they establish a connection. This is analogous to making a phone call, say to a friend in California. A connection is established when you dial the number and get a response from the other side. TCP guarantees that when data is sent from one end of the connection, it reaches the other end in the same order. Otherwise, an error is reported.

### *IP*

Information in a network is transmitted in the form of packets. It is the task of IP to send a packet from one computer to another. It, however, does not verify that the packet actually reaches its destination, or that it reaches error free and in the correct order.

Technically, IP corresponds to the Network layer (Layer 3) in the OSI model, whereas TCP corresponds to the Transport layer (Layer 4) in the OSI model (a discussion on the OSI layers is out of scope for this Unit).

(a) State TRUE or FALSE

  (i) Internet is simply a series of computers linked to one another around the world.

  (ii) LAN connects two or more computers over large areas like across the city.

  (iii) Bluetooth technology is a wireless medium using low power radio frequency to share information across devices.

  (iv) TCP/IP is a set of communication protocols used by the Internet.

(b) What are the various connectivity options available to connect to the Internet?

## STARTING THE INTERNET

Before you start using the Internet, it may prove useful to understand some common terminology used in context with the Internet.

### World Wide Web (www)

Commonly known as the 'Web' it consists of Internet servers that are connected through hypertext. Related text, organized into units by the user, that can be activated using a link is termed as hypertext. The documents are formatted in a language called HTML (HyperText Markup Language) which supports links to other documents, as well as graphics, audio and video files. Such documents are associated with the hyperlink in such a way that when a user clicks on the link, information on that topic is displayed. Thus, hyperlinks allow the user to navigate from one document to another without having to worry about the actual location of the document (which could be the same or another server located miles away). Thus, the World Wide Web has made it possible to share information between disparate users, computers and operating systems.

### Website

The web can be understood as a collection of thousands and millions of information locations connected to each other. Each such location is called a *website.* A website comprises *web pages* – an electronic page like any other computer document, created using HTML (HyperText Markup Language). Web pages can contain pictures, sound files, videos in addition to text, thus allowing multimedia applications.

A website can be created by an individual or an organization and is a virtual location on the web. An Uniform Resource Locator (URL) defines the address of a Website and is used to point to the Website's *homepage.* The homepage is the first page that is displayed when the website is accessed and serves as a reference point containing pointers or links to additional HTML pages or links to other websites.

## HyperText Transfer Protocol (HTTP)

HTTP can be defined as a protocol (set of rules) for exchanging text, image, sound, video and other multimedia files across the Internet. It typically consists of a HTTP client programme at one end, and a HTTP server programme on the other. It is the most important protocol used in the World Wide Web.

## Uniform Resource Locator (URL)

An URL defines the address of a site on the Internet. It is an abbreviation of Uniform Resource Locator, and states the global address of documents and other resources on the World Wide Web.

For example:

**http://msoft.com/index.html**

**ftp://www.freesoft/loadsoft.exe**

The first part of the address indicates the protocol to be used, and the second part specifies the IP address or the domain name where the resource is located. Above, the first URL specifies a web page to be fetched using the HTTP protocol, while the second URL specifies an executable file to be fetched using the FTP (File Transfer Protocol) protocol.

## BROWSER FUNCTIONS

Learning a few basic things about browsing the Web, such as how to use the buttons on the Internet Explorer toolbar, will make it fast and easy for you to use the Web.

### Toolbar (Internet Explorer)

The row of buttons on top of a web browser is known as the toolbar. It consists of various icons that can be used to execute functions. In fact, most of the options available through the menu bar are also available through the icons in the toolbar. Some commonly used icons are detailed below:

#### *Back*

The back button allows you to navigate to the page you viewed last. Similarly, the forward button on the toolbar navigates to the current page from the previous page. To see a list of the last few pages visited, click on the down arrow button beside the *Back* and *Forward* buttons.

***Stop***

The stop button can be used to terminate the loading of the current page. This is usually used when you typed the wrong URL by mistake and you want to stop the Web Page from loading or if the webpage takes too long to download.

**Refresh**

As the name suggests, the refresh or the reload button is used to load the current webpage again. In other words, it refreshes the contents of the current page by fetching a new copy of it.

***Search***

Search allows you to find information on the web. You can find information on the web in a variety of ways:

- Click the *Search* button on the toolbar to gain access to a number of search providers. Type a word or phrase in the *Search* box.
- Type *go, find,* or? followed by a word or phrase in the Address bar. Internet Explorer starts a search using its predetermined search provider.

- After you go to a Web page, you can search for specific text on that page by clicking the *Edit* menu, and then clicking *Find* (*on this page*).

**Favourites**

Favourites/Bookmarks is used to record addresses of frequently visited websites. Once a website or a web page is added to the favourites list, it can be revisited by simply clicking on the link in the list. This saves the effort of typing the URL, each time the user wishes to visit the same site.

As your list of favourite pages grows, you can organize it by creating different folders. For example, you could create a folder named 'Technology' for storing information about sites from where you collect some Technology related information.

To organize your favourites into folders:

(a) Click Organize Favourites on the Favourites menu.

(b) Click on Create Folder and press ENTER.

(c) Drag the shortcuts in the list to the appropriate folders.

**History**

History is a record of all pages visited in the last few days, hours, or minutes. Clicking on the history button displays a list of all recently visited webpages and/or websites. To revisit any one of them, simply click on the address.

**Print**

Print button is used to print contents of the current webpage.

**Net Surfing**

Net surfing is a term associated with browsing or exploring a network or the World Wide Web to find places of interest, usually without any specific goal in mind. It is analogous to channel surfing with the TV's remote control.

**SEARCHING**

You can search for information on virtually any topic on the Internet. This is possible by using websites, that provide a Search engine. One of the most popular search engines is

Google. Other commonly used search sites include Yahoo, Rediff, Alta Vista, Hot Bot, AskJeeves, and Khoj.

Google (www.google.com)

Yahoo (www.yahoo.com)

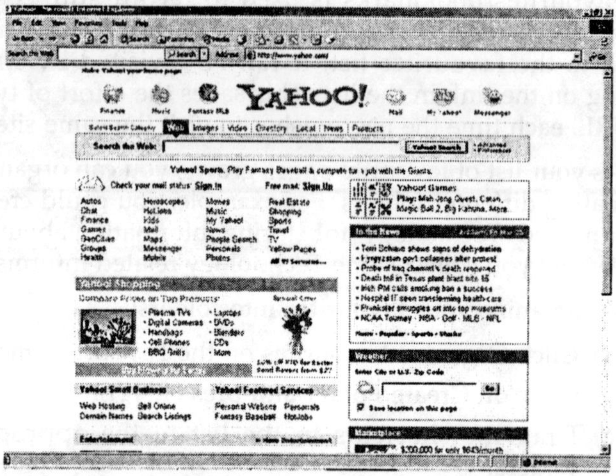


Since different search engines use different algorithms, it will give different results for the same search criterion. The user must, therefore, know which search engine is best suited for his/her specific query.

## E-MAILING

E-mailing is one of the most common and popular uses of the Internet. You can send or receive mails from anywhere in the world, that too in a matter of seconds. Through e-mail, you can send and receive any type of file – image, video, sound, and, of course, plain text. It is a very versatile and open medium with the advantage of being a low cost one.

If you wish to send and receive e-mails, you will need to create an e-mail account for yourself, using a website that offers such services. Various sites provide this facility – some charge for it while others don't. Rediff.com is one of the sites that provide for free e-mail services. Other such sites include yahoo.com,

hotmail.com, lycos.com and many more.

Since we are interested in learning how to use e-mail, let us use services provided by Rediff to do the same.

## Creating an E-mail Account

Type the URL 'http://www.rediff.com' in the Internet explorer to visit the Rediff website. The homepage will be displayed as follows:

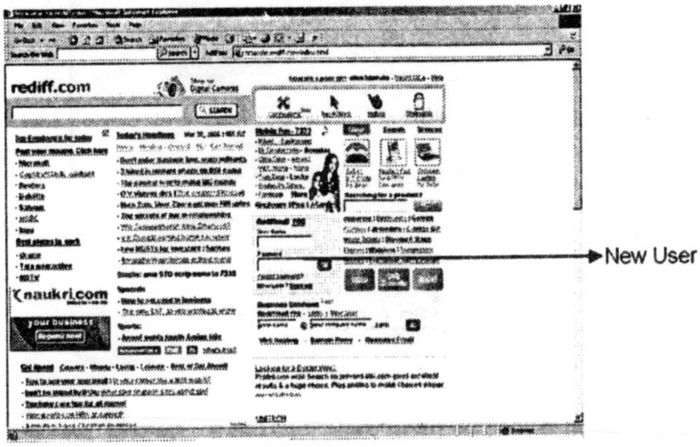


Since you are a new user at this time, you need to Sign Up as a new user.

Click on 'Sign Up 'to create yourself as a new user. A new page will be displayed that will allow you to select the kind of account you want – Free or paid (these differ in the storage space and additional facilities).

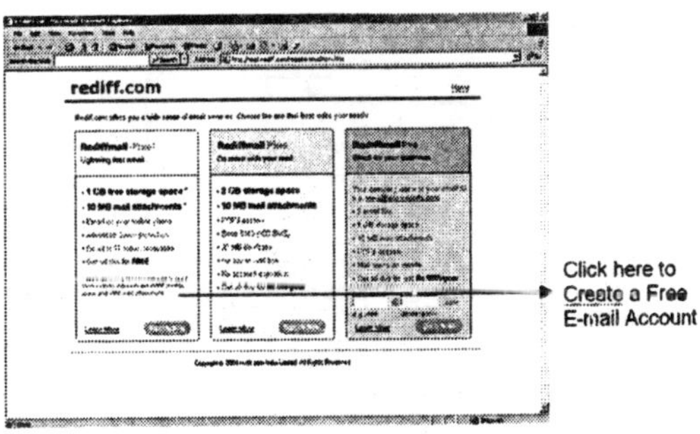


Once you click on the 'Sign Up Now' button, Rediff displays a registration form and requires you to fill some necessary details like a user ID, password, Name etc.

After you register yourself on a website, you become a member and can then simply log into your mail account using the username and password. It is, therefore, very important to remember your username and password because without that you cannot access your e-mail account.

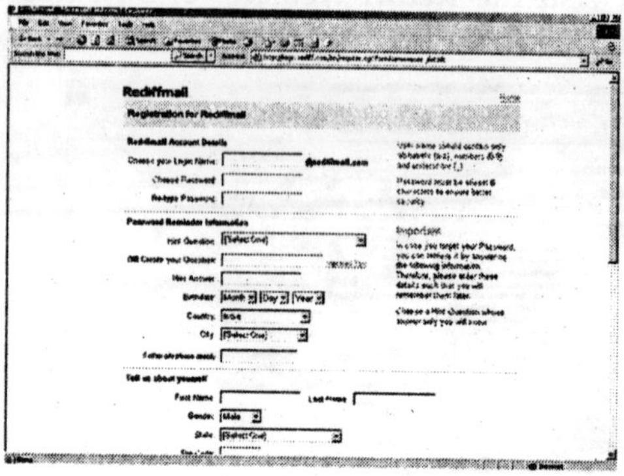

## Checking E-mail

You can access your e-mail at any time by logging into your email.

Type the URL 'http://www.rediff.com' in the Internet explorer to visit the Rediff website.

Enter your username and password in the home page and click on the 'Go' button to take you to your Inbox.

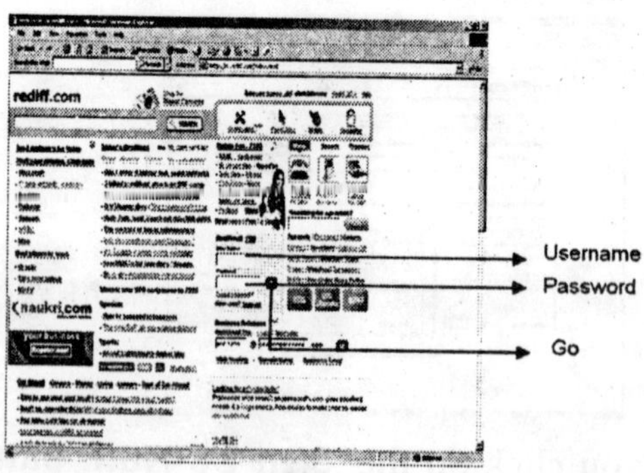


To read an email, simply click on the subject of the mail. This will display the actual text of the mail for you to read.

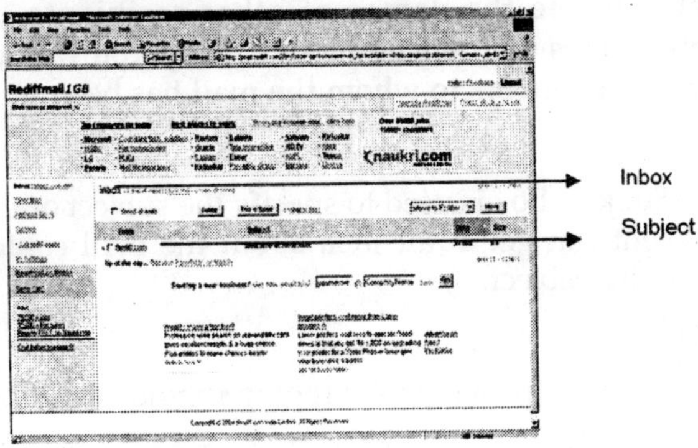


## Sending E-mail

To send e-mail, click on Write Mail. The screen that follows would look like

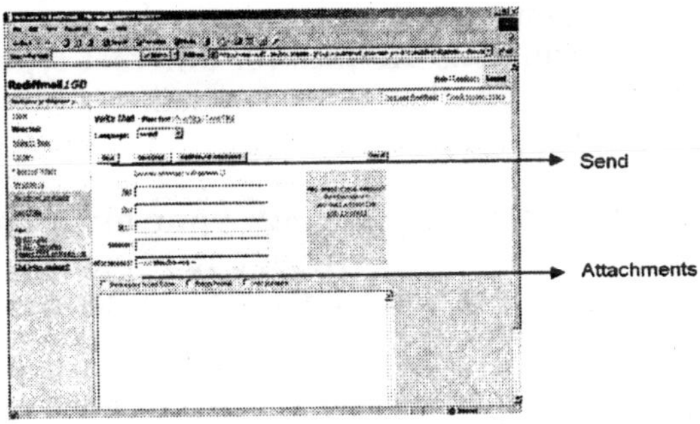


### *To*

In the To box, type the name of the recipient of the form recipient@domain.com. You must enter the correct e-mail ID of the recipient else the message will return to you.

### *Cc*

CC or Carbon Copy is used to send the message to more than one recipient at the same time. Type in the mail IDs of the additional recipients in this box (you can put more than one mail ID in this box by separating the list with commas).

### *Bcc*

Bcc stands for 'Blind Carbon Copy' and is used when you wish to send the message to multiple recipients without them being able to see the names of other recipients. All the recipients' names will remain hidden. Only you would know the names of members to whom the mail has been sent.

### *Subject*

The 'Subject' box is used to specify the subject of the mail. The recipient can get a fair idea about the mail contents by looking at the subject.

### *Message Box*

It is the place provided for typing in your mail message.

Once you have typed in your message, simply click on the **Send** button to send the message to the recipient(s). You will get a message informing you that your mail has been sent.

## E-mail Attachments

You can send and receive attachments with mail messages. Attachments are files (of different types like text, sound, video etc.) attached with the mail.

### Sending Attachments

To send an attachment with your mail, click on the Attachments button while writing a new mail. A screen like below is displayed for you to attach the necessary files.

Clicking on the Browse button opens the standard files selection dialog box. It lets you browse through the files on your disk(s) and select the file you want to attach.

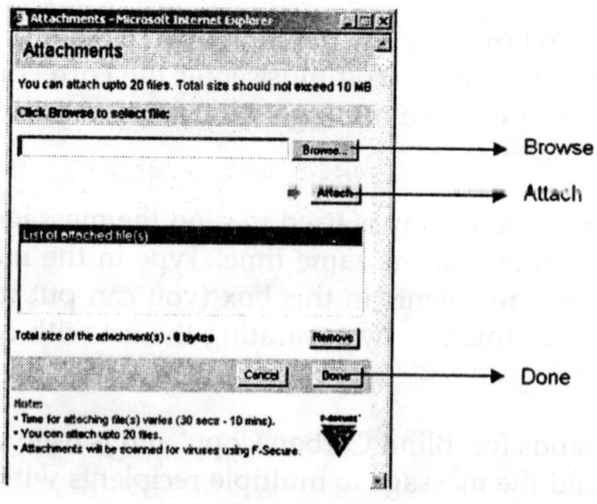

Once you locate the file, click on it and then click on the Open button. You can repeat this process if you wish to attach more than one file with your message. Once you are done with the selection of files, click on Attach button to attach the file to your message. Finally, click on the Done button to return to your message. Now when you Send your message, it is sent along with the attachments (files).

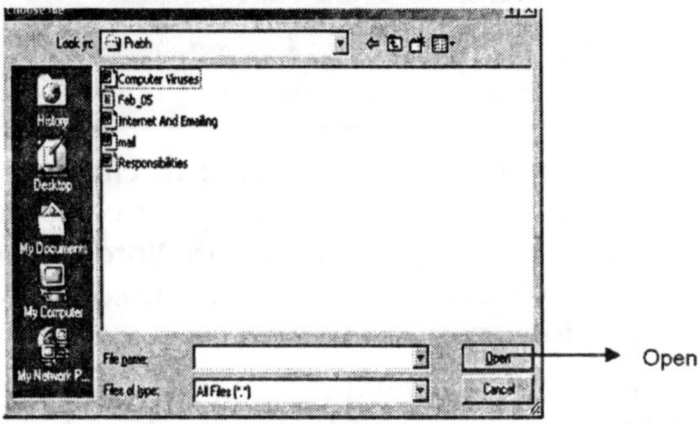


## Opening Attachments

If you receive an e-mail with attachment(s), you can view the attached files on-line and/or save these to your disk and view them later. While reading the received mail, clicking on the Go to Attachments button will display the following:

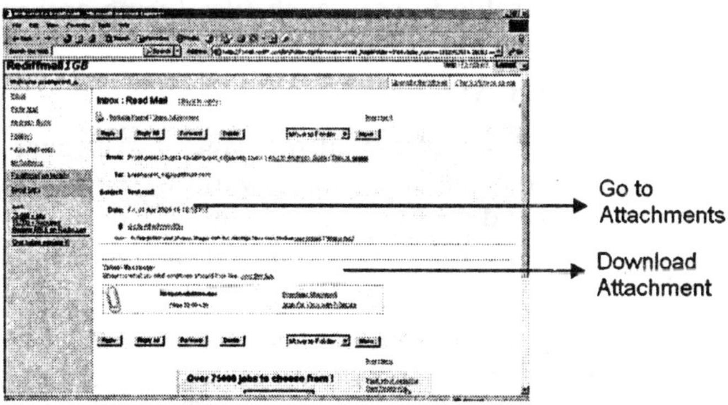


Clicking on Download Attachment will display the following screen:

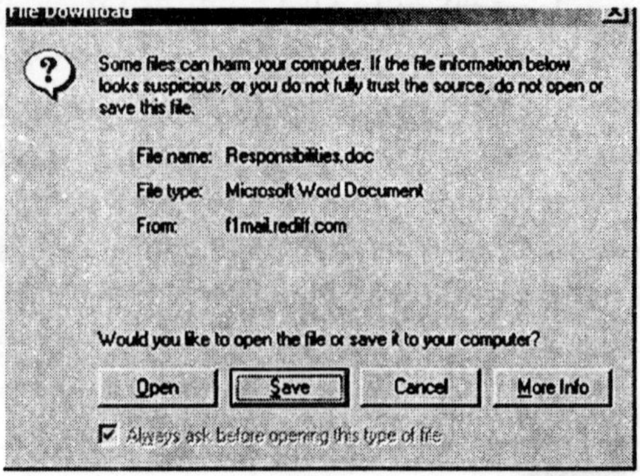


To view the file without saving it, click on the Open button. The file will open (provided your computer has the associated application installed, e.g. MS Word if the document is a word file, MS Excel in case it is an Excel file and so on) allowing you to view the file contents.

Alternatively, you could click on Save to save the file in the desired folder on your disk. You can then view this file(s), whenever you wish, at a later time.

### A Word of Caution

Attachments can prove dangerous to your computer, because these can conceal dangerous viruses or other malicious programmes that may destroy the data on your computer. It is, therefore, advisable to scan such files (using anti-virus software) before opening them.

## SOME TIPS FOR E-MAILING

Each day millions of e-mail messages travel over the Internet. Since each of us contributes towards the large volume of such messages and deal with a large number of them on a daily basis, it may be worthwhile keeping the following tips in mind:

- Arrange your e-mails into different folders (depending on their content). This will organize your mails into different categories, e.g. Travel, Education, Newsletters etc. while leaving only those in your Inbox that require immediate action.

- Periodically scan your messages to delete the old messages and preserve your e-mail account space.
- Always write meaningful subject in your mails.
- You can also set up e-mail filters to avoid cluttering your Inbox. Filters are used to automatically send certain messages (by sender for example) to separate folders.
- Zip your attachments if they are very big.
- Scan the attachments received before opening them.
- Periodically change your password to protect your e-mail account from unauthorized users.
- Do not forward junk mails or chain letters.
- Do not forget to log out of your e-mail account.

**INTERNET CHAT**

In the earlier days, the only medium of online communication with people residing in other cities and countries was a long distance call (STD or ISD). With the Internet gaining popularity, options like Internet Telephony, Internet Chat are also becoming the preferred medium of communication.

Internet Telephony (or IPT) is characterized by transportation of telephone calls over the Internet. All you need is a microphone, earphone and special software on your PC to talk to anyone on the Internet. This makes the telephonic conversation very cheap and is being widely used amongst the Internet society.

Internet Chat (or IRC as it is popularly called) allows you to type in a message, and your friend (anywhere in the world, but logged on to the Net at the same time on the same chat site) would receive it almost instantaneously who can then respond in the same way. Other than the difference of having to type instead of speaking, chatting is almost as good as speaking to another person on the phone.

There are various free chat sites that you can use to communicate with other people – one of the most popular being Yahoo. You can log on to the free chat site, go to the specific chat room where you have agreed to meet the other person, and start chatting by typing your message.

You could go to the Yahoo site by typing the URL 'http://www.Yahoo.com'. Once you have done that, click on Chat from the Yahoo home page.

You can now type in your Yahoo ID and Password and then click on Sign in (in case you do not already have a Yahoo account, you can create one by clicking on 'Sign Up for Yahoo Chat' which will let you create a new Yahoo account).

Once you are logged in you can Enter Chat Room to start chatting.

Clicking on this will take you into a room called Chat Central where you can find many people chatting. You can simply jump in and start chatting. You can also change your chat room by clicking on Change Room to get a list of chat rooms to select from.

**What is the difference between E-mail and Chat?**

In this unit, you have studied the key usages of the Internet, the connectivity options available to connect over the Internet, the most common Internet protocol, and the common terminology used in context of the Internet. You have also learnt how to search the Internet using various search engines available.

This unit also familiarized you with E-mail and Chat, the two most common uses that the Internet is put to. It details, the steps required to create your own e-mail account, thereby being able to send and receive messages to people anywhere in the world.

Chapter 9

# Digital Logic and Boolean Algebra

## INTRODUCTION

We now tackle the lowest of the six levels mentioned in the introduction — the digital logic level.

**Digital:**

means that we are dealing with 'digits', i.e. discrete quantities as opposed to continuous or analogue quantities;

**Logic:**

indicates that the electronics is implementing a form of mathematics based on logic - propositional logic.

First we will introduce propositional logic - 'Boolean algebra'. Then we will show how simple logic (Boolean) functions are implemented in computer hardware.

## LOGIC

## INTRODUCTION

Since at least 400 B.C. human beings have been studying what it means to think and to reason. Two closely related aims can be identified:

- To understand the process of mental reasoning.

- To develop methods to mechanise thinking and reasoning, e.g. to develop procedural methods for doing mathematical proofs, or simply to give procedures by which a thinker could come up with a rational answer to a difficult question, or, more lately, as in the study of Artificial Intelligence, to develop methods by which computers may be programmed to perform tasks that require *intelligence.*

Broadly speaking, logic is the study of the principles and patterns of reasoning, argument and proof. Again generalising, we can say that logic uses a language that is a formalisation of certain types of natural language statements.

You should be aware that there are two distinct but related forms of logic:

- Propositional logic - which is closely related to Boolean algebra. We will have cause to use elements of propositional logic in this course. And, you will come across it frequently in your other courses. Note: in programming, where you will have already come across statements like: if(x == 10 && y == 20) (test the truth of the logic statement *x is-equal-to 10* and *y is-equal-to 20.*
- Predicate calculus, which is at the basis of the Prolog programming language.

## PROPOSITIONAL LOGIC

Propositional logic deals with statements (propositions) which make claims which can be either true or false. Thus, valid propositions are:

- Dublin is the capital of Ireland.
- Belfast has more than 100,000 inhabitants.
- Manchester United are Premiership Champions.
- Joe Bloggs is a first year QUB student.

The test for validity is as follows: you must be able to meaningfully append to the statement "is true" (or "is false").

Thus "Dublin is the capital of Ireland is true".

Notice, however, how "Manchester United are Premiership Champions" may need time/date qualification.

The following are invalid propositions.

- What is the capital of Ireland? (a question)
- Has Dublin a large population? (a question)
- Go now to room 1.15! (a command)
- Will you come to the Botanic Inn with me on Thursday? An invitation - variations on which may be called a "proposition" in everyday language!

**Generalisation/Abstraction: Symbolic Logic**

We can make symbols stand-for any proposition, e.g.

$p$ = "Dublin is the capital of Ireland"

- Hence, in propositional calculus, the 'Boolean' variable $p$ has the truth value *true*.

$q$ = "Belfast has more than 100, 000 inhabitants"

**Compound Propositions**

We can now combine elementary propositions using logic connectives to make compound or complex propositions.

**Conjunction - and**

Dublin is the capital of Ireland and Belfast has more than 100,000 inhabitants is true.

The combined proposition is true if-and-only-if both elements are true.

In this case, let us agree that both are true, so that the statement:

Arsenal are European Champions and Belfast has more than 100,000 inhabitants is false.

The meaning of and can be neatly summarised with a truth-table using abstract symbols:

**Table:** Truth-table for conjunction

| *p* | *q* | *p and q* |
|---|---|---|
| *F* | *F* | *F* |
| *F* | *T* | *F* |
| *T* | *F* | *F* |
| *T* | *T* | *T* |

Other symbols for conjunction are: ∧ (looks like an A), and, in C/C++/Java, &&.

## Disjunction - or

Note that or has two natural language meanings: exclusive-or, only one of the statements can be true at any time; inclusive-or, only either one or the other needs be to be true, or *both*; without any qualification, *or* generally means inclusive-or.

The meaning of or is given by the following truth-table:

**Table:** Truth-table for disjunction

| *p* | *q* | |
|---|---|---|
| *F* | *F* | *F* |
| *F* | *T* | *T* |
| *T* | *F* | *T* |
| *T* | *T* | *T* |

Other symbols for disjunction:, and, in C/C++/Java,.

## Negation - not

If a proposition *p* is true, then not(*p*) is false.

The meaning of not is given by the truth-table:

**Table:** Truth-table for negation

| *p* | *not q* |
|---|---|
| *F* | *T* |
| *T* | *F* |

## SET THEORY

The propositional calculus on truth values is equivalent to (*isomorphic* with) the calculus of set operations:

$$\begin{aligned} \textbf{and} &\leftrightarrow \cap \text{ (intersection)} \\ \textbf{or} &\leftrightarrow \cup \text{ (union)} \\ \textbf{not} &\leftrightarrow \sim \text{ (complement)} \end{aligned}$$

## DIGITAL LOGIC

Digital computers are constructed from switching circuits which implement propositional calculus - Boolean algebra; indeed, the term *switching algebra* is sometimes used. 'Switch-on' might be associated with true and 'off' with false. However, equally, so long as everyone is agreed as to the convention, 'on' could be associated with false and 'off' with true.

Likewise, the physical entities representing the values could be {voltage-low, voltage-high} or {light-off, light-on}, or whatever. Very often, we use {0, 1} - the binary digits - to represent {false, true}.

The essence of Boolean algebra is that we have only two allowable values, which we can label whatever we like, usually: {false, true}, or {0, 1}, and the two *binary* operations mentioned above: *conjunction* (and), and *disjunction* (or), together with the *unary* operation *negation* (not). There are other binary operations, but they can be expressed in terms of these three.

Let us now examine these operations or functions - to emphasise that they are functions, we write them in *prefix* notation, remarking, however, that the *infix* notation conveys exactly the same meaning. In addition, we use the value set {0,1}, recalling that the set {false, true} is entirely equivalent.

**Conjunction - and**

and (0,0) = 0

and (0,1) = 0

and (1,0) = 0

and (1,1) = 1

Of course, this is the same thing as Table.

Because there is a slight analogy with numerical multiplication, and is sometimes denoted by the infix '.', or just concatenation of the input variables; also, and itself is often written in infix form. Thus, for Boolean variables *p*, *q*, and *r*, the following are equivalent:

$$r = \text{and}(p, q)$$

$$r = p \text{ and } q$$

$$r = p \wedge q$$

$$r = p.q$$

$$r = pq$$

$$r = p\&q$$

**Disjunction - or**

and (0,0) = 0

and (0,1) = 0

and (1,0) = 0

and (1,1) = 1

Of course, this is the same thing as Table.

Because there is a slight analogy with numerical addition, or is sometimes denoted by '+'. Thus, for Boolean variables *p*, *q*, and *r*, the following are equivalent:

$$r = \mathrm{or}(p, q)$$
$$r = p \text{ or } q$$
$$r = p \vee q$$
$$r = p + q$$

## NEGATION - NOT

not (0) = 1

not (1) = 0

This is the same thing as Table.Because there is a slight analogy with numerical negation, or is sometimes denoted by variations of - and $\sim$. Thus, for Boolean variables p, q, the following are equivalent:

$$q = \mathrm{not}(p)$$
$$q = \neg p$$
$$q = \bar{p}$$
$$q = \sim p$$
$$q = p'$$

**0, 1 are not numbers!**

The analogies with arithmetic (and 'ordinary' algebra) may cause confusion for the unwary; remember that {0,1}stand for {false, true}and that it makes no sense at all to do arithmetic on them - no more sense than, for example, attempting to multiply a Java text String by.

## AND, OR ARE BINARY, NOT IS UNARY AND THE ASSOCIATIVE LAW

Although it is not uncommon to see $p + q + r = p$ or q or r, you must remember that both or and and are *binary* - meaning two parameter functions. Thus, strictly,

$p + q + r = p + (q + r) = \mathrm{or}(p, \mathrm{or}(q, r)),$

just as in Java, if(x==2||y==3||z==4) strictly could be written if(x==2||(y==3||z==4)).

Of course, in 'ordinary' algebra, + and X-, etc. are also binary, but the *associative law,* see section 3.3.2 for these operations allows us to string a series of them together. Note: in 'ordinary' algebra, there are two minuses, a unary one (-1) and a binary one (3 - 1 = 2); always remember that if you have to write an expression evaluator programme.

## EQUIVALENCES OF BOOLEAN ALGEBRA

Just as it helps to know that in ordinary algebra, $a \times x + b \times x + a \times y + b \times y = (a + b) \times (x + y)$, or that $x + (-x) = 0$, it is useful to be aware of the more useful equivalences (or identities or laws) of Boolean algebra. Some of them are shown in Table 3.4. Some of these are intuitive, some not. For each equivalence there are duals - where and is swapped for or and *vice-versa*. For completeness, we show the table in two forms, Table 3.4, using the mathematicians $\wedge, \vee, \neg$ notation, and Table, using the engineers $\cdot, +, \bar{}$ notation.

## LOGIC GATES

Logic gates are the hardware implementation of logic functions. Again, all Boolean functions can be implemented using a combination of and, or, and not gates. The term gate comes from the operation of the and gate, see below, which, if one of its inputs is false, blocks or gates the other input, even if it is true.

Microprocessors, and other digital logic integrated circuits (chips) are simply massive collections of interconnected gates.

Because of a particular twist of fate in the physics of transistors - of which logic gates are constructed - it turns out that real circuits tend to employ nand and nor gates a good deal in preference to and and or:

**Nand:**

$$p \text{ nand } q = \text{not}(p \text{ and } q)$$

**Nor:**

$$p \text{ nor } q = \text{not}(p \text{ or } q)$$

## TRANSISTOR IMPLEMENTATIONS

For completeness, we show transistor implementations of not (also called an *inverter*), nand and nor. Again for completeness, we give the following model of a transistor when it is operated in so-called *switching* mode.

### Transistor as a Switch

There are three connections - collector, base, and emitter. The positive power supply (e.g. +5 volts) is applied to the collector via a resistor; the emitter (the one with the arrow) is connected to ground/earth. The input signal is applied to the base. When the input signal is high, say > 3 volts when the power is 5 volts, the transistor switches on, i.e. current is allowed to flow down to the emitter and out to ground. When the input signal is low, the transistor switches off i.e. little or no current is allowed to flow.

The net effect of the transistor in Figure switching on is that the output is connected to ground and $V_{out}$ takes the voltage of ground - $\sim 0$ volts. Thus high input ($V_{in}$) - logic 1 - yields low output - logic 0; thus, not, inversion.

The net effect of the transistor switching off is that the output takes on the voltage $\sim V_{cc}$ volts. Thus low input ($V_{in}$) - logic 0 - yields high output - logic 1; thus, not, inversion.

With this model in mind, it is easy to verify that the circuits in Figures do in fact operate as nand and nor.

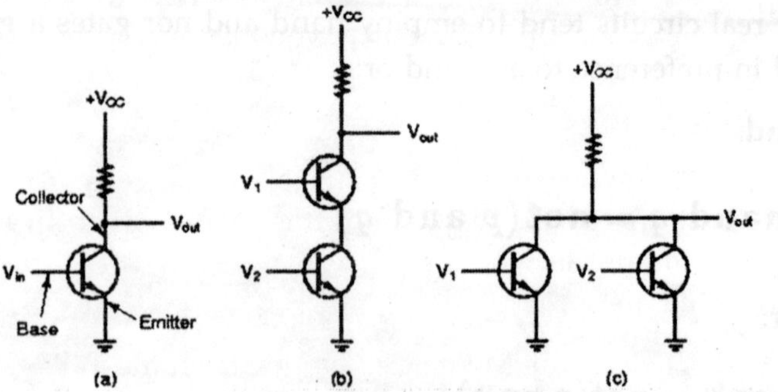


**Figure:** (a) Not (b) nand (c) nor

If you would like to see mechanical implementations of gates (levers, also water valves), see [Hillis, 1999].

### Symbols for Logic Gates

Figure shows the symbols, and truth-tables, for the five basic logic gates.

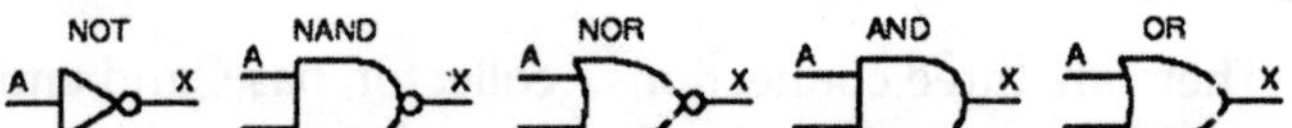


(a)

| A | X |
|---|---|
| 0 | 1 |
| 1 | 0 |

(b)

| A | B | X |
|---|---|---|
| 0 | 0 | 1 |
| 0 | 1 | 1 |
| 1 | 0 | 1 |
| 1 | 1 | 0 |

(c)

| A | B | X |
|---|---|---|
| 0 | 0 | 1 |
| 0 | 1 | 0 |
| 1 | 0 | 0 |
| 1 | 1 | 0 |

(d)

| A | B | X |
|---|---|---|
| 0 | 0 | 0 |
| 0 | 1 | 0 |
| 1 | 0 | 0 |
| 1 | 1 | 1 |

(e)

| A | B | X |
|---|---|---|
| 0 | 0 | 0 |
| 0 | 1 | 1 |
| 1 | 0 | 1 |
| 1 | 1 | 1 |

**Figure:** Symbols and truth-tables for (a) not (b) nand (c) nor (d) and (e) or

The circles denote negation - not, inversion. It is possible to have negation on inputs too.

### LOGIC CIRCUIT ANALYSIS

There are two fairly distinct activities in working with digital logic, analysis, and synthesis.

**Analysis:**

given a circuit, what does it do? i.e. what Boolean function does it implement.

**Synthesis:**

given a Boolean expression, produce a circuit that implements it - preferably using a minimal number of gates. This is synthesis or design.

This section covers analysis.

| A | B | C | M |
|---|---|---|---|
| 0 | 0 | 0 | 0 |
| 0 | 0 | 1 | 0 |
| 0 | 1 | 0 | 0 |
| 0 | 1 | 1 | 1 |
| 1 | 0 | 0 | 0 |
| 1 | 0 | 1 | 1 |
| 1 | 1 | 0 | 1 |
| 1 | 1 | 1 | 1 |

(a)

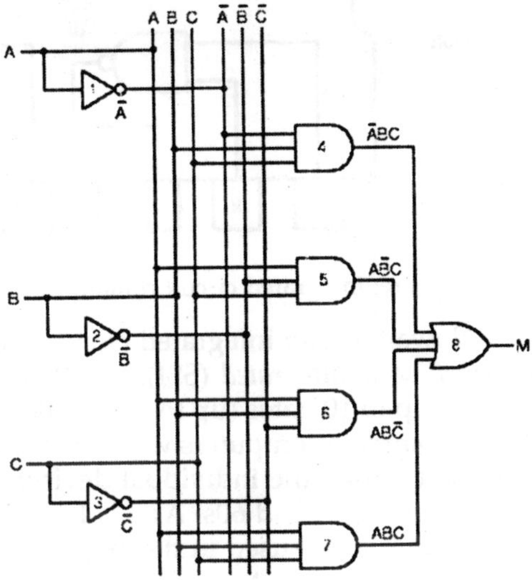


(b)

**Figure:** Truth-table (a) and circuit (b) for majority of three circuit

It takes a majority vote over the three inputs.

Exercise. Verify the truth-table in Figure by creating an expanded truth table containing columns for. Note: starting from scratch, and not knowing the answer, this is the way you would normally do it - you cannot hope to work out column *M* in your head.

## GENERATIONS OF INTEGRATED CIRCUITS

Integrated circuits started to appear in the late 1960s. A typical single chip of that age - but still available to buy today - is shown in Figure; it contains four nand gates and has 14 pins.

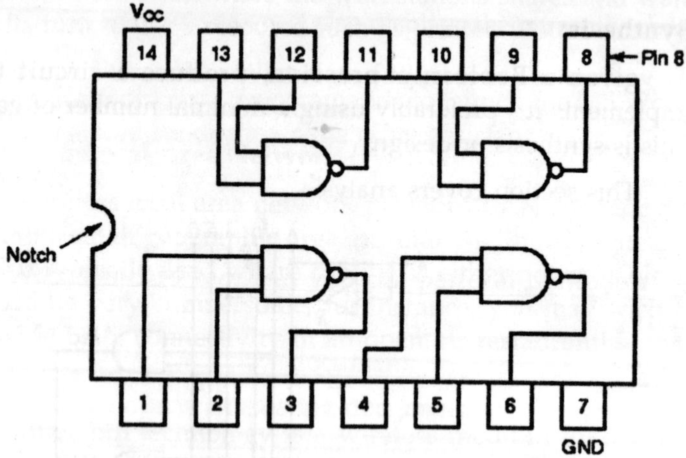


**Figure:** Integrated circuit containing just four nand gates

Nowadays, an integrated circuit such as Figure is said to be *small scale integrated* (SSI). Small scale integrated circuits contain up to 10 gates (up to about 100 transistors). In the late 1960s, complete computers were made from SSI; still, this was a lot better than the individual devices (transistors, resistors, etc.) of the 1950s and 60s. And, a fantastic improvement over the vacuum tubes used in the 1940s.

You will still find SSI circuits, e.g. Transistor-transistor-logic (TTL) 74xx00 quad 2-input nand used on the periphery of computer systems, and as the 'glue' which connects the more complex circuits/chips together.

In SSI chips, as many gates of a given type as possible are put in the package (chip). The number of gates is limited by the number of pins, and to a lesser extent by the ability to dissipate the heat generated by the circuit. On the 74xx00 you have: power 2 pins + 4 *x* (2 *inputs* + 1 *output*) = 3 for each NAND gate = total of 14 pins. An additional consideration is the area taken up by such an SSI chip, roughly. 2.5 *Cm*× 1*Cm*

In the case of early TTL each chip would consume about 10 milliWatts of power.

Later medium scale integrated (MSI) circuits began to appear - containing 10-100 gates. Later on large scale integrated (LSI) containing 100-100,000 gates. The first microprocessors

(1971 - the 4 bit Intel 4004) would have been classified LSI. Now we have very large scale integrated (VLSI), and beyond. The latest Pentium III contains in the region of 10,000,000 transistors.

A great many very complex complete components are now available on single chips - microprocessors, disk controllers, modems,.... On the other hand, there is still a need to design circuits from simple gates. But, building large circuits from SSI is simply impractical - it would take too much space and consume too much power. Hence, programmable logic arrays (PLAs) and field programmable gate arrays (FPGAs).

**Programmable Logic Arrays**

A programmable logic array contains a large array of not, and gates and or gates on a single chip. The user can connect certain gates by breaking certain (fuse) connections. Figure contains an example.

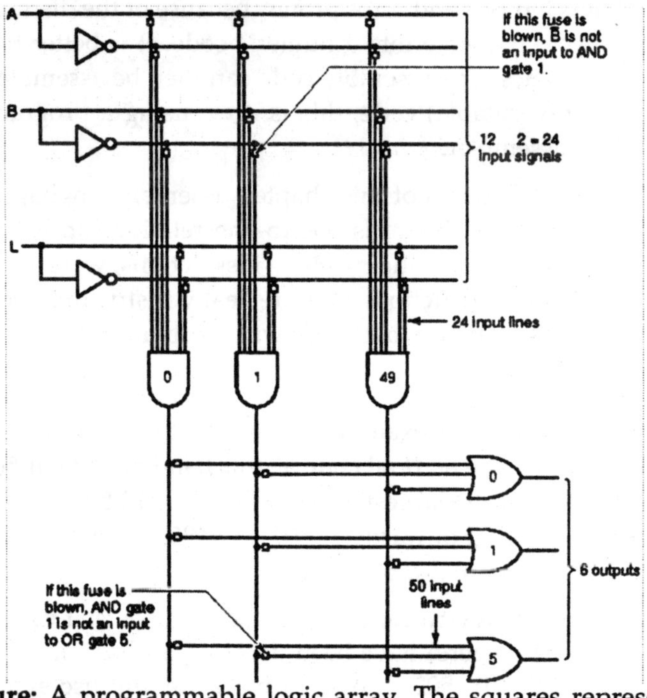


**Figure:** A programmable logic array. The squares represent fuses which can be blown to disable connections, and so determine which function is implemented, i.e. programmed

# Chapter 10

# Assembly Language Programming

## PROGRAMMES IN ASSEMBLY CODE

We now want to write some programmes for the Mac-1A. For completeness, We can write in binary machine code, but, that is tedious and error prone - because of the distraction of having to translate into a numeric code. It is better to use the mnemonics. The assembly code can then be assembled to machine (executable) code; this is done using a programme called an assembler.

For the purposes of this chapter, assembly language is a language in which there is one-to-one relationship between symbolic instructions and machine instructions; we will come across pseudo-instructions that are really instructions to the assembler programme, but these will be obvious.

## CONVENTIONS

In the following examples, if we need to mention actual addresses, we will start all code at 100*H* and all data at 500*H*. Note again that the largest address is *FFFH* (12 bits). Also, be careful with *FFFC* onwards ($4092_{10}$ to $4095_{10}$, which are used for memory-mapped input-output,

Often, for brevity, we will assume variables that variables a0, a1, a2... (integers) have been declared and are already in locations 500, 501, 502,.... Alternatively, we will use symbols for data. Use these assumptions in the exercises where appropriate.

## SIMPLE PROGRAMME - ADD TWO INTEGERS

Programme. Add the integer in `a1` to the integer in `a0` and put the result in `a2`, i.e.

```
a2 = a0 + a1;
```

In assembly code:

```
Start: LODD a0 /get a0 into accum.
 ADDD a1 /accum. gets a0+a1
 STOD a2 /store result in a2
```

There are four fields in an assembly instruction:

### Label

Optional, only necessary if you need to jump to that instruction; can also be useful as comment, e.g. above. Always followed by ':', otherwise assembler will try to interpret it as an instruction.

Instruction mnemonic.

### Operand

I.e. address of thing to suffer the operation. Either:

- Symbolic name, e.g. above.
- Symbolic label, or numeric address, to jump to.
- Constant - for immediate addressing.

### Comment

Comments are even more important for assembly language programmes than the are for high-level language programmes. Make your code maintainable by someone else!

## DECLARING VARIABLES

For a real assembler, we would have to declare all variables. And, tell it where to start main programme at. E.g. in the example above,

```
DW a0 10H /a0 is a WORD type, initialised to
10H
```

```
DW a1 22H /these are not executable
instructions
DW a2 /but pseudo-instructions
/ie. directives to the assembler to allocate
/storage and associate names with that
storage
/ just like you declare variables in Pascal
ORG 100H /start prog. at 100H
```

**IF-THEN**

**High-level language**

```
if(a0==a1) a2 = a2 + 1;
else next instructions...
```

**Assembly language**

```
If: LODD a0
  SUBD a1
  JZER Then
  JUMP Next
Then: LOCO 1 /load constant 1
  ADDD a2
  STOD a2
EndThen: JUMP Next /Unnecessary
Next:...
```

**IF-THEN-ELSE**

**High-level Language**

```
if(a0==a1) a2 = a2 + 1;
else a2 = a2 + 2;
//next instructions...
```

## REPETITION

### High-level language

```
//sum first n integers
int sum=0;
int i=0;
while(i<=n){
sum= sum + i;
i++;
}
```

### Assembly Language

```
init: LOCO 0
  STOD sum
  STOD i
loop: LODD n
  SUBD i
  JPOS loopend
loopbody:
  LODD sum /load sum into accumulator
  ADDD i /add i to it
  STOD sum / and don't forget to store the
result!
incr: LOCO 1
  ADDD i
  STOD i
  JUMP loop
loopend:...
```

It is straightforward to define deterministic loops, for example,

```
for(i = 0; i<n; i++)
{sum= sum + i;}
```

in terms of `do-while`. Likewise `do-until` - the continuation test is merely carried out at the end of the loop, instead of at the beginning for `do-while`.

## MACHINE CODE, MEMORY MAPS

Let us see how the If-then-else from the previous section would *assemble* into machine code. We use Figure to translate.

For ease of understanding, we show the assembly language in the table. Assume that, initially, `a0` contains 8, `a1`, 4 and `a2`, 2.

Thus, we can identify two separate sections of memory: (a) programme, (b) data. Of course, there is nothing really separating these, and there is nothing to stop assembly programmers modifying instructions as data, nor, for that matter, runaway programmes attempting to execute data!

Actually, as shown in Figure, in a C or C++ programme, we can identify four sections of memory. Exact implementation detail may differ depending on compiler, machine architecture and operating system. In some contexts, Figure is called a memory map.

## THE ASSEMBLY PROCESS

Assembly is the process of translating the symbolic assembly code into (numeric) machine code.

### Example

Assemble (translate) the following assembly programme into binary machine code. Assume a0, a1... at 500, 501 etc. Start code at 100.

### Two-Pass Assembler

This section describes how a two-pass assembly programme works. We said that one assembly language instruction maps to one machine instruction; thus, it would appear natural to run through the list of assembly instructions and translate them.

This works fine until we get to `JZER Then;` what address is Then?

*You don't know until you have assembled up to* `Then`.

Therefore, we must have a symbol table - - which is a list of (symbol, address) pairs. If a symbol has been entered in the table, then you can look up its value. Initially, the table is empty.

Also we must have an operation-code (op-code) table - similar to the symbol table, only it is fixed, and contains a table relating instruction code (LODD, STOD,...) to the 4-bit op-code part of the instruction (0001, 0010,...). In general, this should also contain the length of each instruction, or some means of calculating it. Unlike most machines, Mac-1a has a single fixed instruction length of one; most machines have instruction lengths which vary according to the instruction.

## MANUAL ASSEMBLY

Here in a slightly less formal way, is a recipe for assembling manually. We do it in a table, first write down the assembly code, the make two columns, one for address, the other for instruction or data. Then translate using Figure .

Do it in two passes. Leave Jump addresses blank first time round - you don't know the Jump destination addresses until after you have coded the Jump destination.

Use Hexadecimal for the machine code. If necessary, separate the binary fields in Figure into groups of four - one for each Hex. digit, and add another column to Figure to contain the Hex. representation of the operation code (op-code).

## LINKING AND LOADING

If the programme above was viable to work on their own, it would be possible to load it into the addresses given: 100 to 107 for programme and 500 to 50b for data, set the PC to 100, and the programme would run.

Unfortunately, programmes are usually made up from more than one module, and the results of each module translation - object files - must be linked together to produce an executable programme.

Essentially, at the end of pass two, there will be symbols for which you do not have an address; these will refer to subprograms that are contained in other modules. Also, the ILC will need to contain relative addresses, not absolute addresses as above.

In linking and loading the main jobs to be done are:

- Resolve references to external objects (symbols for which you have no value after pass two), these will be given in the symbol tables of another module.

Relocate relative addresses to yield absolute addresses.

## FURTHER ASSEMBLY PROGRAMMING

The instruction set (Mac-1a) introduced was severely limited - particularly in its inability to call subprograms. We now extend our coverage to the remainder of the Mac-1 instruction set, and attempt some more ambitious programmes.

Firstly, we will introduce the additional instructions - especially those based on the stack; we will explain the purpose of a stack and its use for handling subprograms.

In addition, we will describe the memory addressing modes found on most general purpose computers. Next, we will show how some more real programmes can be constructed, from simple three or four liners, to subroutines, input-output and interrupts.

Although this chapter is entirely about Mac-1, the presentation is such that the principles of general-purpose computers are emphasised. Thus, someone who follows this chapter will have little difficulty in understanding Motorola 68000, Intel 80x86 series, or virtually any conventional computer.

## ADDRESSING - GENERAL

In a computer, memory locations can hold instructions or data. In addition, as we shall see the data can be interpreted either as a plain value, e.g. 100, or as an address or reference to another data item. Those of who are familiar with C/C++

will recognise pointers; and Java people will recognise references.

In general, machine instructions usually take zero, one, or two operands (e.g. in lodd a0; a0 is the single operand; lodd is the operation;

Actually Mac-1 has no multi-operand instructions. For a start, it is an accumulator machine, i.e. in instructions like addd, lodd, the second - implicit - operand is AC, the accumulator.

Operands can be data, or can refer to data - i.e. address of data, or can be labels - which translate to addresses - of instructions, e.g. for jumps.

The question of addressing is concerned with how operands are interpreted. In the case of data the operand can be:

- A so-called immediate constant, e.g. LOCO 10;
- A value held in a register - no example in Mac-1;
- A value held in memory, e.g. LODD a0;
- In addition we can *qualify* the operand to say in which mode it should be interpreted:

**Immediate:**

When an operand is interpreted as an immediate value, e.g. LOCO 5, it is the actual value '5' that is put in the accumulator. In the case of Mac-1, the value '5' is part of the instruction: `LOCO 5; 0111 0000 0000 0101;`

**Direct:**

The specified name or number is the 'direct' address of the intended operand, e.g. LODD a0, which is the same as LODD 501 - if our usual definitions apply -, so that the contents of memory cell '501' are loaded into the accumulator. Thus, `0000 0101 0000 0001; lodd 501;`

**Register:**

The number or name of a register is given, which contains the real operand; conceptually similar to direct except that the register name/number is substituted for memory address;

**Indirect:**

the specified name or number contains the address of the operand, i.e. the operand is the 'indirect' address of the true operand, e.g. let us invent LODI 501, so that the *contents of the contents of* memory cell '501' are loaded into the accumulator. Thus, `xxxx 0101 0000 0001 lodi 501`; if memory cell 501 contains '50a', and memory cell 50a contains '3'.

**Indexed:**

Lets us assume that we have an integer array stored in an array of N (= 9, say) contiguous locations starting at location 1230 (say), and we want to successively add them into the accumulator:

```
    \lodd 1230
loop: addi 1230+SI;ac<- [ac]+m[1230+si]
    \inc SI
    \...test for end
    \jump loop
```

Of course, because Mac-1 has no index registers, I have had to invent one (SI), and an addressing mode for add: addi - add direct using SI as an index; also I had to invent an 'increment instruction. Indexing is a bit like running your finger along a table of figures. The instructions 'lodl'...'subl' introduced below are a bit like indexed - but they use a very special index register called the stack-pointer (SP).

Addressing modes look complicated, but if you are careful to analyse what a construct means - by drawing a diagram, if necessary - then there are no real pitfalls.

Also, for those who are not specialists in assembly programming, you should keep to the simple modes and only use the complex modes when they are absolutely essential.

## MAC-1 INSTRUCTION SET EXTENSIONS

The Mac-1 instruction set extended to the full repertoire, we do not bother with the binary version of the instruction since we will not be assembling programmes using the additional instructions, nor writing them in machine code.

## THE ADDITIONAL JUMPS

```
jneg x Jump on negative if ac<0: pc <- x
jnze x Jump on nonzero if ac!=0: pc <- x
```

These save some of the trouble encountered using just `jpos` and `jzer`; however, as we have seen, they are not essential.

## THE STACK

In Mac-1, the register SP is the stack-pointer and is dedicated to maintaining the stack; the stack itself - the data *pointed-to* - is actually part of main-memory.

The stack is a memory into which values can be stored and from which they can be retrieved on a last-in-first-out (LIFO) basis. Ideally, you store with a PUSH and retrieve with a POP. It may help to think of an analogy such as a spring loaded canteen tray dispenser, or a bus conductor's coin dispenser; the main point is that you can only put on the top (PUSH), get from the top (TOP) or remove the value at the top (POP). In spite of its simplicity this device has a remarkably large impact on the computational capability of a computer. A stack gives us a *sort-of* indirect addressing and also a *sort-of* indexed addressing via a the stack pointer; but a stack does much more than that, it is the basis of the implementation of functions and procedures, and blocks in block-structured high-level languages. SP points to the top of the stack - i.e. to the memory location where the last value was pushed.

In the case of Mac-1, the stack grows from high memory towards low memory. PUSH increases the size of the stack by one and places a value in the new memory cell (at the top). POP exactly reverses the process, i.e.. retrieves the last value written (the top) and decreases the size of the stack. PUSH followed by POP has exactly NO effect. And, as usual with Mac-1 most things are done through the accumulator (AC); PUSH pushes the number in the AC, and POP retrieves the top of the stack into the AC.

PUSH operates as follows:

```
PUSH;sp <- sp - 1;SP decremented, NB. this INCREASES
    size of stack.
    ;m[sp] <- ac;put contents of AC into the memory
    cell that SP POINTS TO
```

POP:

```
POP;ac <- m[sp];get contents of cell pointed to by
    SP, into AC.
    ;sp <- sp + 1;decrease size of stack.
```

Note carefully again that the stack actually grows downwards, one word at a time - actually this is the case on a great many machines. Normally, in Mac-1 programmes, we will assume that SP starts off pointing at memory cell 4020.

## STACK INSTRUCTIONS

### Direct Accumulator-Stack Instructions

```
push Push onto stack sp <- sp-1; m[sp] <- ac
pop Pop off stack ac <- m[sp]; sp <- sp+1
```

### Indirect Accumulator-Stack Instructions

```
pshi Push indirect sp <- sp-1; m[sp]<-m[ac]
popi Pop indirect m[ac] <- m[sp]; sp <- sp+1
```

Thus, the AC is used 'indirectly' - see indirect addressing mode, section 7.2; i.e. the value that is contents of the memory cell that is *pointed-to* by [ac] is pushed and popped.

### Call and Return - CALL and RETN

CALL and RETN are used for CALLing subprograms (methods or functions in Java) and RETurning from them.

## CALL

```
call x Call procedure sp<-sp-1; m[sp] <-
pc; pc <- x

get stack (save pc) (put jump

ready)   address

in pc)
```

CALL causes all of the following to happen:

1. Decrement the stack pointer - so that we will not overwrite last thing put on stack,
2. The contents of PC - which is pointing to NEXT instruction, the one just after the CALL - is pushed onto the stack, and,
3. Jump to 'x', which is the address of the start of the subprogram is put in the PC register, this is all a jump does. Thus, we go off to the subprogram - just as in JUMP label, but the important difference is that we remember where we were in the calling programme, i.e. we must remember where we came from, so that we can get back there again.

## Retn

```
retn Return from proc. pc <- m[sp]; sp <- sp
+ 1
```

RETN causes all of the following to happen:

1. Pops the stack, to yield an address/label; if correctly used, the top of the stack will contain the address of the next instruction after the call from which we are returning; it is this instruction with which we want to resume in the *calling* programme;
2. Jump to the popped address, i.e. put the address into the PC register.

## INPUT-OUTPUT INSTRUCTIONS

As stated earlier, there are no *direct* instructions for input-output; instead Mac-1a uses memory-mapped input-output, whereby some memory cells are mapped to input-output ports; for simplicity we assume that there are only two ports, one connected to a standard-input device, the other connected to a standard-output device:

- Input, mapped to 4092 (0FFCHex); status 4093 (0FFDHex).
- Output, mapped to 4094 (0FFEHex); status 4095 (0FFFHex).

**Input from standard-input device**

A read from address 0FFCHex yields a 16-bit word, with the actual data byte in the lower order byte. There is no use in reading the input port until the connected device has put the data there: so 0FFDH is used to read the input status register; the top bit (sign) of 0FFDH is set when the input data is available (DAV).

Thus, a read routine should go into a tight loop, continuously reading 0FFDHex, until it goes negative; then 0FFCHex can be read to get the data. Reading 0FFC clears 0FFD again.

**Output to the standard-output device**

Output, to 0FFE, runs along the same lines as input. A write to 0FFE will send the lower order byte to the standard-output device. The sign bit of 0FFFH signifies that the device is in a ready to receive (RDY) state; again there is no use writing data to the output port until the device is ready to read it.

## MORE ASSEMBLY LANGUAGE PROGRAMMING

This section further illustrates the use of assembly language with some simple examples.

Note: in none of the following examples have I tried to optimise the code or to be *clever*; assembly coding is difficult enough without that.

**Multiply Two Numbers**

Mac-1 has no multiply or divide - not even for integers - so we have to do it all with adds and subtracts.

Note. we will assume that the result will fit into 16-bits; Q. what general check on the two operands will ensure this? Ans. if the multiplication is `z = x * y;` then if `x <= 127` and if `y <= 127`, the result will certainly be less than 32767, which is the largest positive number that can be stored in 16-bit twos complement.

**Divide**

Again, we assume that both numbers are positive, and that it is sensible to divide them - again we will leave out some of the bullet-proofing details.

```
z = x / y;
```

We use the algorithm in Figure , i.e. we count how many times we have to subtract 'y' from 'x' to get to a remainder less than 'y'.

At the end (`end:`) the result is in 'z'. Of course, the result is 'integer' divide, e.g. we could modify this code to give you `per cent` (modulo - or 'remainder after division').

**Iterate over an Array**

Assume that `a0, a1, a2,... a9` are stored contiguously in 500, 501,...509, and we want to treat them as an array `arr[10]`; we require to sum them and put the result in `sum`. We will assume that all the numbers are sensible, i.e. that overflow isn't a problem.

We *could* address each of them individually:

```
init loco 0
  addd a0
  addd a1
...
  addd a9
  stod sum
```

but that wouldn't be too clever for very long arrays.

## Chapter 11

# Programming Languages

Sun CEO Scott McNealy has a lot to say about everything: what 21st century IT should look like, Microsoft and the DOJ, national security, and the economy. But nothing sticks out in my mind more than the one thing he repeated over and over during our recent interview; "There are only two multi-million developer bases out there. That's it."

He's right. It has all come down Java vs..NET. Plenty of other battles for supremacy are raging in our industry: Databases. Operating Systems. Corporate Portals. Chips. Mobile. Security. Outsourcing. Not one of them looms larger than Java vs. Windows.

In fact, all are simply caught in the draft of Java vs..NET. While we struggle to make strategic technology decisions that are little more than calculated bets on the winner, Sun and Microsoft are in a desperate race for the same brass ring: transactional user IDs. As McNealy put it at Gartner Symposium/ITxpo in October "The big war is that he or she who dies with the most rich and/or smart people in their online directory wins. Every bank, every retailer, everybody is trying to get the most rich and/or smart people into their online directories before their competitors do. Microsoft has figured this out."

### MAILING LISTS ALL OVER AGAIN

History is repeating itself. It's mailing lists all over again. Businesses have long understood that the key to winning is finding and contacting people who have their wallets out. That idea gave birth to the special interest publication whose main business proposition to advertisers is its mailing list — a targeted demographic ready to spend money on something specific. Why else would they be reading the special interest publication? They must be looking for something to buy. Millions of businesses exist solely for the purpose of assembling and distributing these targeted lists.

Before the Internet came along, however, list impurity was a major issue. The older a list, the more likely it was that the list's members had put away their wallets, and the less valuable the list became. But the Internet is enabling businesses with real-time lists with a purity that's nearly 100 percent. These lists immediately answer the question of who has money to spend, who is about to spend it, when they'll spend it, and who is willing to spend it online. It's the 21st century version of a customer list, a.k.a. McNealy's online directory of transactional IDs.

Assembling these directories has put the war between Java and.NET ahead of all other battles, because in the future no transaction will be completed without the presence of one of these technologies in the customer's hands.

### Who do you bet on?

While both technologies could co-exist for the foreseeable future, Sun and Microsoft appear hell bent on disintermediating the other. If either company succeeds, virtually everybody who bet on the wrong horse — businesses, IT managers, programmers, and vendors — would be sent back to the drawing board. This is a potentially devastating setback, because deciding on one technology forces you into making so many other decisions across your entire solution matrix.

For example, thousands of mobile phones and credit cards are already entering the market with Java preloaded. While Web services standards like XML and SOAP should make it possible for these Java clients to conduct a transaction with a server driven by either Java or.NET, the odds of the transaction completing successfully and securely are increased when the same technology is on both ends of the network.

Furthermore, popularity of one technology over the other could create a vicious circle. Merchants who see more potential customers using Java-enabled devices will develop for Java. If more merchants develop for Java, then more mobile phone makers will put Java into their phones. If one technology develops enough momentum over the other, the game could be over.

To keep that from happening, Sun and Microsoft are waging a war that includes smear campaigns, innuendo, personal attacks between the executives, litigation, entire technology and development platforms, and, most interestingly, a no-holds-barred effort to marry those platforms to the most transactional IDs.

The focus of this struggle has now turned to the part of Java and.NET that promises to allow customers to move seamlessly from one site to another without having to use separate user IDs and passwords. In Microsoft's world, this is called Passport. Sun's implementation is called Project Liberty. Getting users to adopt one or the other is one way to complete the aforementioned marriage. To do this as quickly as possible, and to claim bragging rights for the most number of transactional IDs, Microsoft and Sun are taking two completely different approaches.

Microsoft is busy gating virtually every service it runs with Passport. Not a week goes by where I don't find some clever trick that Microsoft uses to convert another one of its constituencies into a clan of Passport holders. A Passport is now required to access all the reseller areas on Microsoft.com. The same goes for Hotmail users.

Last week, my son got a new computer from eMachines. Using a huge rebate, Microsoft subsidized 75 percent of his Internet service costs in exchange for using MSN as his ISP. As an MSN user, he automatically becomes a Passport holder.

So does his mother, thanks to Windows XP's multi-user support. Get the picture? Just yesterday, I attempted to play with Microsoft's UDDI directory. (UDDI is a white pages standard that will play an important role in the future of Web services.) I couldn't get in without a Passport. A freshly installed version of Windows XP asks you to sign up for Passport no fewer than five times. The wording of the request is very disingenuous. I showed the message to several less computer-literate people and all were misled into thinking that they wouldn't be able to access the Internet unless they signed up for a Passport.

**The power of partners**

Sun on the other hand has no existing services or products that people are registered to use. As a result, Sun has no way of doing what Microsoft has done: converting over 165 million constituents into Passport holders. However, according to McNealy, the number of transactional IDs that use Liberty will blow right past Passport once his 34 partners in the Liberty Alliance start enabling their customers. VodaFone's hundreds of millions of customers, says McNealy, will be authenticating with Liberty. If other Alliance members — Fidelity, Bank of America, American Airlines, Sprint — follow suit, the number of transactional IDs suddenly married to Java could easily dwarf the universe of Passport users. For example, American Airlines could require a smart card enabled with Sun's JavaCard technology that authenticates the cardholder against a Liberty-based authentication server before that person is allowed to board a flight.

At the Gartner conference, Microsoft CEO Steve Ballmer said, "Liberty has zero probability of mattering." Considering the way Microsoft has its pedal to the metal in order to work. NET into as many transactional hands as possible, I'm not so sure. Sun has managed to get Java into just about every digital device out there. The company has focused on the market leaders: some form of Java is on smart cards from American Express, Visa, and MasterCard. It's still in almost all Windows-based devices (except for recently shipped XP systems and

Pocket PC). The world's leading mobile phone, digital TV, set top box, and gaming system manufacturers have all included Java. When I asked Richard Green, Sun's Vice President of Java and XML Software, what he charged everyone for that, he wouldn't say. My bet is pennies. For pennies, no one had anything to lose. And Sun had everything to gain.

Considering how Java's tentacles have extended into everything everywhere, it should come as no surprise to see Microsoft working hard to catch up. To get more transactional customers, Microsoft's goal is to get the.NET equivalent of Java into as many of those devices as possible, even if it has to make them itself. Can you say "XBox?" The gaming constituency wouldn't be a bad group to turn into Passport holders, would it?

At Fall Comdex 2001, I asked John Montgomery, Microsoft's.NET Developer Platform group product manager, what the company calls that piece of.NET they're trying to put into all those devices out there and how Microsoft plans to get it there. Montgomery calls it the ".NET Framework." He says Microsoft will soon announce three huge partners for the mobile version that they want to put into phones to compete with J2ME, the micro-edition of Java. Earlier this week, I learned that Microsoft's code name for this is ".NET Compact" and my bet is that Microsoft will do a lot more than give it away in order to disintermediate J2ME. I have no idea who the partners are, but only a handful of phone manufacturers matter. My guess is Microsoft has found three of them willing to manufacture a new model based on Windows CE for mobile phones (code-named Stinger). In that scenario, Stinger would come with.NET Compact built-in. Another scenario is where Microsoft ports.NET Compact to the existing OS from Symbian that's used by many existing smart phones.

## Chapter 12

# Fractions and Floating Point

## INTRODUCTION

Often, the quantities we want to represent and compute are not integers. Furthermore, the intermediate results in a computation may not be integer.

To represent non integers, the following are required:

1. Representation of the digits of the number - on both sides of the 'point';
2. Representation of the position of the 'point'.

In a fixed point representation, the point is assumed to be in some fixed position - and, since it is fixed, the position need not be stored. In a floating point representation, the position of the point can be varied according to the size of the number. Floating point is by far the most common and useful on general purpose computers.

## FIXED POINT

To represent fractional numbers, we simply extend the positional system, introduced in section 2.3.1, to include digits corresponding to negative powers. We do this by introducing a *point* '.'; the integer number is as before, and is shown to the left of the point; the fraction part is shown to the right of the point.

Therefore, generalising what was given in section 2.3.1, a number which includes a $q$bit fractional part - for a total of $p+q$ bits - is written:

$$d_{p-1}d_{p-2}\ldots d_2d_1d_0.d_{-1}d_{-2}\ldots d_{-q+1}d_{-q}$$

and its value is:

$$value = d_{p-1}\times b^{p-1} + d_{m-2}\times b_{p-2} + \ldots d_2\times b_2 + d_1\times b + d_0$$
$$+ d_{-1}\times b_{-1} + d_{-2}\times b_{-2} + \ldots + d_{-q+1}\times b_{-q+1} + d_{-q}\times b_{-q}$$

Thus, $123.45_{10}$,

$$\begin{aligned}123.45_{10} &= 1\times 10^2 + 2\times 10^1 + 3\times 10^0 + 4\times 10^{-1} + 5\times 10^{-2}\\ &= 1\times 100 + 2\times 10 + 3\times 1 + 4\times 0.1 + 5\times 0.01\\ &= 100 + 20 + 3 + 0.4 + 0.05\\ &= 123.45\end{aligned}$$

In binary,

$$\begin{aligned}0.1 &= 1\times 2^{-1} = 1\times 0.5 = 0.5\\ 0.01 &= 1\times 2^{-2} = 1\times 0.25 = 0.25\\ 0.001 &= 1\times 2^{-3} = 1\times 0.125 = 0.125\end{aligned}$$

Example. Convert $11.101_2$ to decimal.

$$\begin{aligned}11.101 &= 1\times 2^1 + 1\times 2^0 + 1\times 2^{-1} + 0\times 2^{-2} + 1\times 2^{-3}\\ &= 2 + 1 + 0.5 + 0 + 0.125\\ &= 3.625\end{aligned}$$

The the magnitude of the number depends on the fixed position of the point. The problem arises that sometimes we want most of the digits after the 'point', i.e. small numbers, sometimes we want most of them before the 'point', i.e. large numbers. A single fixed-point representation cannot do both.

Other methods that have been proposed for storage of fractions:

- Store the number as a logarithm - actually, logarithms are peripherally involved in floating point representation;
- Store the number as a pair (*a*,*b*) representing a rational number.

But, floating point is the widely adopted solution.

## FLOATING POINT

A floating point number is composed of two parts:

1. The digits of the number, the fraction; the fraction is often called the mantissa, but, strictly, this is an abuse of the term.
2. The position of the point - the exponent.

The floating point representation is similar to the 'scientific', or 'exponential' representation of very large and very small numbers on some calculators and in books; e.g. 123.56 = 0.12345 E + 03, i.e. $0.12345 \times 10^3$. In this scientific representation, you can think of the exponent as representing the 'point' position.

In fact, the exponent is the integer part of the logarithm to which the base must be raised in order to place the point in the right position.

Examples of decimal floating-point with five digit fraction and three digit exponent are shown in Table.

**Table:** Examples of floating-point

| fraction | exponent | floating-point | fixed-point |
|---|---|---|---|
| 12345 | 003 | $0.12345 \times 10^3$ | 123.45 |
| 12345 | 002 | $0.12345 \times 10^2$ | 12.345 |
| 12345 | 001 | $0.12345 \times 10^1$ | 1.2345 |
| 12345 | 000 | $0.12345 \times 10^0$ | 0.12345 |
| 12345 | -001 | $0.12345 \times 10^{-1}$ | 0.012345 |

## BINARY FLOATING POINT

We will explain binary floating point using a total of 8 bits (1 for sign, 3 for exponent, 4 for fraction); most practical systems use 32 bits, but the following explains the principles without the confusion of many bits. The bits are arranged as follows,

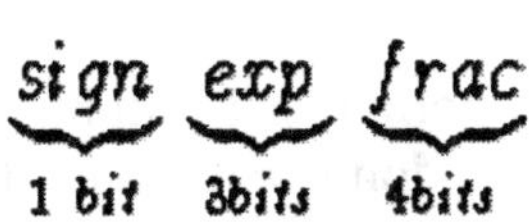

The fraction (mantissa) is just a straight fraction, i.e. the (virtual) point is at the left hand side of the four bits. The exponent is stored as a signed number, using excess 4 (biased by 4) representation, i.e. biased by 4 - recall Table. Thus, the bit patterns in the exponent represent values as shown in Table .

**Table:** 3-bit, excess 4

| bits | 111 | 110 | 101 | 100 | 011 | 010 | 001 | 000 |
|---|---|---|---|---|---|---|---|---|
| value | 3 | 2 | 1 | 0 | -1 | -2 | -3 | * |

Of course, you don't have to look up Table, simply subtract 4 from the stored number.

The value, *v*, of the stored floating point number is given by eqn. 2.2.

$$v = f \times r^{e}$$

where *f* is the fraction, *r* is the radix (base) of the exponent and *e* is the exponent.

Or, to make the excess in the exponent more explicit,

$$v = f \times r^{e-q}$$

where *q* is the excess.

**Normalisation**

Unless otherwise stated, *f* is bounded as follows:

$$.1000 \leq f \leq .1111 f \times r^{e-q}$$

i.e. the top bit of the fraction is always set.

The most common practical floating point number system (IEEE Standard 754, single precision) uses 8 bits for exponent, 23 for fraction - including 1 for sign; a total of 32 bits. There is a double precision format at 64 bits and extended precision at 80 bits.

**Hidden Bit**

Notice that, in a normalised number, eqn 2.4, the top bit is always set; thus, we don't really have to store it - this is a trick that the IEEE standard uses to 'steal' an additional bit for the fraction; actually, they work it so that the top bit is assumed to be just to the left of the 'point'. We will adopt this trick for our floating-point-byte system. Finally we end up with eqn. 2.5, where we show the hidden bit, and make the sign explicit,

$$v = (-1)^s \times 1.f \times r^{e-g}$$

**Denormalised Numbers**

In special circumstances, IEEE 754 allows numbers to be stored with a denormalised fraction; for such cases they use exponent 000 which flags the special case. The major advantage is that we can store a 'pure' zero.

Henceforth, we will call this small floating point number system flob - floating-point byte.

Example: Stored representation is 01101011, what is the value?

Sign 0→+ Stored exponent = 110 = $6_{10}$, actual exponent = +2. Fraction = 1011, i.e. with hidden bit, 1.1011. Therefore,

Example: Stored representation is 10111100, what is the value?

Sign 0→– Stored exponent = 011 = $3_{10}$, actual exponent = –1. Fraction = 1100, i.e. with hidden bit, 1.1100. Therefore,

$$\begin{aligned} v &= -1.1100 \times 2^{-1} \\ &= -.11100 \times 2^{0} \\ &= -.11100 \\ &= -(0.5 + 0.25 + 0.125) \\ &= -0.875 \end{aligned}$$

None: In the following we will assume that the only allowed denormalised number is 0; i.e. 0000000→0; there is no other allowable case where stored exponent can be 000.

## ROUNDING AND TRUNCATION

As mentioned in the introduction, section 2.2.4, the real numbers form a continuum. However, instead of infinity of them, exactly 225can be represented in flob. In flob there are three legal regions on the real line, and four illegal.

```
-infinity -15.5     -0.125          0          0.125      15.5 +inf
-----------+----------+-----------+----------+----------+-------
             ...........                      ...........
-----------+----------+-----------+----------+----------+-------
  illegal   | legal     | illegal   | illegal | legal      | illegal
 (1)            (2)       (3)       (4)   (5)       (6)          (7)

  Negative    Negatives Neg.        Zero Pos.    Positives Pos.
  Overflow        "     Underflow        Underflow         Overflow
```

**Figure:** The Seven Regions of The Real Number Line.

The dots (...) in Figure are meant to show that, even within the legal regions, we do not have a continuum, but a discrete set of numbers. So, in reality, there are many other *illegal* regions, besides those mentioned above.

For actual numbers, we must compromise and represent them with a close legal number; this entails *rounding* or *truncation.*

=

Rounding is probably the best - it takes the closest; e.g. in a one digit representation, 0.34→0.3, 0.36→0.4; therefore, the maximum error = 0.05, i.e. half the step between legal numbers (0.1).

### Truncation

Truncation chops off the insignificant digits, e.g. 0.34→0.3; in this case, the maximum error is 0.09.

## ADDITION AND SUBTRACTION IN FLOATING POINT

Here, we merely show the principle; and, to avoid some detail we use a decimal format.

Example. $2\times10^6+13\times10^3$. Ans. $2.031\times10^6=2013\times10^3=2013000$.

The general method for addition and subtraction, (*A*+/-*B*) is:

1. Line up points by making exponents equal:
   a. Identify the operand with the smaller exponent, say A - *expA*;
   b. Do. Successively shift A's fraction right while increasing its exponent;
   c. until *expA* = *expB*.
2. Add (or subtract) the fractions.
3. Normalise the result.

Example. $0.28\times10^1+0.12\times10^0$.

$0.280\times10^1$
$+\ 0.012\times10^1$
$=\ 0.292\times10^1$

Example. $0.28\times10^2-0.24\times10^2$.

$0.280\times10^2$
$-\ 0.240\times10^2$
$=\ 0.040\times10^2$

$=\ 0.400\times10^1$ after normalisation

## MULTIPLICATION AND DIVSTRANGELY, THESE ARE EASIER THAN ADD AND SUBTRACT.

### MULTIPLICATION

1. Multiply the fractions;
2. Add the exponents;
3. Normalise the result.

### DIVISION

1. Divide the fractions;
2. Subtract the exponents;
3. Normalise the result.

$$x = f_x \times r^{ex}$$

$$y = f_y \times xr^{ey}$$

$$x \times y = \left(f_x \times f_y\right) \times r^{\left(e_x + e_y\right)}$$

$$\frac{x}{y} = \frac{f_x}{f_y} \times r^{(e1-e2)}$$

Example. $0.120 \times 10^1 \times 0.253 \times 10^2 = 1.2 \times 25.3 \cdot$

$0.120 \times 10^1 \times 0.253 \times 10^2 = 0.030360 \times 10^3,$

$= 0.030 \times 10^3$

$= 0.300 \times 10^2$

## FIXED VERSUS FLOATING POINT

**Speed:**

Where there is no dedicated floating-point hardware, fixed - point arithmetic can be performed faster and easier, see below;

Ease of Implementation:

Fixed point may be easier to implement easier; in the past, many computers - like the one we encounter in later chapters - have only integer arithmetic units, and so must use software (using algorithms like those shown above) to do floating point. Up to the Intel 80386 series - great-great-grand-daddy of the Pentium III - you had to have a special purpose floating-point co-processor (the 80387) for Intel XX86 microprocessors; modern digital-signal-processors (DSPs) may not have any floating-point;

**Ease of programming:**

Generally, floating point saves the programmer any worry about over/under-flow;

**Range:**

Fixed point limits the range of the numbers being represented. Floating point gives greater range - at the cost of resolution; see below for definitions of range and resolution.

## ACCURACY

Strictly speaking, accuracy is not a feature of the number system. Accuracy is determined by the error inherent in the production of the number, for example, the error in reading a metre. Thus, $12.34 \pm 0.01$; this indicates that the actual number could be anywhere between 12.33 and 12.35. It might be possible to include better *resolution* e.g. express it as 12.34567, but, due to the *accuracy* limitation, the 567would be meaningless.

## Chapter 13

# Common Number Formats Used in Computers

### VARIOUS SIZES OF INTEGERS AND THEIR RANGES

Table shows some commonly used integer formats and their ranges.

**Table:** Commonly Used Integer Formats

| Size | Name in Java | Minimum | Maximum |
|---|---|---|---|
| 8-bit signed | byte | -128 | 127 |
| 16-bit signed | short | -32768 | 32767 |
| 32-bit signed | int | -2,147,483,648 | 2,147,483,647 |

### FLOATING POINT

IEEE single precision (32 bits): $\pm 1.2 \times 10 - 38$ to $3.4 \times 10^{38}$, 7 significant digits.

$$value = (-1)^{s} \times 1.f \times 2^{exp-127}$$

*bit 31=sign, bits 30 to bit 23 = 8 bitexponent, bits 22 to bit0 = fraction*

IEEE floating-point uses the hidden bit trick mentioned above.

## BITWISE LOGICAL OPERATIONS

In most assembly languages, and in C and C++ there are binary operations which logical operations on each corresponding pair of bits.

**AND**

$$\begin{aligned} a &= 0011\ 0000 \\ b &= 0101\ 0111 \\ a\ \&\ b &= 0001\ 0000 \end{aligned}$$

**Masking**

Let us say that we have two four bit numbers packed into a byte. How do we disentangle them. Take the byte 1001 01111; the two four bit numbers are 7and 9. First, the lower four bits; here we mask with 0000 1111.

$$\begin{aligned} a &= 1001\ 0111 \\ lowMask &= 0000\ 0111 \\ a\ \&lowMask &= 0000\ 0111 \end{aligned}$$

For the higher four bits, we shift right by four bits and use the same mask.

**OR**

$$\begin{aligned} a &= 0011\ 0000 \\ b &= 0101\ 0111 \\ a\ |\ b &= 0111\ 0111 \end{aligned}$$

**SHIFT**

$$\begin{aligned} a &= 0011\ 0000\ (= 16 + 32 = 48_{10}) \\ a \text{ shiftleft } 1 &= 0110\ 0000\ (= 96_{10}) \text{ i.e. } 48 \times 2 \\ a \text{ shiftright } 1 &= 0001\ 1000\ (= 24_{10}) \text{ i.e. } \frac{48}{2} \end{aligned}$$

Thus, you sometimes find assembly language programmers using shift for multiplying (shift left) and dividing (shift right) by powers of two.

**ROTATE**

$$\begin{aligned} a &= 1011\ 0000 \\ a \text{ rotateleft } 1 &= 0110\ 0001 \\ a \text{ rotateright } 1 &= 0101\ 1000 \end{aligned}$$

Rotate is like shift, only bits can wrap-around.

**ALPHANUMERIC CODES**

Text characters, as well as numbers must be binary coded to get them into a computer memory. A code that copes with alphabetic characters, {a...z, A...Z} as well as digits {0...9 } is called alphanumeric.

Up to recently, the most frequently used code was the ASCII (American Standard Code for Information Interchange) code; ASCII uses 7-bits, (0 to 127); this includes printable and control characters.

Table 2.6 gives some codes worth remembering.

**Table:** ASCII table

| Name | Hex | if control |
|---|---|---|
| Bel | 07 | ctrl-G |
| line-feed | 0a | ctrl-J |
| carriage-return | 0d | ctrl-M |
| blank-space | 20 | |
| Digits | | |
| 0 | 30 | |
| ... | | |
| 9 | 39 | |
| alphabetic upper-case | | |
| A | 41 | |

| | |
|---|---|
| ... | |
| Z | 5a |
| alphabetic lower-case | |
| A | 61 |
| ... | |
| Z | 7a |

## UNICODE

ASCII has proved adequate for English text. But what about languages with accents? And those with funny shaped characters? UNICODE is a new international standard, governed by the UNICODE consortium, aimed at allowing a richer character set. In fact, Java uses UNICODE a 16-bit code - so that Java char type is 16-bit, compared to 8 bit in C and C++. According to [Tanenbaum, 1999] the total of known characters in the world's languages number some 200,000 - thus, there is already pressure on UNICODE.

## TYPES

41*H* could be 'A' or the number 41*H*. "AB" together in a 16-bit word could be part of a string, or the number 4142*H*, or part of an instruction, or.... The computer programme must know beforehand what each memory cell represents - thus, types.

## ERROR DETECTION

When information is transferred between various parts of a computer system it is possible that errors may be introduced. These errors take the form of transmitted 0s inadvertently being received as 1s or vice-versa.

Parity provides single error detecting capability. The scheme involves appending an additional bit to the string of 1s and 0s - the parity bit. Depending on the chosen convention, the appended bit is chosen so that the total number of 1s in the string is always even even parity or always odd odd parity.

Bit 7 is often used - pure ASCII uses 7 bits, bits 0...6...

Example.. ASCII character 'A' using odd parity.

*A* = 41 = *P*100 0001 = 1100 0001with odd parity bit placed in bit 7.

## Chapter 14

# Subroutines

### INTRODUCTION

As mentioned above, CALL and RETN are used for CALLing subroutines and RETurNing from them. One objectives of subroutines is to avoid having to repeat large chunks of code.

Side-Note: On modern machines and particularly when block-structured languages like Pascal, C, or Modula-2 are used, subroutines via a stack are essential. Older machines often used a JUMP-and-STORE type of call: the return address was stored in a memory address somewhere amongst the code of the subroutine.

### Subprograms without arguments

That is, we use global variables to pass values to and from the subprogram.

Recall the multiplication programme above:

```
z = x * y;
```

using the following algorithm:

```
z = 0;

for(i=1; i<=x; i++){

z = z + y;}
```

This is fine, but have a look at the assembly code; it is not the sort of thing you want to be bothered with each time you want to multiply two numbers. The code for the multiply will never change, only the names of the variables (x, y, z).

Say you wanted to do the following:

```
c = a * b;

d = e * f;

g = c + d;
```

A simplistic solution would be:

1 Load two operands (a, b) into variables x, y respectively;

2.Jump to 'mult';

3.'Mult' will run and put the result in 'z'; thus, 'z' is a global variable - it has global scope;

4.Copy 'z' to 'c', i.e. `lodd z; stod c;`;

5.Then, similarly, compute 'd', etc.

```
startprog:

lodd a (assume at location 200)

stod x

lodd b

stod y

jump mult   204

** lodd z   205

 stod c   206
```

But, without subprograms, the is a major problem: the programme never gets to '**', because when it's finished the multiply programme it continues on to the next instruction after 'mult' (end: i.e. 115H), not 205H as desired.

Note, however, there is nothing to stop you (at 115H) JUMPing to 205 - but this means that 'mult' programme is only useful for this one multiply; later down at 20aH (say) when we want to multiply 'e' and 'f', we want to JUMP back to a different place.

This gets us to one of the crucial differences between JUMP and CALL (subprogram). With JUMP, it's a one way ticket, you don't ever come back! With CALL you can remember where you came from and JUMP back there (using RETN) when you're finished in the subprogram.

Figure shows how we can make the multiply programme into a a procedure 'mult' (just add RETN at the end) and how to use it.

There is no explicit use of the stack, all PUSHes and POPs are done implicitly by CALL, RETN.

## SUBPROGRAMS WITH PARAMETERS

The procedure 'mult' above has no parameters; effectively we used global variables x, y, z for the parameters and return value. In C++ this would look like Figure.

This is alright, but I'm sure your Programming courses up to now have warned you against the evils of global variables.·

So, we now write 'mult1' that looks like this:

```
 int mult(int x, int y)
{
return x * y;
}
```

and is called like: `c = mult(a, b);`

To do this we need to make explicit use of the stack: we PUSH onto the stack the two values to be multiplied - the arguments, then CALL, finally when we RETN we retrieve (POP) the result from the stack. We can make the multiply programme into a proper procedure 'mult1' (just add RETN at the end) with parameters and return values, see Figure. We will also change 'mult' slightly to ensure that it uses only two local variables - the only reason for this is to make it a bit more like the one in [Tanenbaum, 1990].

## SUBPROGRAMS WITH RETURN VALUES

Above, we used the trick of passing the result back in the AC. This is alright for a single 16-bit result, but, if the result was more than one word (e.g. 32-bit floating point stored in two words, or a record), we would have to use the stack.

The usual solution is to allocate space for the return values just before the return address.

## OTHER USES FOR THE STACK

Most computers (eg. 80X86, 680X0, VAX) have a multitude of general purpose CPU registers - just as if Mac-1 allowed the assembly programmer access to registers A, B,...F.

Therefore, as well as storing the return address - which we could term 'storing the callers PC', it may be necessary to store these registers as well before going off to a procedure. This is because, inevitably, the procedure will overwrite some or all of the registers and on return, we want to be able to 'restore' the registers and carry on where we left off. This pair of processes is called 'saving' and 'restoring' the 'environment'.

Alternatively, a more common practice is to leave it up to the procedure to save whatever registers it will overwrite - and restore them just before returning.

Here, of course, we are concentrating on subprograms; there is nothing to stop a programmer using the stack as a general temporary storage area, or for a purpose like the swapping mentioned above.

### Stack Frame

In connection with procedures, there are four uses for the stack:

1. Passing parameters:
   (a) Passing parameters to the subprogram;
   (b) Returning values from the subprogram.
2. Storing the return address;
3. Saving the environment (registers);
4. Finally, all local variables are created on the stack.

### Local Variables

```
int a, b, c;

a = 25;
```

```
b = 159;
c = mult1(a, b);
a = 0
(*...etc*)
```

See section 7.9.2 for 'mult1' in assembly:

```
int mult1(int i, j);
```

**Analysis of 'Call' to mult1**

The interesting action happens after 'b:=159;'.

1. Assume SP starts off at 4020, and instruction corresponding to 'a = 0;' is at address 210; assume the first executable instruction in 'mult1' is at address 100;
2. The value a (=25) is pushed: [sp]<-401f, [401f]<-25;
3. The value b (=159) is pushed: [sp]<-401e, [401e]<-159;
4. 210 - the return address is pushed: [sp]<-401d, [401d]<-210;
5. Jump to 100 - start of 'mult1';
6. Here, we could save the AC, just to make the general point of register saving, but to retain compatibility with [Tanenbaum, 1990], we'll leave it out. At this point the stack looks like:

```
Addr.     Contents
4020      ?
401f      25
401e      159
401d      210 <- SP (SP now points at
401d)
```

But we're still not done. We must allocate space for the two local variables on the stack. We could do this by:

```
loco 0
push
```

```
push
```

i.e. push two zeros onto the stack, but a quicker way is

```
desp 2
```

i.e. decrement the SP by 2, in which case the stack looks like

```
Addr.       Contents
4020        ?
401f        25
401e        159
401d        210
401c        ?*
401b        ?* <- SP (SP now points at 401b)
```

Note that the space for the local variables is now uninitialised, i.e. 401c and 401b contain whatever was last put in them. This is why you can never assume that a local variable is initialised to 0.

## RECURSIVE SUBPROGRAMS

If you called the procedure `mult1` recursively three times - or, indeed, there were three nested calls of different procedures - the situation would look like Figure

In this way a procedure can call itself again and again, without one call interfering with the other; the only limit is the size of the stack.

Earlier machines, and languages, like FORTRAN, did not use a stack. Parameter passing, return addresses and local storage was all mixed in with the procedure code area - and there was only one copy - so any recursive calls, if they were allowed, would have overwritten the local data area etc. of the previous call.

## PARAMETERS PASSED BY VALUE

In the scheme mentioned in the previous two subsections, parameters are passed by by value, or by copy. Thus, procedure `mult1` can do whatever it likes to the memory location that contains the `25` - the copy of a (the parameter) and a itself (the argument) are separate and so the argument a - in the caller - will never change.

## MACROS

As indicated above, a non-procedure solution could have been used to repeat the `mult` code as many times as a multiply was required. As well as making the programme bigger, this would have introduced the greater problem of three pieces of code to debug/maintain, instead of just one.

Now, if we are content to accept the increase in programme size, use of a macro avoids the second problem (i.e. maintenance of separate copies of the same code).

Essentially, you declare a macro containing the working bits of the subroutine (no need for the housekeeping bits at the top and bottom) and then insert the macro code wherever the CALL appears.

Macros are used whenever you want to trade memory for speed - you waste no time PUSHing and POPping the stack; however, avoid if possible - they make a programme difficult to read, think about and, consequently, hard to test.

## INTERRUPTS

The scheme of polled input and output indicated in sections 7.6.2 and 7.6.3 is fine for many cases, especially if the computer is just reading data from a single source.

However, consider the case of the keyboard and GUI interfaces with a mouse. In Windows and other operating systems the keyboard is read even when the computer is away running another part of the programme. This is done with a special type of subroutine call - an interrupt.

When you hit a key on the keyboard, something like the following happens:

**Hardware Actions:**

(invisible to programmer)

1. The keyboard controller detects the key hit;

2. It asserts an interrupt line on the system bus;
3. As soon as the CPU is prepared to handle the interrupt, it sends an acknowledge signal to thc controller;
4. The kb. controller sends a small integer - and interrupt vector to identify itself; note that there could be many interrupting devices;
5. The CPU reads and stores the interrupt vector;
6. The CPU PUSHes the PC and the flags (N,Z) onto the stack;
7. The CPU constructs the address of the interrupt service routine from the interrupt vector;
8. The interrupt service routine i CALLed (but implicitly).

**Software Actions:**

1. Save all registers on the stack;
2. Read the input port - in the normal way; if things are designed properly the device will always be ready after it has generated an interrupt;
3. Put the data in a buffer, and maintain the buffer pointer; all this means is 'put the input character somewhere where the programme can get at it';
4. The interrupt service routine may need to tell the controller that you have completed servicing the interrupt;
5. Restore (POP) all saved registers;
6. Execute a return-from-interrupt (IRET on an 80x86); IRET restores flags and POPs return address.

A key factor is the transparency of the interrupt. The interrupt causes the service routine to run, but when that routine is finished, and IRET executed, the executing programme should be none the wiser - except, maybe, it notices that an instruction took 20 or 30 microsecs to run, instead of just 1 microsec; and, of course, there will be another character in the input buffer.

## DIRECT MEMORY ACCESS (DMA)

Mass storage devices like disk or tape require very rapid data transfer of data from the device to memory and vice-versa. A typical hard disk transfers data at about 1 byte per 2 microsecs (1993); neither polled nor interrupt-initiated input-output could cope with this.

In addition, if you look at the system diagram in Figure, you will see that both the disk (for example) and memory are connected to the system bus. Hence, there may be little requirement for the CPU to get involved in a data transfer, except to initiate it. Typically, a third device will be connected to the bus - a DMA controller - which mediates between the two data transfer devices and ensures an orderly use of the bus.

In DMA, the only effect on the CPU and executing programme is slight slowing down, because the DMA must *steal* bus cycles — so called cycle-stealing — for the data transfer. For example, recalling Mac-1a, and memory read/write: during a LODD, for example, Mac-1a would place the address to be read in MAR, and issue an RD; if a DMA byte transfer was happening, the DMA would have to be able to tell the CPU to wait for a cycle or two.